Arab Women's Lives Retold

Gender, Culture, and Politics in the Middle East
miriam cooke, Simona Sharoni, and Suad Joseph, *Series Editors*

SELECTED TITLES FROM GENDER, CULTURE, AND POLITICS IN THE MIDDLE EAST

Faith and Freedom: Women's Human Rights in the Muslim World
MAHNAZ AFKHAMI, ed.

Gendering the Middle East: Emerging Perspectives
DENIZ KANDIYOTI, ed.

Intersections: Gender, Nation, and Community in Arab Women's Novels
LISA SUHAIR MAJAJ, PAULA W. SUNDERMAN, AND THERESE SALIBA, eds.

Intimate Selving in Arab Families: Gender, Self, and Identity
SUAD JOSEPH, ed.

Missing Persians: Discovering Voices in Iranian Cultural History
NASRIN RAHIMIEH

Muslim Women and the Politics of Participation: Implementing the Beijing Platform
MAHNAZ AFKHAMI AND ERIKA FRIEDL, eds.

No Shame for the Sun: Lives of Professional Pakistani Women
SHAHLA HAERI

Voices from Iran: The Changing Lives of Iranian Women
MAHNAZ KOUSHA

War's Other Voices: Women Writers on the Lebanese Civil War
MIRIAM COOKE

Women of Jordan: Islam, Labor, and the Law
AMIRA EL-AZHARY SONBOL

Arab Women's Lives Retold

Exploring Identity Through Writing

Edited by
Nawar Al-Hassan Golley

With a Foreword by
miriam cooke

Syracuse University Press

First Edition 2007
12 13 14 15 6 5 4 3

Permission to reprint the following text in chapter 9 is gratefully acknowledged: (1) Poetry of Mohja Kahf. Reprinted with permission of the University Press of Florida; (2) Poetry of Suheir Hammad. Reprinted with permission of Suheir Hammad.

∞ The paper used in this publication meets the minimum requirements of the American National Standard for Information Sciences—Permanence of Paper for Printed Library Materials, ANSI Z39.48–1992.

For a listing of books published and distributed by Syracuse University Press, visit our Web site at SyracuseUniversityPress.syr.edu.

ISBN-13: 978-0-8156-3122-4 (cl.) ISBN-13: 978-0-8156-3147-7 (pbk.)
ISBN-10: 0-8156-3122-7 ISBN-10: 0-8156-3147-2

Library of Congress Cataloging-in-Publication Data

Arab women's lives retold : exploring identity through writing / edited by Nawar Al-Hassan Golley with a foreword by Miriam Cooke. — 1st ed.
p. cm. — (Gender, culture, and politics in the Middle East)
Includes bibliographical references and index.
ISBN 978-0-8156-3122-4 (hardcover : alk. paper) — ISBN 978-0-8156-3147-7 (pbk. : alk. paper)
1. Women—Arab countries—Biography. 2. Autobiography—Women authors. 3. Feminists—Arab countries—Biography. I. Golley, Nawar Al-Hassan, 1961–
CT3748.A73 2007
920.72089'927—dc22 200702217

Manufactured in the United States of America

To my beloved mother and father

To my darling children, Jinan and Cézanne

To my beautiful niece, Shahrazad

To my sisters and brothers

To my soul mate

To my special students

at the American University of Sharjah

Let those who may complain that it was all on paper remember that only on paper has humanity yet achieved glory, beauty, truth, knowledge, virtue, and abiding love.

—BERNARD SHAW, preface to *Ellen Terry and Bernard Shaw: A Correspondence*

Contents

Illustrations

Foreword

MIRIAM COOKE

Not so long ago in the West, Arab women were thought not to write. Courses in European and U.S. universities covered Arab men's writings, with perhaps one or two classes devoted to women's. In the 1970s, the exceptional women were the Lebanese Layla Baalbaki and the Syrian Colette Khuri and sometimes the Egyptian Nawal el-Saadawi. To include these women in a syllabus was a sign that one was progressive. In the 1980s, the situation began to change when translators of Arabic literature turned their attention to women. The first International Feminist Bookfair in London in 1986 featured the Lebanese Hanan al-Shaykh's *Story of Zahra* and the Egyptian Alifa Rifat's *Distant View of a Minaret,* both books garnering considerable critical acclaim.

It was almost as though gates had been opened into a world unknown until then. The realization that Arab women had been writing for some time in literary centers like Beirut and Cairo sent researchers to other less likely places such as Saudi Arabia, the countries of the Arabian Gulf, and the Maghreb. It appeared that women in Riyadh, Kuwait, and Rabat were writing in newspapers but also publishing their own creative works. They were part of the local literary scenes, and some, like the Kuwaiti Layla al-'Uthman, were well known in Arab intellectual circles.

Literary critics published analyses of individuals' writings, and some were surprised that women were not just writing about homes and families and that some were as socially and politically engaged as their male colleagues. With their pens, Lebanese women were fighting the civil war (1975–92) in the hope of bringing about peace through reason and art. Palestinian women such as Sahar Khalifa and Raimonda Tawil were critiquing men's ways of fighting against the Israeli occupiers and demonstrating, through their heroines and their own lives, that women's strategies and tactics were more successful and less lethal than the men's. Arabian Peninsula women integrated questions of technology and oil-driven modernization into their life writing, their fiction, and their poetry. Egyptian women were linking class, patriarchy, and religion in their creative writings.

During the 1980s and 1990s, the French writings of women in the three countries of the Maghreb (Morocco, Algeria, and Tunisia) came to be seen as part and parcel of Arab women's literary production. Women whose books had found readers in Paris and sometimes in their home countries were drawn into the broader circle of global Arab literature. The autobiographical quartet by Algeria's Assia Djebar has become a reference for women thinking about writing their lives wherever they might be. The Moroccan Fatima Mernissi wrote her life in English, thereby allowing herself liberties she might have eschewed had she written in French or Arabic.

It was during this period also that Arabs in exile began to publish, and their writings were increasingly read in the Arab world. The Syrian Ghada al-Samman, who left her chosen home of Beirut for Paris during the civil war, wrote semiautobiographical stories about her life in France and the challenges facing Arabs in the French nation regardless of their class and religion. Arabs in the United States after the 1991 Gulf War, made newly aware of their ethnicity and difference, started to write their lives. Some targeted readers back home, whereas others wrote to be read only in exile so that they might be free to express themselves as they wished. The poetic life reflections of Mohja Kahf and Suheir Hammad are brilliant examples of this trend.

In the 1990s, a new kind of writing, some of it autobiographical, began to emerge: Islamic feminist discourse. An increasingly fundamentalist turn in Muslim countries had its impact on women, who were expected in dress and behavior to represent their culture and their religion. Public intellectuals like el-Saadawi and al-'Uthman were attacked for their blasphemous writings and taken to court. Each turned her encounters with religious vigilantes into autobiographical essays. The Egyptian prison memoirs of the Muslim Sister Zaynab al-Ghazali (1977) and of the feminist activist el-Saadawi (1984) enjoyed a new popularity.

Nawar Al-Hassan Golley has collected studies in Arab women's autobiographical writings that bring the lives of these writers in from the margin and show their variety. They take the reader through critical moments in twentieth-century Arab literature when creative women were reflecting on their situations and sharing their insights with the world. This volume is an important book that insists on the centrality of women's literary and intellectual contributions to the Arab literary canon.

Acknowledgments

This book would not have been possible without the cooperation of the scholars who contributed to making this book a reality; my profound gratitude to one and all. I would also like to extend my appreciation to Frances and Annette for their efficient editorial help.

I also wish to thank the American University of Sharjah, in particular the Graduate Studies and Research Office, for its continued support of research and professional development. Grateful thanks to Nabeel and Naji, the information-technology experts at the American University of Sharjah, for their kind assistance and technical support. Working on this book with Syracuse University Press (SUP), especially Mary Selden Evans, has been an enjoyable professional experience. Thank you, SUP.

On a more personal level, I continue to be eternally grateful to my family and particularly my two lovely children, Jinan Petra and Cézanne-Jawad, who have always been understanding and extremely patient with me. I am always inspired by their youthful excitement and enthusiasm. I am equally indebted to the confidence that my good friends and loyal students have continually showed in me. I thank them all.

Finally, I hope that this book, which encompasses the labor of so many, will deepen the understanding and broaden the acceptance of Arab women writers by readers around the world.

Contributors

BERNADETTE ANDREA is associate professor of English at the University of Texas at San Antonio, where she is also chair of the Department of English, Classics, and Philosophy. Her research focuses on women's writing from the sixteenth through the eighteenth centuries, with an emphasis on Western European interactions with the Ottoman Empire. Her recent publications also focus on twentieth-century Algerian, Egyptian, and Turkish women writers. Her book *Women and Islam in Early Modern English Literature* is scheduled to be published in 2007.

MIREILLE ASTORE is an artist, poet, and art scholar. In 2003 she won Australia's National Photographic Purchase Award and a University of Western Sydney Ph.D. scholarship. She is now completing "Missing Lebanon: Art and Autobiography," her Ph.D. thesis in contemporary arts. Her videos have been screened at numerous film festivals, as well as at art galleries in the United Kingdom, Denmark, and Italy, including the Leeds City Gallery; Focal Point Gallery; Freud Museum; Copenhagen Contemporary Art Center; Museum of Contemporary Art, Roskilde; and the Casoria Contemporary Art Museum, Naples. She is published widely in Australia, the United States, and Europe.

MRINALINI CHAKRAVORTY received her B.A. in English from the University of Colorado at Boulder and her M.A. and Ph.D. from the University of California at Irvine. Her research and teaching interests include postcolonial literature, critical theory, and gender and sexuality studies, as well as the various intersections among these areas. Her book project *Managing Modernities: Postcolonial Collectives in Twentieth-Century Anglophone Literature* examines the social, political, and literary intersections of modernity, sexuality, and collectivism in postcolonial film and literature from South Asia and the Middle East. Having previously taught at Kenyon College, she is currently assistant professor of English at the University of Virginia.

KARINA EILERAAS is a Mellon Postdoctoral Fellow in women's and gender studies at Carleton College. She received her B.A. from Wesleyan University in 1993 and a Ph.D. from the University of California at Los Angeles (UCLA) in 2003. Her interests include feminist postcolonial theory; Francophone diaspora studies, especially pertaining to the Middle East and North Africa; autobiography; visual culture; and performance studies. She has published articles in various anthologies and journals, including the *Drama Review* and *Modern Language Notes,* and is currently working on revisions for the forthcoming publication of her dissertation.

CAROL FADDA-CONREY received her Ph.D. in American literature from Purdue University in 2006. Her dissertation, "Racially White but Culturally Colored: Defining Contemporary Arab-American Literature and Its Transnational Connections," situates Arab American literature within the U.S. ethnic canon while underscoring the transcontinental and cross-cultural Arab American connections to the Arab world. Her research interests include Arab American studies, ethnic and postcolonial literature, and women's literature. Her work has been published in *Al-Jadid, Studies in the Humanities,* and the *Encyclopedia of Multiethnic American Literature.*

KEITH FELDMAN is a doctoral candidate in English literature at the University of Washington. His dissertation looks at the question of Palestine, imperial sovereignty, and racial politics in U.S. culture. Among his publications are "The (Il)legible Arab Body and the Fantasy of National Democracy" and a review of "The Black Panther" comic book series, both published in the *Journal for Multi-Ethnic Literatures of the United States* (2007).

NAWAR AL-HASSAN GOLLEY is associate professor of literary and critical theory and women's studies in the Department of English at the American University of Sharjah, where she teaches courses in literature, literary theory, and women's studies. A Syrian by origin, Golley obtained her Ph.D. in critical theory at the University of Nottingham. Her research interests include literary and critical theory, especially feminism and women's studies, postcolonial studies, cultural studies, and autobiography, and she has published numerous essays in these areas. She is the author of *Reading Arab Women's Autobiographies: Shahrazad Tells Her Story* and has translated the literary and critical works of Adonis, Edward Said, and Etel Adnan.

DAPHNE M. GRACE received her Ph.D. in English literature from the University of Sussex. She has taught twentieth-century and postcolonial literature at Eastern Mediterranean University (North Cyprus), the University College of the Bahamas, and the University of Sussex. Her book *The Woman in the Muslin Mask: Veiling and Identity in Postcolonial Literature* was published in 2004. She has also published in the fields of women's studies and feminist ethics and has presented widely at international conferences. Her next book, *Relocating Consciousness: Diasporic Writing and the Dynamics of Literary Experience,* is to be published by Rodopi in the series Consciousness, Literature, and the Arts.

AHMAD AL-ISSA is associate professor of English and linguistics in the Department of Language and Literature at the American University of Sharjah. A Jordanian by origin, he completed his studies in American universities and is a member of several international organizations. Al-Issa obtained his Ph.D. in rhetoric and linguistics from Indiana University of Pennsylvania. His research interests are in the areas of intercultural communication, language and culture, and sociolinguistics. Al-Issa has presented many papers at national and international conferences and published many articles in international journals such as the *International Journal of Intercultural Relations, Intercultural Communication Studies,* and the *Journal of Behavioral Research Methods.*

JAMIL KHADER is associate professor of English at Stetson University, where he teaches postcolonial literature and international feminisms. His article on the Palestinian poet Al-Mutawakel Taha appeared in *Al-Sharq: A Literary Quarterly* (1991), and his article on Rudolfo Anaya's proletarian novel, *Heart of Aztlan,* appeared in the *Journal for Multi-Ethnic Literatures of the United*

States (2002). He has also published a few articles on U.S.–third world women writers in *Ariel* (Calgary); *African Literature and Its Times; FS: Feminist Studies; College Literature;* and most recently *Global Neo-imperialism and National Resistance: Approaches from Postcolonial Studies.* He is currently working on a book tentatively titled "Global Visions, Postcolonial Futures: Gender, Ideology, Transnationalism."

BENAOUDA LEBDAI is a senior lecturer at the University of Angers, France. He is a specialist in African literature written in English. He obtained his Ph.D. in 1987 from the University of Essex on Ngugi wa Thiong'o and Rachid Boudjedra. His critical studies deal with the relations between literature and history, gender, and postcolonial theory through the works of Edward Said, Frantz Fanon, Homi Bhaba, and Rimmon-Kenan. He published *Signes et symbolique de la révolte existentielle à travers les personnages des romans d'Ayi Kwei Armah, Lille, Septentrion* (2000) and *Post-independence African Literature: Boudjedra/Ngugi* (1992).

FILIZ TURHAN-SWENSON earned her doctorate in English literature at New York University and is currently associate professor of English at Suffolk Community College. She is the author of *The Other Empire: British Romantic Writings about the Ottoman Empire* (2003) and an essay on Shelley and De Quincey in the essay collection *Interrogating Orientalism* (2006). In addition to British romanticism, her research and teaching interests focus on contemporary world literature.

PAULINE HOMSI VINSON is adjunct assistant professor in the Women's Studies Department at the University of South Florida, Sarasota-Manatee. She has taught at several universities in the United States and abroad. Most recently, she was at the American University in Sharjah. She has published several articles on Arab women writers. A number of her articles and translations on Arab cultural issues have appeared in the magazine *Al-Jadid,* of which she is a contributing editor. She is a native of Lebanon.

Introduction

Contemporary Arab Women's Autobiographical Writings

NAWAR AL-HASSAN GOLLEY

The idea for putting together an edited anthology of studies of contemporary Arab women's autobiographical writings was instigated by the favorable and encouraging responses to the publication of my previous book, *Reading Arab Women's Autobiographies: Shahrazad Tells Her Story* (2003). The book filled a gap in the field of Arab women's writings, as it studied autobiographical and fictional-autobiographical texts together with anthologies of interviews with women examining the sociopolitical backgrounds of the texts in addition to the tradition of narrative theory. The field of Arab women's autobiographical writings remains underresearched and in need of further investigation. The available critical readings do not match the number of autobiographical writings that Arab women are producing. This book, *Arab Women's Lives Retold: Exploring Identity Through Writing,* will, I hope, encourage further critical and theoretical questioning of Arab women's modes of self-representation and personal narratives.

In the past century, Arab countries underwent fundamental sociological, economic, and political changes, as they progressed from colonial rule through nationalist movements to independence. Over the past couple of decades, as the various countries have sought to find an identity in the postmodern, postcolonial world of the twenty-first century, attitudes regarding women have changed at a phenomenal rate. One positive aspect has been that Arab women of all classes and denominations and from all Arab countries have been reaping the benefits of increased and improved access to education and employment opportunities. However, throughout these changes, the

Western stereotype of Arab women remains that of an invisible and silent woman shrouded in mystery. Neither discourses on orientalism nor studies within feminism have managed to dispel this myth. However, if we examine the autobiographical writings of Arab women themselves, we find that they have been courageous and creative in both the lives they have lived and the ways in which they have written about them. They have played a full part in political struggles and developed many different modes of writing the self. In this sense, Arab women's autobiographical writings serve as more than a means by which to create images of the self through the writing act, but rather they have served as a way to find a voice—whether private or public—through which to express what cannot be expressed in any other form.

In 2001, in *Interpreting the Self: Autobiography in the Arabic Tradition,* which covers the period "from the ninth to the nineteenth century (including a small number of texts written or published in the early twentieth century)," Dwight F. Reynolds stated that "only three [Arab] women autobiographers can be identified with certainty" (6, 8). However, the profuse production of autobiographical works by Arab women throughout the twentieth century, and especially in the past two decades, as evidenced in this book, shows the increasing role and contribution of Arab women writers to autobiographical writings. Although Syrian, Lebanese, and Egyptian women have been known as writers for centuries, today women writers from every Arab country are making their mark. Naturally, these writers have produced texts in all literary genres (poetry, drama, and fiction). In addition, these writers have also developed new and different forms and modes of writings, with self-writing being one of the modes in which Arab women have produced a substantial number of creative texts.

As I have noted in my previous book, Arab women's autobiographical writings are embedded in a long literary tradition of writing the self in Arab culture. Such writings relate directly to the relationship among self, society, and history; to established social values; and to the possible modes of personal, political, and intellectual expression. This book examines late-twentieth-century autobiographical writings by Arab women writers in their social, political, and rhetorical contexts, exploring the ways in which Arab women have portrayed and created themselves within differing social environments.

The female authors whose texts this book studies are either Arab or of Arab descent; they come from various Arab countries stretching from the

Mashreq of the Middle East (a term that refers to countries such as Syria, Lebanon, Palestine, Iraq, and Egypt) to its Maghreb (countries such as Libya, Tunisia, Algeria, and Morocco); and they reside in Arab or Western countries (the Mahjar or the diaspora). Their texts are written originally in English, French, or Arabic. As autobiographical expressions can take many forms, the texts analyzed in this book cover the whole spectrum—from autobiographies to fiction, poetry, memoirs, and even photographs—showing the diverse ways in which Arab women are examining and exploring contemporary issues in terms of their own lives.

Examining a number of contemporary Arab women's various expressions of private and public experiences, this book shows the active and engaged roles of Arab women in determining not only their own lives but also the lives of many others in their societies at large. To this end, it contains analytical studies that are informed by and grounded in theoretical discussions of autobiographical, feminist, cultural, and postcolonial studies. The issues of self and subjectivity, the private and the public, ethnicity, nationalism and transnationalism, and postcolonialism intersect, setting up a polyphony of readings that overlap, challenge, and digress from each other. The autobiographical writings are analyzed in relation to the discourses of feminism, postcolonialism, nationalism, socialism, hybridity, and religion—discourses that have also dominated the autobiographers' experiences.

Covering a variety of subjects ranging from the most private and personal to the most public and political, the autobiographical writings studied here include such themes as the conflicting roles of woman as wife, mother, daughter, sister, and lover; women's predicaments in societies that make a firm distinction between a "man's world" and a "woman's domain," that is, between the domestic and the public sectors; women who find through autobiographical writing a means to survive childbirth, disease, and the deaths of loved ones; the creation of images of self through the act of writing; finding a voice through creative forms of expression; outspoken women resisting patriarchal definitions to open up new opportunities for professional and personal development; the creation of interracial, anti-imperialist, and antisexist solidarities; the ambivalent impact of cultural hybridity; the question of cultural identity in a postcolonial world; a critique of the Euro-American nation form; transnational circuits of cultural exchange; recovering submerged histories; reexamination of literary standards and traditions; and the negotiation of language and textual practices. With difficulty, I have picked four of these themes—cultural hybridity, transnationalism, communal identity, and the personal and the political—as the most dominant issues into which to divide this book.

PART ONE: "AUTOBIOGRAPHICAL WRITING AND CULTURAL HYBRIDITY"

In chapter 1, "Passage Through the Harem: Historicizing a Western Obsession in Leila Ahmed's *A Border Passage: From Cairo to America—a Woman's Journey*," Bernadette Andrea, tracing the etymological and historical genealogy of Western ethnocentric perceptions of the harem, sees that Leila Ahmed's *Border Passage* (1999) charts the geographical, ideological, and political movements constituting the liminal-subject position of a Muslim Egyptian woman whose memories are shaped by the waning Ottoman Empire, the intrusive British Empire, and the nascent neoimperialism of the United States. Andrea places Ahmed's influential intervention as an Islamic feminist into American women's studies in dialogue with her representation, in *A Border Passage,* of multiple harems from both the Arab world and the West. Dwelling within—and then upon—these contiguous women's communities, Ahmed, according to Andrea, delineates a transcultural model of the harem that contests patriarchal and feminist orientalist projections.

Karina Eileraas, in chapter 2, "Dismembering the Gaze: Speleology and Vivisection in Assia Djebar's *L'amour, la fantasia,*" examines the semiautobiographical novel (1985) in which Djebar pays particular attention to the ways in which identities are impacted by the colonial politics of language. Eileraas demonstrates that Djebar foregrounds cultural hybridity as the necessary mise-en-scène of identity in order to create a powerful narrative, or "countermemory," of French colonization and the Algerian anticolonial revolution from a woman's perspective. Djebar devotes much time in her work to articulating the interwoven strands of her identity: born in Algeria, she attended French colonial schools, spent summers with cloistered girls in the countryside, and left Algeria during the revolution to attend university in Paris. As French was imposed as the "official language" of Algeria during colonization, whereas Arabic became the official language during and after revolution, Djebar describes how this battle of tongues had a salient impact on her identity—even the most intimate aspects of her existence, notably her ability to express love. Eileraas explores how Djebar conceives female identity and sexuality in relation to French colonial and Algerian nationalist images and histories.

In chapter 3, "Yasmina, an Autodiegetic Character: *Her*story and History," Benaouda Lebdai tests the questions of identity, history, and reconciliation in the autobiographical novel *Garçon manqué* (2000) by Nina Bouraoui, a French Algerian woman, in order to show how writing one's life through fiction can be used to understand larger historical contexts. Bouraoui's text raises the question of hybridity in race, culture, religion, language, and history. This chapter tackles the question of identity and gender through a postcolonial perspective where "construction" and "deconstruction" of one's personality, entity, and identity are of utmost importance. For a better understanding and full acceptance of "history," Lebdai draws on Frantz Fanon's theories and argues that such writings necessitate an investigation of broader historical contexts, looking into the particular rapport between history and fiction.

PART TWO: "AUTOBIOGRAPHICAL WRITINGS AND TRANSNATIONALISM"

Keith Feldman examines national belonging in transnational contexts in the autobiographical works of contemporary Arab American women's writings, such as *The Indian Never Had a Horse, and Other Poems* (1985) by Etel Adnan and *Born Palestinian, Born Black* (1996) and *Drops of This Story* (1996) by Suheir Hammad. The aim of chapter 4, "Poetic Geographies: Interracial Insurgency in Arab American Autobiographical Spaces," is to examine the particular production of a minority discourse—Arab American diasporic belonging in a transnational context—by tracing the rhetorical strategies in the previously mentioned works. These strategies negotiate the apparent contradiction of the simultaneous critique and transvaluation of the nation form. Feldman reads these strategies as a mode of revaluing "Arab" as a transnational category through which to forward specific literary projects in order to imagine a viable and inclusive Arab society built in a transnational context and through transnational solidarities. By considering the transnational—circulations beyond the nation—as a key form of Arab American autobiographical production, contradictions in citizenship within the nation can be clarified, and broad transnational solidarities produced through reflections on the diaspora can be creatively imagined.

Chapter 5 is grounded in a transnational framework that reads *My Home, My Prison* (1980) by Raimonda Tawil, a Palestinian writer and journalist, within and against transnational networks of cultural, political, and theoretical production, be it Western feminism (Simone de Beauvoir), U.S. global hegemony, or postnational theory. Jamil Khader examines the material conditions of the oppression of Palestinian women as both Arab women and Palestinian nationals living under Israeli military occupation and Zionist settler colonialism. Khader reads Tawil's autobiography as contesting and problematizing the dominant thematics and tropes of Arab women's literary tradition that valorize the metanarratives of nationalism, oppositional consciousness, and unified community.

In chapter 6, "A Muslim Woman Writes Back: Leila Abouzeid's *Return to Childhood: The Memoir of a Modern Moroccan Woman,*" Pauline Homsi Vinson explores the ways in which self-representation in Abouzeid's life narrative is inextricably linked to questions regarding the transnational reception of postcolonial texts, especially those works written by women. At the same time, the chapter addresses the ways in which Abouzeid weaves female oral history into her written native while also transforming her personal memory into a political history of her native country. This chapter examines the uses of autobiography by Arab women writers as a strategic intervention in transnational discourses about Arab women. As Vinson illustrates, Abouzeid links her personal story to the lives of other Moroccan women and to the political history of her country while also offering a corrective to Western stereotypes regarding Arab, and specifically Moroccan, women.

PART THREE: "AUTOBIOGRAPHICAL WRITINGS AND COMMUNAL IDENTITY"

Filiz Turhan-Swenson establishes a lineage or history of Muslim women's writings, asserting that the proliferation and popularity of such texts will likely help to express the diverse experiences of women across the Muslim world.

Drawing on feminist theories of autobiography and postcolonial literature in order to analyze Fatima Mernissi's memoir, *Dreams of Trespass: Tales of a Harem Girlhood* (1995), she establishes connections between Mernissi's characteristic use of a polyphonic narrative voice and the voices of other women poets, writers, and memoirists. In doing so, Turhan-Swenson shows that although Mernissi condemns harem life, she also seeks to present alternative forms of feminist resistance enacted by the harem inhabitants.

In chapter 7, "Voices Across the Frontier: Fatima Mernissi's *Dreams of Trespass: Tales of a Harem Girlhood*," Turhan-Swenson shows how *Dreams of Trespass* not only characteristically presents Mernissi's own individual experiences but also very keenly contextualizes her personal development within the social constraints of her time. In the process of telling her personal story, Mernissi simultaneously creates a rhetorical construction of her nation and asserts that a true and authentic Islam does not in fact call for the stifling or eliding of the female voice and the cloistering of her body. Such practices, Mernissi argues, have instead been the reactionary tools of patriarchal societies to assert a strong Islamic, postcolonial identity in which the status of women in society is seen to be the defining and distinguishing characteristic.

Mrinalini Chakravorty examines Ahdaf Soueif's *In the Eye of the Sun* (1992) and focuses on the issues of Pan-Arabism and gender, especially as they are inscribed within frames of individual and collective responses to imperialism in contemporary Arab contexts. Chakravorty engages the work of Frantz Fanon, Edward Said, Saree Makdisi, and Leila Ahmed to set up a theoretical claim for Pan-Arabism as a mode of cultural translation and political empowerment within contemporary Anglophone Arab fiction. In chapter 8, "To Undo What the North Has Done: Fragments of a Nation and Arab Collectivism in the Fiction of Ahdaf Soueif," Chakravorty looks at how in *In the Eye of the Sun,* Soueif, an Anglophone Arab woman writer, self-inscribes a secularist Pan-Arab identity that disrupts Western, and even Islamist, stereotypes of Arabs as united only by religion. She explores the alliances among neglected Islamic treatises on Pan-Arabism, Nasser's socialist program for Egypt, and attitudes of solidarity toward migrant women workers in Soueif's fiction.

Carol Fadda-Conrey makes a close analysis of the autobiographical elements in the work of two contemporary Arab American poets: Suheir

Hammad's *Born Palestinian, Born Black* (1996) and Mohja Kahf's *E-mails from Scheherazad* (2003). She argues in chapter 9, "Weaving Poetic Autobiographies: Individual and Communal Identities in the Poetry of Mohja Kahf and Suheir Hammad," that writing for women is both self-discovery and self-making and that in Kahf's and Hammad's works, these writings extend beyond self to emphasize through poetry a collectivity of the Arab American experience, a gesture that develops into a complex act of creation and discovery since it involves the unpeeling of historical and cultural layers.

PART FOUR: "THE PERSONAL AND THE POLITICAL IN AUTOBIOGRAPHICAL WRITINGS"

Daphne M. Grace uses postcolonial theory to problematize notions of life writing, addressing how writing autobiography can both heal and hurt: the process can be an exercise in both anodizing and exposing pain. In chapter 10, "Arab Women Write the Trauma of Imprisonment and Exile," Grace looks at recent autobiographies (Haifa Zangana's *Through the Vast Halls of Memory* [1991] and Nawal el-Saadawi's *Daughter of Isis* [1999] and *Walking Through Fire* [2002]) by writers who were incarcerated without trial as "political" prisoners under the governments of Iraq and Egypt in the 1970s and 1980s. Grace analyzes the production and effect of writing autobiography, its role as both a cathartic and a didactic process, and the problems of exposure for Arab women writing their personal experience when that writing assumes the role of political and social criticism.

Ahmad Al-Issa and I explore a different mode of autobiographical writing, political memoir, specifically Queen Noor's *Leap of Faith: Memoirs of an Unexpected Life* (2003). In chapter 11, "A Journey of Belonging: A Global(ized) Self Finds Peace," we look at an Arab American who assimilated into Arab life, making a leap in the opposite direction from the one taken by some Arab women studied in this book who assimilated into American or European life. Already a multicultural person, Queen Noor took a sense of alienation with her to an Arab country where she fell in love with the man with whom and with whose culture and religion she adherently identified and found peace.

An account of a transition from an ordinary person to a player on the international stage, Queen Noor's memoir also represents the cultural empowerment of the maternal stance. In a very modest style, she tells of a series of sacrifices and exemplary achievements.[1] In the context of globalization and postcolonialism, taken as broadly cultural phenomena, Al-Issa and I argue that the most positive aspect of these two phenomena can be best represented by Queen Noor's personal and political narrative, as she comes through as one of the most culturally complex yet genuinely understanding, adaptable, and assimilable global personalities.

In chapter 12, "Art, Autobiography, and the Maternal Abject," Mireille Astore, an Australian of Lebanese origin, explores human emotions and their environment in her own photographic work. Through the experience of becoming a mother, she asks what it is to be human and contextualizes her experience within the framework of contemporary discourses. Through the Maternal Abject photographic series, Astore attempts to construct a visual narrative of contemporary nuclear motherhood as perceived by an Arab woman living in the West. In Astore's images, the dismantling of spontaneity, systemic isolation, and cultural invisibility merge with the surrender of the self.

There could be no better time than ours for a book such as this one. In spite of increasing globalization, recent political developments have encouraged popular culture to reinforce existing negative stereotypes about Arab women as victims of gender oppression, escapees of their intrinsically oppressive culture, or pawns of Arab male power (Kahf 2000). This book aims to challenge the passive, limited image that continues to be publicized about Arab women

1. In the same year that Queen Noor's memoir appeared (2003), Elibron Classics published two volumes titled *Memoirs of a Babylonian Princess (Maria Theresa Asma), Daughter of Emir Abdallah Asmar,* which was written in London, May 1844. In 1993, E. J. Brill (Leiden, the Netherlands) also published another very interesting book translated from the German, titled *Emily Ruete/Princess Salme bint Said ibn Sultan, an Arabia Princess Between Two Worlds: Memoirs, Letters Home, Sequels to the Memoirs, Syrian Customs and Usages.* Emily Ruete, who was Sayyida Salme bint Said ibn Sultan, princess of Oman and Zanzibar, was born in Zanzibar on August 30, 1844. After fleeing in 1866 to Aden, she took the Christian name Emily when she was baptized in 1867. After her marriage to the German Rudolph Heinrich Ruete, she moved to Germany. Ruete wrote her memoirs between 1875 and 1886. It is my intention to look at these memoirs together with Queen Noor's memoirs in a forthcoming study.

and to show instead the active, multiple nature of their identities and the roles they play in their societies.

From this book, *Arab Women's Lives Retold: Exploring Identity Through Writing,* it can be seen that the metaphoric and uncharacteristic unveiling by these Arab women writers, undertaken both to refute the West's view of them as passive victims and to expose the discrimination within their own societies, often at the risk of censorship and punishment, is a courageous act that reveals Arab women writers as contributors to the future of their societies.

Artistic Works Discussed

AUTOBIOGRAPHY, FICTION, AND MEMOIR

Leila Abouzeid (Moroccan). *Return to Childhood: The Memoir of a Modern Moroccan Woman* (1998). Chapter 6.

Leila Ahmed (Egyptian). *A Border Passage: From Cairo to America—a Woman's Journey* (1999). Chapter 1.

Nina Bouraoui (Algerian). *Garçon manqué* (2000). Chapter 3.

Assia Djebar (Algerian). *L'amour, la fantasia* (1995). Chapter 2.

Fatima Mernissi (Moroccan). *Dreams of Trespass: Tales of a Harem Girlhood* (1995). Chapter 7.

Queen Noor (Arab American). *Leap of Faith: Memoirs of an Unexpected Life* (2003). Chapter 11.

Nawal el-Saadawi (Egyptian). *Memoirs from the Women's Prison* (1986). Chapter 10.

Ahdaf Soueif (Egyptian). *In the Eye of the Sun* (1992). Chapter 8.

Raimonda Tawil (Palestinian). *My Home, My Prison* (1980). Chapter 5.

Haifa Zangana (Iraqi). *Through the Vast Halls of Memory* (1991). Chapter 10.

POETRY

Etel Adnan (Arab American). *The Indian Never Had a Horse, and Other Poems* (1985). Chapter 4.

Suheir Hammad (Arab American). *Born Palestinian, Born Black* (1996). Chapters 4 and 9.

Mohja Kahf (Arab American). *E-mails from Scheherazad* (2003). Chapter 9.

VISUAL ARTS

Mireille Astore (Arab Australian). *Body Map* (2001). Chapter 12.

———. *DeadBird Mary* (2001). Chapter 12.

———. *Endoscopic Journey* (2001). Chapter 12.

PART ONE

Autobiographical Writings and Cultural Hybridity

Central to self identity . . . is the capacity to sustain and in some sense reconcile multiple and often conflicting identities. . . . The experience of lack of self is the familiar dark side of a culture characterized by increasing pressure for self-identity under conditions of increasing fragmentation. . . . [T]he development of self-identity requires the cognitive capacity to reflect on who I am and what matters to me, and to organize diverse identities, and identity-attributes, into some sort of meaningful narrative or constellation.

—Allison Weir, *Sacrificial Logics: Feminist Theory and the Critique of Identity*

1

Passage Through the Harem

Historicizing a Western Obsession in Leila Ahmed's *A Border Passage: From Cairo to America—a Woman's Journey*

BERNADETTE ANDREA

Leila Ahmed's *Border Passage: From Cairo to America—a Woman's Journey* (1999) charts the geographical, ideological, and political movements constituting the liminal-subject position of a Muslim Egyptian woman whose memories are shaped by the waning Ottoman Empire, the intrusive British Empire, and the nascent neoimperialism of the United States (Ahmed 1999a).[1] This memoir, premised on the titular image of "a border passage," complicates the metaphorics of boundaries constituting not simply the imperialist discourses Ahmed examines but perhaps more so the anticolonial nationalism epitomized by Gamal Abdel Nasser as the champion of the third world.[2] That she specifies her passage as "a woman's journey" enables this challenge to the persistent hierarchies of oppositional anti- and postcolonial models, which nevertheless maintain—and sometimes even establish—principles of subordination based on gender and minority status.[3] Her movement into the emergent space of women's studies in American academe further complicates this journey, as the historical specificities of race cut across the solidarity of gender to produce

1. In *Women Claim Islam: Creating Islamic Feminism Through Literature,* miriam cooke (2001, 80) mentions Ahmed's *Border Passage.* For more sustained analyses, see W. Hassan 2002; and Shereen 2003.

2. Ahmed explicates Nasserism in "Egypt: The Background" (1999a, 3–31).

3. Ahmed confronts this contradiction in "On Becoming an Arab" (1999a, 243–70).

Ahmed's influential essay "Western Ethnocentrism and Perceptions of the Harem" (1982).[4]

In this chapter, I propose to place Ahmed's influential intervention as an Islamic feminist into American women's studies, epitomized by "Western Ethnocentrism and Perceptions of the Harem," in dialogue with her representation in *A Border Passage* of multiple harems from both the Arab world and the West.[5] In chapters exploring the traditional domestic harem of her childhood, Ahmed establishes this woman's space as the font of ethical Islam, which she contrasts with the official legalistic Islam perpetuated by a male-authored tradition—one embraced by the West in its own official discourses.[6] Ahmed stresses, moreover, the similarities between the space of the harem in her Egyptian home during the early twentieth century and the space of the English women's college she entered in the late 1950s. Her final intervention into discourses of the harem occurs as she moves from Abu Dhabi in the United Arab Emirates to the United States, specifically into the emerging academic space of women's studies during the 1980s. Dwelling within—and then upon—these contiguous women's communities in the Arab world and the West, Ahmed delineates a transcultural model of the harem that contests patriarchal and feminist orientalist projections.[7] The patriarchal orientalist view, which still dominates Western imaginary, casts the harem as a site of phallocentric excess premised on the exclusive access of one man to numerous women in a primarily sexual context. The feminist orientalist position critiques the phallocentric control fantasized in this scenario but does not contest the view of the harem as the primary locus of unmitigated gender oppression. For the feminist orientalist, a political stance embedded in Western liberal feminism from its inception, women in the harem must be rescued from Islam in order to be liberated as women. As Ahmed stresses in

4. "Western Ethnocentrism and Perceptions of the Harem" was first published in *Feminist Studies* in 1982 and has been frequently cited since.

5. In *Women Claim Islam,* cooke outlines "Islamic feminism" (2001, 55–64).

6. Ahmed addresses the Western academic world's privileging of "textual Islam" over "alternative oral forms of lived Islam" (1999a, 129–30).

7. I analyze the "genealogy of feminist Orientalism" in my forthcoming book, *Women and Islam in Early Modern English Literature* (Cambridge Univ. Press).

"Western Ethnocentrism and Perceptions of the Harem," American women of Christian and Jewish descent did not demand a rejection of their similarly patriarchal cultures as part of their feminist commitments. It is "colonial feminism" in relation to the Islamic world, Ahmed concludes in her extended study *Women and Gender in Islam,* that produces this dual distortion of the harem in dominant patriarchal and oppositional feminist discourses (1992, 151). Before examining Ahmed's multiple harems in *A Border Passage,* therefore, we must assess Western ethnocentric perceptions of the harem against the root meaning of the term. This clarity regarding its etymological and historical roots will form the basis for evaluating Ahmed's radical displacement of the harem into the Western context.

THE ETYMOLOGICAL AND HISTORICAL ROOTS OF THE HAREM

The phallocentric Western fantasy of the harem remains, distressingly, all too familiar. Already, I wager, for most readers the word evokes, to follow Alain Grosrichard's seminal analysis in *The Sultan's Court: European Fantasies of the East,* "that walled space, forbidden to the gaze, saturated by sex and structured by it—the seraglio" (1998, 119). In the classic Ottoman context Grosrichard references, however, "the term 'harem' did not connote a space defined exclusively by sexuality" (Peirce 1993, 3). To draw further on Leslie Peirce's revisionist history of "the imperial harem," the word *harem*—"derived from the Arabic root *h-r-m*"—fundamentally signifies "to be forbidden or unlawful, and to declare sacred, inviolable, or taboo" (3, 4). Thus, a "harem is by definition a sanctuary or a sacred precinct" (4): the holy cities of Mecca and Medina are considered *haram,* as were the precincts of the Ottoman sultan. As N. M. Penzer emphasizes in his earlier study *The Harem,* "In its secular application the word [harem] was used in reference to that portion of a Muslim house occupied by the women, because it was their *haram,* or sanctuary" (1937, 16). Indeed, the Italianate term *seraglio* that came to be applied to this space, whose Western etymology suggests a "cage" or being "shut up," erroneously attaches the connotation of imprisonment to the Arabic roots of *haram.*

To establish the women's quarters of a household as *haram,* then, connotes neither male sexual mastery nor female imprisonment, as in the Western fantasy, but defines safeguards for women's space that restrict the movement of men into, as well as women out of, that space. Indeed, as western European women began to enter the space of the harem as writers from the early eighteenth century onward, they emphasized their appreciation of the women's space the harem enabled against their own experience in gender-integrated societies, which involved the complete absence of a space not contingent on the male gaze.[8] It is exactly this privileging of women's space in a gender-integrated society, even when it may be more dependent on patriarchal structures than the gender-segregated spaces of the Islamic world, that Ahmed asks her colleagues in women's studies to reconsider in "Western Ethnocentrism and Perceptions of the Harem." As she stresses, although "the harem can be defined as a system that permits males sexual access to more than one female . . . it can also be defined, and with as much accuracy, as a system whereby the female relatives of a man—wives, sisters, mother, aunts, daughters—share much of their time and their living space, and further, which enables women to have frequent and easy access to other women in their community, vertically, across class lines, as well as horizontally" (1982, 524). Particularly in the context of emerging women's studies in the United States, which in its "radical" strains stressed separatist communities of women apart from the male-dominated culture, Ahmed's emphasis on the harem as perhaps the prototypical women's community foregrounds the persistent blind spots and contradictions of contemporary feminist orientalism (Douglas 1990).

THE DOMESTIC "HAREM" IN *A BORDER PASSAGE*

Importantly, the nineteenth- and early-twentieth-century upper-class Egyptian harems Ahmed discusses were *domestic* harems, as distinct from the imperial or "sultan's" harem, incorrectly labeled a "seraglio" in Western discourse. As Margot Badran indicates in her introduction to *Harem Years: The Memoirs of an Egyptian Feminist* (the autobiography of the pioneering Egyptian *nisa'iyah* Huda Shaarawi [1879–1947]), "the word *harem,* which to Western eyes usually conjures up a host of exotic images, was simply the portion of the house where women and children conducted their daily lives." As Badran continues, the "harem also signified a man's wife or wives, and it connoted

8. Billie Melman (1992) documents this gendered perspective.

respect" (Shaarawi 1986, 7).[9] Notably, Shaarawi, the founding president of the Egyptian Feminist Union (1923), occupies a central place in Ahmed's first chapter, "Harem" (1999a, 93–134), not only because Shaarawi's upbringing in a traditional harem reflects the lives of Ahmed's mother's generation but also because her challenge to the confining cultural norms of childhood marriages, cloistering, and complete veiling—all of which Shaarawi stressed are not inherently Islamic—launched the autochthonous feminist movement that informed Ahmed's generation. This chapter thus weaves together Shaarawi's famous memoir with the unrecorded life of Ahmed's mother as imagined by her feminist daughter.

As Ahmed realizes, "I know my father's date of birth, November 13, 1889, but not my mother's" (93). This effacement of her maternal history impels Ahmed to explore the places, rather than the dates, that shaped her mother's life: "Benisweif . . . her grandfather's estate," "Cairo, in the house that I knew," and "her father's estate in al-Fayyum, the rich, fertile oasis a hundred miles or so southwest of Cairo" (93). Though she came of age in an era when "change for women was well under way in Egypt" under the aegis of anticolonial nationalism (93–94), Ahmed's mother, from the landed feudal class, remained bound by the traditions of the harem. Given the contradictions of the traditional harem, which simultaneously presented an empowering woman's space and a space of effacement for women, Ahmed as a postcolonial feminist must grapple with the retrospective assumption that "the ethos of the world whose attitudes survived into my own childhood"—a world premised on the institutions of slavery and concubinage—"must have been an ethos in which women were regarded as inferior creatures, essentially sex objects and breeders, to be bought and disposed of for a man's pleasure" (100). Such views have been reiterated for centuries as part of the Western ethnocentric view of the harem; Ahmed also suggests such prejudices may have dominated masculine views in Egypt during her mother's era. However, she realizes while recovering her mother's history that her "memories do not fit with such a picture" (100). In fact, from her perspective, the inviolable space of the traditional domestic

9. See also Badran's 1995 study, where she clarifies the use of *nisa'iyah* as "feminist" (19–21, 91). Nawar Al-Hassan Golley (2003, 35–52) resites the 1986 edition of *Harem Years,* edited by Margot Badran, vis-à-vis the Arabic manuscript.

harem—into which no adult male outside the natal family could enter and in which even the master of the family (her grandfather) had to accede to the nonrelated women who might be visiting his female relatives (107)—represented not simply a sanctuary for the women of her extended family apart from the dominant patriarchal society. Instead, it constituted an active space of consultation, even theorizing, for these women whose responsibilities encompassed the upbringing of children and the upkeep of households that sustained numerous servants and other domestic workers.

This gendered distribution of space leads Ahmed to propose that, "living differently and separately and coming together only momentarily, the two sexes inhabited different if sometimes overlapping cultures, a men's and a women's culture, each sex seeing and understanding and representing the world to itself quite differently" (100–101). In "Western Ethnocentrism and Perceptions of the Harem," Ahmed uses the analogous situation in late-twentieth-century Saudi Arabia to argue that such harems, in which women's space is inviolable (whereas the public sphere of men, requiring the presence of women if only as domestic workers, is not), might offer a prototype for the "radical" separatists of the 1960s and 1970s women's movement in the United States. As she declares, "To believe that segregated societies are by definition more oppressive to women, or that women secluded from the company of men are women deprived, is only to allow ourselves to be servilely obedient to the constructs of men" (1982, 531).

Still, as she closes her first chapter in *A Border Passage,* Ahmed acknowledges the patriarchal boundaries that ultimately defined women's spaces in her mother's era, which are presented most tragically in the suicide of her aunt Aida, who was persistently denied the divorce she sought by her husband, her father, and perhaps even her mother. Although, as Ahmed stresses, her aunt had every right to this divorce under Islamic law, the customs of her patriarchal era nonetheless restricted her to a situation so intolerable that she sought release by jumping out of a fifth-story window (1999a, 133).

Ahmed's recollection of the traditional domestic harems of her childhood therefore seeks to mitigate the effacement of women's histories in the larger patriarchal culture; however, this depiction does not lead to the rejection of Islam as inherently patriarchal, as feminist orientalism assumes. Rather, Ahmed adduces her personal experience to support the thesis, previously developed in *Women and Gender in Islam,* that "there are two quite different Islams, an Islam that is in some sense a women's Islam and an official, textual Islam, a 'men's' Islam" (1992, 123). Her warning to Westerners pursuing "gender studies" of the latter paradigm, which is incorrectly taken to be representative of Islam as a whole, is to interrogate the women's spaces—both literal and literary—that challenge this hegemonic assertion of an ultimately masculinist discourse (129).

"THE HAREM PERFECTED" IN GIRTON COLLEGE, CAMBRIDGE

As a border crosser, Ahmed similarly complicates those binary oppositions constituting patriarchal and feminist orientalism in the second of two chapters highlighting the harem, the first of which focused on the domestic harem of her childhood. Provocatively titled "The Harem Perfected" (1992, 179–94), this chapter begins, "I loved Girton from the moment of my arrival on a day in early October as dusk was falling" (179), Girton being the women's college in Cambridge, England, that Ahmed entered in the late 1950s at the age of eighteen. During the same decade, British and Israeli war planes bombarded Egypt in response to Nasser's nationalization of the Suez Canal, a bombardment Ahmed experienced in "the basement of Zatoun," her paternal grandfather's feudal estate (169). As an "English Schooler" (170)—her upper-class status enabled her to be educated in the British missionary system (along with Jean Said, the sister of Edward)[10]—Ahmed became conscious at this time of the split subjectivity characterizing the colonial subject who represents the traditional ruling class. Her nascent colonial and class consciousness accordingly introduces a note of dissonance into her otherwise enthusiastic description of Girton, as she realizes "the college cleaning women" are known as "gyps," which the *Oxford English Dictionary* traces to "Gypsy: 'a wandering race . . . believed to have come from Egypt'" (179). As an eighteen-year-old, however, Ahmed's colonial and class consciousness remains in the realm of cognitive dissonance (188–90), and her enthusiasm for England—an imaginary construct she had patched together out of books during her education as

10. Ahmed refers to Jean Said in "School Days" (1999a, 135–57). For her critique of Edward Said's *Orientalism* (1978), see 240–42.

an "English Schooler"—continues to grow as she embraces its contradictory cultural and physical landscape.

Evoking one of the English texts that had the greatest influence on her during her early schooling—Virginia Woolf's feminist classic *A Room of One's Own* (1929)—Ahmed stresses another startling similarity between her Egyptian and English experiences: "I found myself living, just as I had in Alexandria, in a place where women, presiding over the young in their charge, were the authorities. This is how it had been from when I first came into the world, and here it was, the same underlying reality, at Girton. Girton, that is to say, was a version of the community of women—the harem—as I had lived it every summer in Alexandria" (181). As she reiterates, "In some ways, indeed, Girton represented the harem perfected. Not the harem of Western male sexual fantasy or even the harem of Muslim men, fantasy or reality, but the harem as I had lived it, the harem of older women presiding over the young" (183; cf. 191). Woolf's book *A Room of One's Own,* whose embedded audience consists of a similar women's college, addresses the issue of gendered space at the close of its introductory chapter, focusing on "how unpleasant it is to be locked out; and . . . how it is worse perhaps to be locked in" (1977, 24). The sex that is "locked in," ironically, consists of men who have barred Woolf as a woman from their libraries, and hence their tradition. It is this sex that is nevertheless prosperous in the context of Woolf's imaginative essay, whereas the women of the college she addresses remain poor materially (they drink water, whereas the men drink wine) and intellectually (they lack the "tradition" Woolf deems necessary for literary production) (26).

Importantly, Woolf recognizes that the poverty of the English women's college system resulted from centuries of common law, whereby English women once married could not own or distribute property—a situation that did not change until the end of the nineteenth century, when the Married Women's Property Act was passed (107). The Islamic context presents a significant contrast, in that women have always been entitled to own and distribute property; they therefore used their personal wealth to endow institutions that specifically benefited women (many instances of which Shaarawi documents in her memoirs). Although Ahmed does not highlight this difference between English and Muslim women's access to material resources in *A Border Passage,* she does stress this contrast in her essay "Western Ethnocentrism and Perceptions of the Harem," with the early-eighteenth-century English traveler Lady Mary Wortley Montagu testifying to the relative liberty of Muslim women of the Ottoman Empire when compared with her countrywomen (1982, 525). Such a historical awareness, of course, completely counters the feminist orientalist assumption that Muslim women are invariably more oppressed than Western women.

Returning to Woolf, and particularly to Woolf's incisive questions about the drawbacks for women of their incorporation into schools and professions instituted by men, Ahmed confirms the value of the knowledge produced in the "harem" as a woman's space, whether in the domestic harems of Egypt or the de facto harems of England's women's colleges. As she further emphasizes, the fallacy that when women speak they produce only "idle gossip" was applied not just by Western men but also by Western women (many of whom called themselves feminists) when considering the harems of the Islamic world (1999a, 192). A case in point, Ahmed cites Harriet Martineau, a prominent nineteenth-century English woman writer, whose visit to the harems of Egypt produced a prototypically feminist orientalist response, focusing on "how ignorant these Muslim women were and how worthless and mindless their harem talk" (193). Yet, as Ahmed points out, "Martineau spoke no Arabic. And the harem women, naturally, spoke no English" (193). Martineau relied, therefore, on her orientalist prejudices in representing these women, and thus was "just one of a steady stream of Europeans who looked down on and thought of Muslim harem women as mindless" (193). Ahmed characteristically refuses to except herself from this critique of feminist orientalism and of traditional patriarchy, as she recalls she "too internalized the low regard in which Westerners and also traditional men of the local culture at large held women and the activities of women" (193). Ahmed accordingly closes her chapter "The Harem Perfected" with this assessment: "The only escape from this [the life of her mother in the traditional domestic harem], the only way out, I must have concluded at some level, would be for me to grow up to become either a man or a Westerner" (194). With this self-reflexive conclusion, she links Woolf's materialist approach with her own emerging double consciousness as a postcolonial subject to establish the basis for an Islamic feminism that provocatively and productively engages women's studies in the West.

WOMEN'S STUDIES "FROM ABU DHABI TO AMERICA"

Ahmed's final chapter continues to explore this expanded sense of the harem by tracing a trajectory from the Islamic world, though from a locale that situates her as a "foreign Arab" (273), to the United States. Specifically, after receiving her doctorate from Cambridge University, where she wrote a dissertation on the British orientalist Edward Lane, Ahmed accepted a post in Abu Dhabi, the modernizing hub of the newly oil-rich emirates in the Persian Gulf (Ahmed 1978). Here she found herself on a committee of other "non-local Arabs" (271)—all men—crafting recommendations for the emirates' newly established school system. As a woman in a highly gender-segregated society, Ahmed was assigned the task of surveying the local notables' wives to get their assessment of this educational initiative. Her experience of confronting her own hidden prejudices about traditional women in a gender-segregated society consequently leads her to an understanding, if not an endorsement, of western European women traveling to the similarly dissonant cultural space of Egypt in the nineteenth century (287). For instance, Ahmed on first glance dismisses women who wear the full veil of the region as unimportant, and she initially assumes these women will spout male-supremacist doctrines (274). What Ahmed learns, however, is that the traditional Bedu culture produced strong, determined, intelligent women who "were firm and passionate about the importance of education for women" (275). Indeed, their responses to her survey indicate these women believed all professions should be open to their daughters, particularly the "hard" sciences—a tendency confirmed elsewhere in the Islamic world, which produces significantly more women architects, doctors, and engineers than does the United States, where girls are still discouraged from the sciences. Moreover, these women of the United Arab Emirates evoked Islamic law to support a woman's "right . . . not to be married without her consent and the right to an education" (275). Furthermore, the men of this traditional society were fully behind the women's aspirations to be educated in a wide range of professions. Shockingly for Ahmed, it was the modernizing "foreign Arab" men who attempted to block the development of the equitable educational system the women and men of the emirates desired. Ahmed's access to the harem, where she was able to inform influential local women of these men's prejudices, thus functioned to undermine the imposition of modernity's more thorough forms of male supremacy.[11] As Ahmed recognizes, the man who hired her, a native to the region, placed her on this committee precisely because he recognized the power of the harem to pressure for progressive change in his community.

The final women's space that Ahmed occupies in *A Border Passage* involves "the transition to America and to women's studies," which she frames with the comment, "It was no easy transition" (291). In fact, it was in Abu Dhabi as she confronted the prejudices of modernizing men and observed the possibilities and restrictions for women in traditional Arab and Islamic communities that Ahmed began to have her "consciousness raised as a feminist" (288). During her summer vacation in England before returning to the United Arab Emirates, Ahmed immersed herself in works by feminist writers such as Kate Millet (1969), Elaine Showalter (1977), Patricia Spacks (1975), Adrienne Rich (1979), and Mary Daly (1973), among others (288). In the American context, first-wave feminism focused on the struggle for the vote during the late nineteenth and early twentieth centuries; second-wave feminism emerged in the 1960s as women in the civil rights movement seeking justice for U.S. racial minorities realized their struggles for gender justice were deemed irrelevant to the larger cause; and third-wave feminism resulted when U.S. minority women, and other "women of color," protested the intransigent racism in the mainstream Anglo-American feminist movement.[12] Ahmed's initial immersion in feminist writings thus situated her at the cusp of second-wave feminism, with the influences she cites all white, middle-class American women of Christian and Jewish descent. These writers focus primarily on literary feminism, with the controversial theologian Mary Daly extending her reach to cultural criticism more broadly. Hence, as with her initial conception of "England," Ahmed's first encounter with

11. For modernity's male supremacy as it emerged in a Western context, see Pateman 1988.

12. On the feminist critics Ahmed cites in the context of this extended history, see Robbins 2000. Rich and Daly, who identify as lesbians, participated in the critique of the heterosexism of second-wave feminism. The designation of three "waves" for American feminism is, of course, diagnostic only. It does not foreclose the complexities of this movement at any given moment.

"women's studies" was entirely textual. Her eventual transatlantic journey, which brought her to the University of Massachusetts in 1980, nevertheless quickly revealed the limits of the second-wave feminists who had facilitated her entry into this field.

Unlike the implicit cognitive dissonance Ahmed experienced when she encountered structural racism at Cambridge, her immersion into women's studies while a part-time lecturer at the University of Massachusetts propelled her explicit challenge to the contradictions of mainstream American feminism in the groundbreaking essay "Western Ethnocentrism and Perceptions of the Harem."[13] The gist of this essay, which I have already referenced, results from Ahmed's experiential and intellectual encounter with emergent women's studies: "Although Western feminists have succeeded in rejecting their culture's myths about [Western] women and their innate inferiority and irrationality, they continue to subscribe to and perpetuate those myths about Muslims, including Muslim women, and about harems, as well as to assume superiority towards women within them" (1982, 526).

During this time, Ahmed became aware of the burgeoning critique from feminists of color who were concurrently unmasking white privilege in the mainstream movement. An intervention paralleling her own, she discovered, had been voiced by Audre Lorde in her 1976 address to a largely white feminist conference, subsequently published as "An Open Letter to Mary Daly" (1984a).[14] Like other feminists from the Arab world, Ahmed shifted her identification from the false universal of "whiteness" to the politicized model of "woman of color" upon confronting the deeply ingrained anti-Arab and anti-Muslim attitudes of mainstream American feminists.[15] Yet in linking Egyptian feminists such as Huda Shaarawi, English feminists such as Virginia

13. Ahmed subsequently became a professor of women's studies and Near Eastern studies at the University of Massachusetts in Amherst, where she served as director of the Near Eastern Studies program from 1991 to 1992 and as director of the Women's Studies Program from 1992 to 1995. She moved to the Harvard Divinity School in 1999 as the first professor of women's studies in religion and was named Victor S. Thomas Professor of Divinity in 2003.

14. Similar interventions from this decade include Hull and Bell-Scott 1982; Moraga and Anzaldúa 1981; and Spivak 1987.

15. This response is echoed in Joanna Kadi's 1994 study, especially Lisa Suhair Majaj's chapter, "Boundaries: Arab/American" (65–86). For a related collection, see Darraj 2004.

Woolf, "white" American feminists from Kate Millet to Mary Daly, and U.S. "women of color" feminists such as Audre Lorde, Ahmed not only challenges the orientalism that mars mainstream Western liberal feminism. Rather, she elaborates, with other Islamic feminists, the counterparadigm of "the western women's harem" to enable a truly radical transcultural feminism (Mernissi 2001, 208–20).

2

Dismembering the Gaze

Speleology and Vivisection in Assia Djebar's *L'amour, la fantasia*

KARINA EILERAAS

> Images of Algerian women are not displayed in homes, they are kept to themselves. We cannot be feminist except by circulating things among ourselves.
>
> —Assia Djebar, lecture at UCLA, May 2001

> The fourth language, for all women, is that of the body: the body which male neighbours' and cousins' eyes require to be deaf and blind, since they cannot completely incarcerate it; the body which, in fits of hope and despair, rebels, and unable to read or write, seeks some unknown shore as destination for its message of love. . . . Every language is a dark depository for piled-up corpses.
>
> —Assia Djebar, *Fantasia: An Algerian Cavalcade*

BURNING IN

Assia Djebar, one of North Africa's most esteemed writers, has spent more than twenty years composing a projected quartet of works that she describes as an attempt, trace, or aspect of autobiography ("apparence d'autobiographie"). Thus far, Djebar's gesture at autobiographical expression has lasted roughly twenty years and has incorporated extensive revision. Her bursts of literary production have been punctuated with gaps, most notably when Djebar returns to her Algerian homeland in times of political crisis. "J'ai eu plusieurs parentheses" (I've had several parentheses), explained Djebar in a lecture at UCLA in 2001. These "parentheses," including her relative absence from the literary scene in the 1970s, attest to Djebar's commitment to the indivisibility of personal, political, and artistic life. I will focus here on Djebar's *L'amour, la fantasia,* the first and most celebrated volume of her autobiographical quartet (1985), translated into English and published in 1993 as *Fantasia: An Algerian Cavalcade.* Highlighting both the material and epistemic violence of colonization, *Fantasia* frames the colonial gaze as a catalyst for traumatized yet creative visions of identity.

Fantasia highlights the potency of images that have been handed down throughout history, especially orientalist and nationalist representations of women. Yet Djebar is not content to disavow colonial fantasies of sexual and racial otherness. Instead, she orchestrates an autobiographical economy that challenges the ideals of singularity and equivalence as necessary foundations for identity. If the orientalist imagination is, in Edward Said's words, "based exclusively upon a sovereign Western consciousness" (1978, 8), then Djebar problematizes this sovereign subject, especially its primacy within autobiographical projects. By so doing, she seeks not to return the colonial gaze but to dismember[1] its very conditions of possibility.

In order to revision Algerian experiences of colonization, domesticity, and revolution, *Fantasia* engages in a painful odyssey of re-membering, or "a putting together of the dismembered past to make sense of the trauma of the present" (Bhabha 1986, xxiii). Djebar pays particular attention to the images of women that circulate within orientalist discourse. Her efforts to radically reconfigure images of Algerian women compel her to "go under" in a Nietzschean sense in order to excavate the minor or unseen details of national memory, historiography, and colonized subjectivity.

Infused with this spirit of genealogical inquiry, *Fantasia* is haunted nonetheless by a profound suspicion of origins. The narrator of *Fantasia* refers to herself by alternating between the first and third persons and continuously reflects on the impossibility of claiming an authentic or stable identity within the context of colonization. In this sense, Djebar's project "will never confuse itself with a quest for 'origins.' On the contrary, it will cultivate the details and

1. With this term I mean to evoke a sense of both physical or bodily tearing apart (dismemberment) and a critical engagement at the level of representation that acts as an interruption, interference, or "disservice" to national memory or "official" history or both.

accidents that accompany every beginning. Where the self fabricates a coherent identity, the genealogist sets out to study numberless beginnings. To follow the complex course of descent is to discover that truth or being does not lie at the root of what we know and what we are" (Foucault 1984, 80–81). Ultimately, *Fantasia* stages an "unfounding" of nationalist and orientalist historiography. Positioning herself as a "warrior of knowledge," Djebar confronts a long history of imagery in order to express the complex interface between national political identity and female sexuality.

As Djebar traces the descent of colonial and nationalist representations, her genealogical project constantly spills over, or contaminates, the topos of the body. Like Foucault, Djebar regards bodies as the primary sites of inscription for discourses that seek to establish truth and regulation. Throughout her work, the wounding or empowering potentials of representation linger in bodily surfaces, contours, and cavities. Djebar probes the female body as a terrain especially ravaged by competing projects of representation and descent. Not a fully colonized territory, however, the female body in *Fantasia* also houses the subversive potentials of the voice and, in particular, the cry.

Part 1 of *Fantasia* examines the work of French writers and artists who were employed by the state to draft impressionistic accounts of the French conquest of Algeria. Because they so often present Algerian women as exotic objects for colonial contemplation, these images have fracturing implications for female subjectivity and embodiment. In response to colonial images of Algerian women, Djebar tries to imagine the female body apart from the oriental look.

Djebar also challenges the "specular economy" that underlies masculinist nationalist portrayals of women.[2] Privileging masculinity as a standard or universal trait, this economy assigns greatest value to ideals of correspondence, similitude, and self-reference. Women serve as a medium of exchange within the specular economy, wherein what remains most forbidden to and impossible for women is to speak about sexual difference and to "express something of [their] own sexual pleasure" (Irigaray 1985b, 157). As Luce Irigaray writes,

2. A "specular economy" is a system of exchange and valuation theorized by Luce Irigaray (1985a) wherein masculinity is presumed standard and femininity can be understood only in terms of sameness, difference, or deviation.

"The feminine cannot signify itself in any proper meaning, proper name, or concept, not even that of woman. . . . 'She' must only be the shutter set up to allow the eye to frame its view; the path, the *mirror,* which leads back, by a process of repetition, to the recognition of (his) origin for the 'subject'" (1985b, 156 [emphasis in original]; see also 1985a, 239–40).

Notably, a symbolic economy of this sort held sway during the Algerian revolution, when women's bodies became a battleground for French colonial and Algerian nationalist male aggression. Partly because of the intermittent campaigns of rape and forced veiling or unveiling that targeted Algerian women throughout the revolution, those women who wanted to assume substantive roles to support nationalist military objectives were prevented from doing so on the grounds of their intractable "difference." Denied entry to the nationalist movement often had fracturing effects for Algerian women who wanted to mobilize as both women and nationalists. Their experiences testify to the real political effects of an economy prefaced on sameness or indifference to sexual difference.

Djebar's effort to conceive of an alternative symbolic economy that questions the ideals of similitude, correspondence, and reflection constitutes a significant feminist intervention into philosophy, colonial politics, national history, and autobiography. Insisting on the need to create a new language to express female desire, Djebar's work uniquely integrates the gaze (vision), the cry (voice), and the hand (touch). By launching a series of missions to unexplored depths and hidden interiors throughout *Fantasia,* Djebar engages in a novel project of revisioning that can be read as both an effort to see the revolution from a fresh perspective and a feminist act of survival. Djebar hopes to reclaim vision by "seeing difference differently," focusing not on particular images of women but on the ways of seeing that produce those images.[3] Through this project of revisioning, *Fantasia* identifies the female body, desire, and identity as the stakes not only of foundational projects to establish truth and history but also of destructively creative acts of "unfounding" *(effondement/effondrement)* and misrecognition.[4] By so doing, the novel

3. I borrow this notion of revisioning from Adrienne Rich, as discussed by Teresa de Lauretis (1997, 34).

4. By "unfounding" *(effondement),* I refer to the joyfully destructive and creative process

understands postcolonial feminist subjectivity as the site of ambivalent negotiations between image and identity.

In her travels through "memory's subterranean store-house," Djebar foregrounds the intersections between sexuality and war and defaces the borders of the personal and political (1993, 109). As a result, her voyage into the female body is best understood as a revolutionary attempt to express female sexuality and desire within a philosophical and linguistic tradition in which it has forcibly remained underground, unthinkable, and inarticulable. For Djebar, this revolution of the female body is tantamount to the Algerian revolution. Both are profoundly political, personal, and sexualized efforts of decolonization.

The representative economy set in motion throughout *Fantasia* aims to distort, to preclude simple reflection, and *to burn*. Djebar's radical vision emerges from a dichotomy of location that complicates her relationship to language, culture, and politics. By highlighting the kaleidoscopic, traumatized, and ultimately untenable eye/I that inhabits the interstices between warring nations, cultures, languages, and identities, Djebar attempts to map out the cultural and colonial space of the Maghreb and to imagine the specificity of women's positions therein.

Fantasia proposes a subaltern feminist symbolic economy—one in which bodies, voices, and gazes circulate on the basis of fragmentation and misrecognition rather than equivalence, substitution, reflection, or identification. Yet the physicality, musicality, and split subjectivity expressed in Djebar's work cannot be read in purely aesthetic terms; they also need to be understood in the context of postcolonial feminist praxis. To counter years of silence and erasure, Djebar constructs a national past that includes Algerian women's voices as well as their sexual experiences of violation and desire.

---

of challenging the metaphysical foundations of knowledge, truth, and identity; Nietzschean philosophy best exemplifies this art. But I also want to evoke the American legal definition of "unfounding," which refers to the ways in which law enforcement officials routinely discredit or delegitimate women's charges of rape or sexual assault (Catharine MacKinnon, "Sex Equality" [2001], unpublished manuscript). I think this second legal meaning foregrounds a central issue with which this chapter will be concerned, namely, the devaluation and silencing of female voice, cry, and *jouissance* within the specular economy. My chapter will argue that both of these senses of "unfounding" spur Djebar's project to create a feminist symbolic economy in *L'amour, la fantasia*.

GOING UNDER: KNOWLEDGE AND CAVE EXPLORATION

Djebar evaluates Algerian women's oppression from the space of intersection between French colonization and Algerian nationalism. She especially hopes to show how the founding images of both discourses violently brand women's bodies with inflexible truths that limit their possibilities for identification and political mobilization. Highlighting complex negotiations between image and identity, Djebar confronts the "I" as a topos of division, aphasia, aporia, and mutilation.

Remarkably evident in *Fantasia* is a series of difficult choices that Djebar has made in the conception of her work. Foremost among them is Djebar's decision to write in an autobiographical mode, since autobiography is often associated with Western narrative tradition. What does it mean for a postcolonial woman to write autobiography, when that genre is arguably bound up with colonial culture? Djebar engages this question by repeatedly decentering the Cartesian or sovereign subject presumed to be at the heart of autobiographical projects. *Fantasia* strategically positions and lives the "I" in the interstices between first and third persons, subtly interweaving the voices of self and other.

As Gayatri Chakravorty Spivak notes, *Isma*, the name of one of *Fantasia*'s primary narrators, is the Arabic word for "she is called _____" (akin to the French "elle s'appelle _____") (1996, 187). By figuring this improper, unnamed woman as the central voice in her text, Djebar challenges both the stability of identity and the proper name—two of the foundations of traditional Western autobiography. By so doing, she implicitly rejects the "autobiographical pact" or contract of equivalence between self and narrator that has been identified as a hallmark of autobiography (Lejeune 1989).

Yet Djebar also refuses to express herself "appropriately" vis-à-vis traditional Algerian oral culture, that is, through orality alone. By this refusal, she violates a national law of genre that would seem to govern her decolonizing project and launches her narrative into the realm of the impure, improper, and inauthentic. Given the primacy of oral culture and collective expression within traditional Algerian society, Djebar's decision to write an autobiographical text reminds readers of the contingency of her project and the radicalness of her attempt to promote cross-cultural *chocs*, or collisions.

Djebar also chooses to write predominantly in French rather than in Arabic. This choice has debilitating implications for her articulation of the "I" as a coherent identity in *Fantasia*. Djebar's choice of language plunges her text into a dizzying abyss in which the issues of culture, authenticity, and complicity assume agonizing proportions. She inserts fragments of Arabic throughout her text, noting that French alone is insufficient: it often lacks the words, the musicality, and the gestures to accompany her story. By navigating between the languages of oppressor and oppressed, *Fantasia* persistently undermines the presumed singularity of cultural identity, that is, "Frenchness" or "Algerianness."

Language is an especially fraught issue for Djebar: in adolescence, her father transferred her from a traditional Quranic school to a French school in Algeria. Later, during the Algerian revolution, Arabic was declared the official language of the nascent Algerian nation. In response to competing discourses regarding the superiority of the French or Arabic tongue, Djebar centers language not only as a crucial component of her identity but also as an intractable problem that circumscribes the very project of subaltern autobiography. Throughout her work, Djebar strategically deploys French as a playful "bi-langue" in order to contaminate the French language, rendering the "true French" strangers in their own tongue.[5]

In response to the anticolonial nationalist symbolism that figured women as either icons of cultural purity or objects of male sexual aggression and territorialization, Djebar's autobiography restores the complexities of female embodiment to national memory. Ultimately, *Fantasia* foregrounds the problem of representation not only to challenge specular models of identity and autobiography but also—and more crucially—to commemorate the untenable subject positions of Algerian women within the national imaginary.

Djebar's novel asks what it means to represent history: Who decides what counts as historical truth? Who counts as an authentic knower of Algerian society? *Fantasia* is an attempt to do battle with history, especially with the ways of seeing that severely limited the options available to women both during and after colonization and revolution. I want to take seriously the constitutive

5. In addition to Abdelkebir Khatibi's formulations of the "bi-lingue" in various theoretical works such as *Maghreb pluriel* (1983b), see his novel *Amour bilingue* (1983a).

power of the images that Djebar attempts to negotiate and to explore the alternative lines of vision and identification that she enacts in *Fantasia.*

WRITING THE VEIL: PERSONAL UNFOUNDING

As she ventures into the recesses of subjectivity, Djebar disinters the masculinist, orientalist imagery that informs her sense of self. By so doing, she realizes that she is doubly penetrated by the eyes of the French colonizer and her Algerian brother.[6] Djebar experiences her body as if it is physically ensnared; she is at pains to imagine an "I" unmarked by the tattoo of this double gaze.

While spending a childhood summer with three cloistered sisters in a tiny Sahel village, Djebar and her friends excavate some disturbing images from the girls' brother's bookcase. Toward the rear of the dusty shelves, they discover an album of erotic photography and an envelope stuffed with postcards depicting "bare-breasted Ouled-Nail girls, loaded with jewels" (1993, 11). After making this discovery, Djebar and the other girls are "suddenly aware of his uncomfortable presence in those dim siesta hours" (11). They comprehend the girls' Algerian brother as a voyeur who has silently observed their everyday movements from the shadowy recesses of the harem. No longer a stern, paternalistic figure, the brother embodies instead a patriarchal voyeur who is furtively nourished by French orientalist images of Algerian dancers and prostitutes. With this realization, the girls feel violated and sad. But they also feel that their newfound knowledge has somehow catapulted them to the edge of transgression. They perceive themselves as more strategically positioned vis-à-vis their oppressive brother: "We feel we have trespassed into some forbidden territory; we feel we have aged" (11).

Djebar suggests that although encounters with the male voyeuristic gaze are stultifying, they might also provide a starting point for the feminist critique of representation and of women's double colonization by foreign occupiers and nationalist "brothers." Throughout *Fantasia,* Djebar strives to portray Algerian women not as immobile victims trapped in the silent world of the

6. Note that this double penetration is precisely the "double-gaze" that Malek Alloula (1986) does not fully acknowledge or theorize.

harem but as instigators of "unprecedented women's battles" that yield new forms of knowledge and identity (13).

One such battle is a love-letter campaign instigated by the narrator's three cloistered girlfriends. Day after day, the girls write florid love letters to pen pals in distant lands. Unbeknownst to their parents, they daily escape the confines of the harem to post their letters in a mailbox. Covertly dispatched to the outside world, their letters openly circulate before countless male eyes. These girls' "clandestine operation" informs Djebar's imaginary no less profoundly than their brother's pornographic photography. As opposing emblems of oppression and resistance, these contradictory images spark a representational crisis or unfounding of sorts: "Everything is a jumble in my memories: the forbidden pictures in the bookcase and the mysterious letters that arrived by the dozen. In the periods when sleep crept over me I imagined written words whirling furtively around, about to entwine invisible snares around our adolescent bodies, lying side by side across the antique family bed" (13).

Within the love-letter operation, Djebar's narrator figures her girlfriends as political agents or emissaries and recasts the male gaze as an impotent or thwarted attempt at voyeurism. She imagines the postman's feverish wonder and jealousy as he delivers an endless flurry of love letters to the girls—replies from their foreign pen pals. Of the postman, Djebar muses that "the continual arrival of these letters, from every corner of the world, must have weighed upon his mind, feeding some secret frustration!" (12).

Djebar marvels at the audacity of the clandestine love-letter operation. Pen in hand, the cloistered girls commit their first offense, or act of aggression, within Algerian society. By launching their letters beyond the closed doors and blackened windows of the harem to the outside world, they stage illicit passages between private and public spaces. At the same time, their love-letter campaign is an explicit attempt to forsake the native custom of arranged marriage in favor of romance and love-based courtship. Reading their love letters as multilayered texts of resistance, Djebar views the cloistered girls as trespassers, agitators, and cultural mediators par excellence. Her reading provocatively recasts the trope of the foreign correspondent who reports on-site from a war zone.

By reading female engagements with words and images as potentially destabilizing, Djebar dramatically reimagines the space of the oriental postcard as envisioned by Malek Alloula in *The Colonial Harem* (1986). Not content to represent Algerian women as passive victims of the male gaze, Djebar highlights the ambivalence of colonial imagery by recording a series of "imperceptible revolutions" authored by women (1993, 36). Ultimately, she transforms the colonial postcard into an instrument of feminist creativity and resistance.

Fantasia sets in motion a new currency of images—a circulation of eyes, words, and cries with endless potential for travel and resistance. Although Djebar cites oppressive imagery in her work, she continually traces lines of flight from these images—moments at which female voices and visions embrace heterogeneity and difference. These moments erupt in creative symphonies of misrecognition, which work the female body into a countermemory of national, international, and sexual politics.

In her study of imperceptible movement or revolution, Djebar pays particular attention to women's exchange of domestic miniatures, such as jam dishes and children's spoons. *Fantasia* takes an "inventory of tiny objects passed on thus, from febrile hand to fugitive hand" (177). By so doing, the novel traces women's history to an economy of tiny, loving objects transmitted across generations. Djebar's invocation of tiny objects recalls the "daydream of the miniature," which is to reveal a secret history or unexplored interior outside the given field of perception (see Stewart 1984, 54). Within the illusory world of representation, the miniature fosters dialogue between inside and outside, visible and unknown. Likewise, in the interstices between French and Arabic words, bodies, and gestures, Djebar fashions a tongue that restores the "interior" world of female desire to the palimpsest of national political memory.

Djebar locates Algerian women at the sullied intersection of colonialist and nationalist oppression, subject to a "double gaze." This position has splintering effects for female subjectivity and citizenship. As Djebar notes, the image of the warrior woman—war-torn at the crossroads—"prefigures many a future Muslim *mater dolorosa*" (1993, 19). Her words preface political history: during the Algerian revolution, female nationalists were raped by both French and Algerian men. In addition, their revolutionary roles consisted primarily of domestic tasks such as cooking, sewing, nursing, and cleaning. After the revolution, Algeria's new leaders quashed feminist rallies and sent women back to the harem. As Djebar acknowledges, feminist liberation is not easily located within this history. Yet neither is absolute oppression; instead, she highlights nuanced performances of creative misrecognition and recuperation.

ENVISIONING THE FEMALE BODY: GENEALOGY AND VIVISECTION

In many respects, the body provides the ultimate limit, target, and end point of representation.[7] The female body, in particular, bears the marks of a history of intense struggle over its representation. With this thought in mind, I will view Djebar's mission into the depths and crevasses of her body as both a genealogy and a vivisection of female voice, sexuality, and desire.

As Foucault reminds us, the task of genealogy is "to expose a body totally imprinted by history and the process of history's destruction of the body" (1984, 82–83). Djebar's descent into the "dark continent" of the female body is similarly motivated by a desire to understand how female identity and sexuality have been stained, and often precluded, by a long history of nationalist and colonialist imagery (see Freud 1963–1964). Within the pages of *Fantasia,* Djebar enters her body as she would a cave and performs something akin to a feminist speleology or vivisection in order to burn her own images of female subjectivity and sexuality.

As Djebar recalls various moments of her childhood, she realizes that she has lived her body as a kind of snare. Her body emerges as the "dream's navel" that she cannot surpass, a knot of uninterpretability to which she must always return.[8] On one hand, because her "modernist" father sent her to a French school during adolescence, Djebar was able to escape Algerian practices that daily subjected female bodies to unique forms of spatial confinement, such as veiling and seclusion.[9] On the other hand, although her position as a cultural intermediary afforded Djebar an unusual degree of physical mobility, it also exposed her to conceptions of the female body as a vulnerable object to be protected within the private space of "domestic interiors, always interiors"

7. By this statement I mean the following: (1) that the body, as flesh and material, is the diametric opposite or "limit" of representation, but that, nonetheless, (2) the body, as the seat of subjectivity and identity, is always molded by discourse and (3) that representation's ability to impact or engrave the body is enforced by disciplinary regimes of power and regulations of space, which literally force the body into various states of conformity with the "law" of the Symbolic.

8. For a lucid formulation of Freud's concept of the dream's navel, see Sprinker 1980. Freud's own articulation can be found in the standard edition of his work.

9. Yet her guilt at escaping these cultural traditions also sparked a crisis of language and national allegiance.

(1993, 21). For example, Djebar spent her summers in a country house full of cloistered girls. Djebar's experiences of seclusion prompted her to imagine her body as a target for the male gaze, perpetually at risk of rape and violation.

Djebar's serial autobiography attests to the formative effects of these images for her subjectivity. *Fantasia* is littered with voiceless, wounded, or imprisoned bodies "bereft of voices": "To attempt an autobiography using French words alone is to lend oneself to the vivisector's scalpel, revealing what lies beneath the skin. Wounds are reopened, veins weep, one's own blood flows and that of others, which has never dried" (156).

Djebar's "attempt at autobiography" resembles a vivisection; its undertaking in the enemy tongue involves a careful probing of live tissue and membrane and enlists Djebar on a voyage to the deepest cavities of her body. Although she writes in French, Djebar has no choice but to confront the silenced cries and split affinities that inform her identity as an Algerian woman. Frozen cries immobilize her and leave indelible imprints on her body and psyche, as witnessed in *Fantasia.* Furthermore, the incisions of the writer's scalpel unite her body so intimately with the pain of other Algerian women that their blood streams in unison, intermingling in a copulative gesture of intersubjectivity.

GOING UNDER: THE WEDDING NIGHT

The most dramatic leg of Djebar's journey to the hidden depths of her body is prompted by a recollection of her wedding night, or "night of blood" (1992, 141). In the second volume of her autobiography, titled *Women of Algiers in Their Apartment,* Djebar contextualizes the ambivalence of this night by pointing out that a woman's "yes" is, if not unspeakable, irrelevant within Arabic society. During the wedding ceremony, an Algerian woman must affirm her vows ("Yes" or "I do") through a male intermediary who speaks on her behalf. If she fails to do so, the wedding officiator will attribute her hesitation to feminine modesty. In this case, a woman's silence or tears may be construed as legitimate expressions of acquiescence (145). Thus, a woman's formal verbal consent is meaningless; it is "deflowered, violated, before the *other* deflowering, the *other* violation intervenes" (145; emphasis mine). Against the backdrop of this cultural undermining of female consent, Djebar tries to imagine whether or how her body consented to "the other deflowering" that took place on her wedding night.

On the morning after an Arab bride's wedding night, she is expected to provide physical evidence of prior virginity. To fulfill this obligation, she must present a bloodstained sheet to her male relatives. The stained sheet is construed as proof of female virginity, evidence of the rupture of a previously intact hymen. Yet as Nawal el-Saadawi notes, obtaining a stained sheet often requires desperate measures. She points out that a bride's hymen "must be capable of bleeding profusely, of letting out red blood that can be seen as a visible stain on a white bed sheet" stolen from the wedding night (1980, 25). Furthermore, although the hymen often breaks during physical exertion unrelated to sex, this reality is not acknowledged within traditional Islamic practice. Instead, the soiled sheet as evidence of chastity reigns supreme as a cultural-religious symbol and nuptial imperative.[10] As a result, "no girl can be more unfortunate than she who is born with an elastic hymen . . . or whom nature has forgotten to provide a hymen, or whose hymen is so delicate that it is torn away by childhood exercise or accident" (25).

Framed by mandatory bloodstains, passive voice, and silent acquiescence, Djebar's first sexual experience is, above all, an attempt to navigate a complicated web of social and sexual "symbols" (1993, 106). Because it is defined according to masculinist cultural and religious objectives, sex enlists Djebar in a feminist vivisection of sorts. To sort out her feelings of sexual violation and pleasure, she mobilizes the creative powers of vision to decode the meanings of the female body within masculinist discourse. Ultimately, Djebar hopes to live the female body and voice as a means of sexual and social empowerment.

As she recalls her wedding night—performing this vivisection, traveling back in time through bodily memory—Djebar labors to find her own voice. She dissects every timbre of her cry during intercourse, a cry that reveals

10. Of course, this imperative often leads women to devise creative and unofficial "ways around" it. Also, "traditional" Islam, as Leila Ahmed (1989) points out, is by no means "inherently" sexist. Instead, Ahmed distinguishes tradition from phallocentrism by arguing that the Quran is actively *interpreted* in misogynist ways by a male elite.

the profoundest grief and the most intense liberation that her body has ever known. On one hand, Djebar's cry narrates a journey to unprecedented pain. For Djebar, sex is excruciating not only because of the blood that flows but also because of the unspoken "No!" that trembles on her lips. On the other hand, her cry also signifies the ache of silence—a silence that seems to drain all color from the scene as she recalls its intensity.

Because of its painful reverberations, Djebar partly understands her wedding night as an experience of rape; or, rather, she imagines a fine line between consensual sex and rape. What can consent mean when it emerges from a body mired in silence and seclusion, when it is uttered by a voice inessential to the formal exchange of wedding vows? How can a woman imagine the sound or value of her consent when that consent is socially constructed as irrelevant to the personal undertaking of marriage?

By weaving these questions into her narrative, Djebar implicitly situates sex on a continuum with wartime rape. As she notes elsewhere in *Fantasia,* the word *rape* was unspeakable during the Algerian revolution. Even if its euphemism, *damage,* was presented to a rape victim as a question or concern, this question was answered in silence—"swallowed" (202). Djebar's reflections on the meaning of consent shake the very foundations of her being and seem to put her in touch with a "universal truth" of female suffering. As she describes her wedding night, she adopts the interrogative form:

> The cry rises in the air; falling, at its nadir, in multi-layered sediment, lurks an unspoken "No!" Did I feel this refusal tremble on my lips? Travelling on the Metro during the next few days, I stare closely at all the women I see around me. I am devoured with curiosity as if I were some primitive creature: Why do they not say, why will not one of them say, why does each one hide this fact: love is the cry, the persistent pain, which feeds upon itself, while only a glimpse is vouchsafed of the horizon of happiness? (107)

Djebar experiences sexual initiation as an unfounding of both the Imaginary and the Symbolic orders. So acute is this trauma that on the day after her wedding night, she is unable to look in the mirror. Sex triggers a crisis of representation (or an undoing of the accomplishments of the Lacanian mirror stage) and a disorientation of the self characterized by autistic withdrawal and alienation. Although Djebar is shattered by this self-implosion, *Fantasia* effectively integrates traumatic rupture within its narrative of identity by moving beyond a facile understanding of sex as entailing women's absolute oppression or liberation. Instead Djebar asks, "How can this blood be transformed into a ray of hope?" (106). While formulating this question, Djebar begins to imagine feminist potentials for creative misrecognition.

Djebar powerfully transforms "blood to hope" by registering the ambivalence of her cry and the amplitude of its desire. Her cry induces vertigo: "a voice of infinite range in aerial flight, opening onto a vertiginous void and only gradually growing aware" (106). Most important, it propels her into a space without boundaries or physical restrictions. Sex allows Djebar to establish a new relationship with her body and gives her license to explore the invisible details of its pleasurable caverns. Resplendent with words for female desire and *jouissance* (sexual pleasure, orgasm; also connotes legal ownership and property rights), Djebar's cry enacts a new symbolic economy with which to represent the female body, sexuality, and identity. Ultimately, her cry gives birth: "The sharp cry of relief and sudden liberation, then abruptly checked. Long, infinite, first cry of the live body" (106).

As she writes about her ambivalent cry and rebirth, Djebar stages a painful undoing of the self. Yet she also reinvents her conditions of possibility as a subject. If her spelunking mission to the inner depths of the female body initially required a scalpel, she now wields forceps and, as obstetrician, delivers her own birth. After exploring the cave of her body by way of a grueling vivisection, Djebar manages to emerge alive. Yet the "I" of her identity is decentered, for her cry does not mark a moment of self-presence. Instead, it issues from "the brief absence of a woman and a little girl," or the transitional space of becoming (107). In this space that denies closure, autonomy, and specular reflection, Djebar confronts the untenability of the mirror image.

Djebar's story of her wedding night hovers between autobiography, genealogy, and obstetrics and gynecology. Throughout her narration, she employs the speculum or sistrum in order to trace her body's descent; to record its minute "details," such as the clitoris; and to articulate embodied identity within the parameters of a feminist symbolic economy. Misrecognizing the cry as a pure expression of pain, she takes it elsewhere. Djebar restages representation as an orchestral movement rich with expressions for female desire and *jouissance:* "The plaintive moan escapes, then the prolonged song, the drawn-out song of the rich female voice closes round the copulation, follows its tempo and its figures, is exhaled as oxygen, a tumescent twisted coil of *forte* notes hanging in the air" (109).

Djebar's expression of female *jouissance* discounts the Freudian model of female sexual development, whereby a young girl must renounce clitoral pleasure to achieve "normal" (that is, vaginocentric, heterosexual) femininity.[11] With this passage, Djebar fulfills her mission through the female body in order to create a representational economy that "sings and sizzles" female desire.[12]

By apprehending the tiny details of the female body and genitals—especially the clitoris—Djebar's sistrum reframes the feminine within contemporary fields of vision. Interestingly, the Arabic slang for *eye* doubles as a contemptuous word for the female genitals in Algeria. In a parallel and deliberate conflation of female sexuality and vision, Djebar's autobiographical work persistently refers to the female genitals as "the eye-that-is-sex." By so doing, it recalls the perilous links between sexual politics and visual culture.

As she traces the physicality of her cry on its virtual journey from genitals to eyes to larynx to lips, Djebar displaces the privileged gaze of the specular economy. At the same time, she gives to representation precisely what it has historically forbidden: the female voice, body, sexuality, and *jouissance.* With her cry, she exceeds the moment of radical unassimilability and representational break or omission and completes a journey through the live female body in order to "parler pres de, et si possible, TOUT CONTRE: premiere des solidarites a assumer pour les quelques femmes arabes qui obtiennent ou acquierent la liberte de mouvement du corps et de l'esprit" (to speak close to/near and, if possible, right up against: the first solidarity to be assumed by some Arab women who obtain or acquire freedom of movement for the body and spirit) (Zimra 1995, 162; translation mine).

Djebar locates creative potentials for liberation in the moment when the fiction of a unified "I" becomes unsustainable. In this sense, she understands

11. Freud lays out three possible avenues for the development of femininity: neurosis, the masculinity complex, or "normal" femininity (1963–1964, 126).

12. This phrase is a feminist appropriation of Nietzsche's gay science, a philosophy that "sings and sizzles" (1974).

her first sexual experience as a drama of political and sexual awakening as well as disorientation. She concludes the narration of her wedding night with a series of negative affirmations that induce a destructively creative "spiral of refusal": "There were no peeping women. . . . Normally the bride neither cries out nor weeps: she lies an open-eyed victim on the couch, and the closed thighs prevent any cry from escaping. There was no bloodstained sheet on display the following days" (1993, 108).

Significantly, Djebar's use of the sistrum has both feminist and anticolonial implications. With this instrument, Djebar analyzes the descent of intersectional experiences of oppression and takes her gaze and cry to an "elsewhere" in which female desire may be(come) articulable. She conceives of a signifying economy that does not privilege the visual but instead mobilizes the musical potentials of fugue, *fuga,* cadence, and cacophony to trace lines of flight from masculinist and orientalist fields of vision. By searching for new ways to represent women's "barbaric cries," Djebar reminds us that we might think of these cries not only as melancholic traces of bodily violation but also as unauthorized expressions of female *jouissance.* Djebar's rich evocation of her wedding-night cry indulges subversive musicality in order to sing female subjectivity, embodiment, and *jouissance.*

FINAL OVERTURE: OF MUTILATION AND MEMORY

Fantasia closes on the notes of memory, mutilation, and impossible integration. Djebar describes the severed hand of an Algerian woman—a hand that the painter Eugène Fromentin found on a deserted battlefield and was unable to paint or represent. Djebar notes that "later, I seize on this living hand, hand of mutilation and of memory" (1993, 226). She tries to pick up where Fromentin left off: to express the brutality of a war that left women particularly dismembered. What to do with this hand? How to make of it a bridge between past suffering, present narration, and future political mobilization? How to work the specifics of its grotesque violence into a new story or history of the Algerian revolution? How can Djebar rewrite the revolution as a feminist looking "toward the past,"[13] writing in the colonial tongue, and seeing

13. Reference is made to Walter Benjamin's notion of the "angel of history" facing the past,

only potentials for continued violence against women on Algeria's political horizon? Boldly, Djebar seizes on this severed hand that Fromentin was unable to represent. By re-membering national identity as dependent on masculine fantasies of sexual difference, Djebar insinuates women into the cracks, gaps, and fissures of official projects of national representation.

Yet this severed hand resurrected at *Fantasia*'s conclusion symbolizes the ambivalence of Djebar's "attempt at autobiography." Her narrative cannot deliver memory from the anonymous Algerian woman's severed hand, for that hand—like Djebar's sense of self—is fragmented, unspeakable, and radically unassimilable. Thus, the "I" of *Fantasia* coalesces around "a self that cannot accede to an *ego sum,* to the *iste ego sum* of writing" (Spivak 1996, 191). For Djebar, self-representation is necessarily a record of undoing, as well as an opening up to the possibilities for imagining different histories, images, and identities.

Djebar invents new ways of seeing whereby cognitive dissonance, musical flight, and rupture—rather than specularity—determine and permit subversive reworkings of identity. She uses the space of parallax to map selves, in the first and third persons, as dispossessed mosaics that intertwine the familiar with fantasies of the exotic Other. Djebar sculpts passages between silence and voice, omission and representation. Ultimately, she envisions the Orient as an imagined geography of flesh and fantasy, one in which personal fiction provocatively collides with orientalist and nationalist paradigms of identity.

Fantasia challenges us to reimagine the subjects of cross-cultural exchange, to shift the terms of engagement from "this representation disempowers me because it is false" to "I laugh, disrupt, misrecognize, disown." An emphasis on misrecognition can locate the powers of the false and the bastard to force a productive break and critical passages between image and identity. Although a focus on parallax or disjuncture does not suppose that the subject can somehow find an "outside" of power, it does allow one to study the ambivalent traces of the lens and to leverage the self as a decentered eye/I of becoming. By acknowledging the fantasies at play in images of the

---

wanting to stay and repair "wreckage upon wreckage," yet being propelled into the future by the "storm of progress" (1968, 257–58).

self, practices of creative misrecognition force a kind of "stammer" within dominant discourse.[14] We might learn to *think* this stammer in a double sense: first, and most problematically, as a fissure actualized in the postcolonial body and identity,[15] but also, in its most generous sense, as a stimulant for alternative stories and "joyful discoveries, poetic as well as warlike" (de Certeau 1984, xix).

14. For more on this stammer, see Khatibi 1990.

15. I do not want to underestimate this schism. Frantz Fanon powerfully attests to the crippling potential of the image in *Black Skin, White Masks*: "I took myself off from my own presence, far indeed, and made myself an object. What else could it be for me but an amputation, an excision, a hemorrhage that spattered my whole body with black blood?" (1986, 112). Homi Bhabha (1986) similarly refers to colonialism's attempt to "split the soul." Especially vis-à-vis Algerian women's split subjectivity and double oppression, I have looked for answers to Fanon's cry, *"What else could it be for me?"* Throughout this work, I (have tried to) think about this question.

3

Yasmina, an Autodiegetic Character

*Her*story and History

BENAOUDA LEBDAI

And why don't you write? Write! Writing is for you, you are for you; your body is yours, take it.

—Hélène Cixous, "The Laugh of the Medusa"

Today's postcolonial African literature has evolved by including themes such as duality, hybridity, and self-analysis for the ultimate purpose of (dis)covering and defining one's individuality and one's positioning in the course of "History." Such preoccupations have become key issues in numerous novels such as texts by Ayi Kwei Armah, Leila Sebbar, Myriam Ben, Calixthe Beyala, and Nina Bouraoui. Research works ponder such themes, showing that hybridity has become one of the realities in today's "global village." Bill Ashcroft confirms this tendency in *The Empire Writes Back*: "Contemporary accounts . . . are beginning to assert the syncretic and hybridised nature of postcolonial experience" (Ashcroft, Griffiths, and Tiffin 1989, 41). This reality is a consequence of desired and undesired migrations owing to war periods, to political or economic reasons or both. No doubt these migrations provoked physical and psychological pain because of harsh adaptations to new environments. Over the decades, they certainly triggered the telling of painful personal experiences. In France, a new wave of postcolonial writing is mainly led by women writers who tackle those very themes. Nina Bouraoui, who published *Garçon manqué* in 2000, fits in this "new wave" of literary creativity, as she addresses with an impressive punch and openness of mind questions that deal with dual identities and hybridity.[1] Nina Bouraoui, of Algerian origin, moves beyond the colonial topics as she depicts its consequences in today's issues.

The paratext reveals that *Garçon manqué* was announced not as a sixth novel but as a sixth book,[2] and the reader grasps that difference at the close of the story that reads like autofiction, almost like an autobiography. Most of the key facts of the author's life are clearly inscribed and reported in the diegesis, which may imply that this particular work has become vital in the literary development of Bouraoui. A first reading gives the reader an intimate feeling that the whole text comes from the heart, written with emotion and sensitivity. Line after line, the author faces her own life, her own "self," trapped in a complicated world where politics intrudes, where war interferes. The "book" also demonstrates that culture plays a crucial part in the "construction" or, most probably, "deconstruction" of the personality, the entity, and the identity of the writer. My objective in this chapter is not to verify the authenticity of the biographical data but rather to investigate the psychological impact of historical events on Bouraoui's life in order to analyze the questions raised by such writing and thus place them in a broader historical context. It will be significant to stress the way in which this French novelist of Arab origin puts her personal experiences into perspective to find solutions to her inner problems and questions. I hope to show that *Garçon manqué* attempts to acquire a fuller understanding and a better acceptance of "History." I shall also look into the way in which the novelist expresses her anxieties and her doubts through the problematic questions of gender and identity.

The story itself is not straightforwardly linear, as one does not read about the main protagonist's life from childhood to adulthood. The homodiegetic protagonist is called Yasmina, the full first name of Nina, who speaks about her psychological and social development. The connection between Yasmina and Nina is an indicator of the straightforward link between the author and the main character. The route from innocence to maturity, from lack of confidence to acceptance of oneself, reveals that Yasmina's tortuous mind and complicated psychology are written in circles. The diegesis is written in a swift way, with

1. All quotations will refer to this 2000 edition. Further, all quotations are my own translations.

2. The editor uses the French word *livre*.

short and sharp sentences, some unfinished, producing a rather hatched style. Key events and states of mind bring back central events and ideas in a repetitive way. The ingredients one expects to find in an autobiography are included in the text, such as reminiscences of first emotions, first love, first misunderstandings of the world followed by their taming through positive and negative experiences, through discussions and introspections. The novel delves into family alcoves and secrets. Questions, memories, remembrance of people who helped to express the first emotions and opinions are related without any inhibition. This work presents itself as a disturbing account of an author's initiation into the world.

Garçon manqué could have been the initiatory novel of a young writer, but it is not. It is the sixth by a positively acclaimed writer in terms of literary criticism with a readership in France as well as in Algeria. Nina Bouraoui's urge to write a work where burning questions are raised, after having published *La voyeuse interdite, Point mort, Le bal des Murènes, L'age blessé,* and *Le jour du séisme,* annihilates the assumption that she wanted to publish yet another book.[3] Besides, it is too early for Bouraoui to write her own biography. In that sense, *Garçon manqué* tells more than what the story wants to say, as it moves beyond a self-honored autofiction. It is clearly a work of a fracture, as it holds significant implicit meanings, not only for Bouraoui as a person but also for the novelist, for the artist. The whole process of this type of writing influences the evolution of postcolonial literature, nearly forty years after the independence of Algeria, investigating thus the necessity to ponder one's being within today's cross-historical societies, within today's globalized world. This disguised autobiography raises such key issues not only on a personal level but also within the complicated relationships between two countries, France and Algeria, which experienced a tragic war.

In the context of such a relation between these two countries, this postcolonial novel casts the question of hybridity in a violent way. It shows that the concept of hybridity covers not only a mix of people from different countries but also culture, religion, and language, a consequence of the history of these two countries. Nina Bouraoui's "book" addresses these questions from

3. Nina Bouraoui's first novel, *La voyeuse interdite,* received two prizes—Prix du Livre Inter and the Prix 1537 de Blois—in 1991.

the inside through the protagonist Yasmina, born of mixed blood, of mixed cultures, from an Algerian father, Rachid, and a French mother, Maryvonne. Yasmina's experience sheds light on the consequences of biological and cultural hybridity through introspection and self-analysis, which enhance the psychological difficulties in integrating and accepting one's personality within such a reality. The novel reveals step by step the way in which the autodiegetic character is a construct of the living memory within the history of two peoples and two cultures, the French and the Algerian: "A French mother. An Algerian father. My body gathers together two opposed lands—I come from a rare union. I am France with Algeria."[4] Yasmina experiences this dual belonging with extreme anxiety, as the following expressions show: "We are nothing . . . I disappear . . . Who are we? . . . I stay outside the meaning . . . Who am I? . . . Which part of myself shall I burn?"[5] She lives in a postcolonial era, and she bears the attraction and rejection that exist between the two nations because of a common history, because of a war between them, as she keeps feeling: "I am in the Algerian war. I bear the conflict."[6] In a tense and nervous style, Yasmina puts forward the duality of her inner self with openness and responsibility because she tries to come to terms with her existence even if her will to understand underlines the scars of the colonial conflict and its painful psychological effects, as discussed and denounced by Frantz Fanon, who has always pointed to the difficult, almost impossible relationships based on rejections and separation in *The Wretched of the Earth* (1961). The psychological introspection the narrator discloses shows perfectly the impact of "History" and memory on her. The reader learns that Yasmina's strength lies within her thorough knowledge of her personal story, which demonstrates that in her everyday life, therefore through her body and soul, she carries the weight and the burden of that History: "I come from the war. I come from a contested marriage. I bear the suffering of my Algerian family. I bear the rejection of my French family. I bear all these transmissions—There. The violence does not

4. "De mère française. De père algérien. Seul *mon* corps rassemble les terres opposées . . . je viens d'une union rare. Je suis la France avec l'Algérie" (2000, 10).

5. "Nous ne sommes rien . . . Je m'efface . . . Qui sommes-nous? . . . Je reste à l'extérieur du sens . . . Qui suis-je? . . . Quelle partie de moi brûler?" (10, 12, 13, 146, 35).

6. "Je suis dans la guerre d'Algérie. Je porte le conflit" (33).

leave me. It inhabits me. It comes from me. It comes from the Algerian people who invades. It comes from the French people who denies."[7]

The harsh words used in a direct narrative style convey the thought processes of a character in search of equilibrium. Yasmina searches for her personal identity in a desperate way: "I become violent. With myself. With the others. I am looking for my identity . . . I am not defined . . . I am unclassifiable."[8] Such a violence with herself is a consequence of the war. An accepted and serene identity could not be reached without a complete understanding of the past and a full comprehension of the colonial discourse. There is an obvious search for therapy in which words carry weight; as Albert Camus, the other victim of the French and Algerian history, says: "naming despair, is going beyond it" (1951, 320; translation mine). Such a historical search may lead to a peace of mind, which should stop a certain schizophrenia where she continually has to deny her other half, whether she is in Algeria or in France, as she admitted in a recent interview on *France Inter*: "I have betrayed Algeria from the age of fourteen to the age of twenty."[9] In order to reach a balanced personality, Yasmina has to digest the contradictions of her being. She has to go through a review of key historical and psychological states, in order to relieve herself of guilt, the guilt of the Algerian war.

In *Garçon manqué,* "History" is presented in a hazy way, but in some instances it is referred to directly. History puts into context some expressed thoughts, helping us to understand Yasmina's state of mind. History produces sense in her life. The question of "Who am I?" comes back like a leitmotif. Yasmina is torn, as far as her identity is concerned: "Being French is being without my father. . . . Being Algerian means being without my mother."[10] In a metatextual way, the novelist comments on her own act of writing, which should have solved her puzzle, her queries. Becoming a novelist could have helped her

7. "Je viens de la guerre. Je viens d'un mariage contesté. Je porte la souffrance de ma famille algérienne. Je porte le refus de ma famille française. Je porte ces transmissions—là. La violence ne me quitte plus. Elle m'habite. Elle vient de moi. Elle vient du peuple algérien qui envahit. Elle vient du peuple français qui renie" (34).

8. "Je deviens violente. Avec moi. Avec les autres. Je cherche mon identité . . . Je suis indéfinie . . . Je deviens inclassable" (34–35).

9. Nina Bouraoui on *France Inter,* with Brigitte Kernel, August 29, 2002.

10. "Etre française c'est être sans mon père . . . Etre algérienne, c'est être sans ma mere" (22).

transcend the whole problematic issue, but critics and journalists like classifying authors, which accentuates the gap within herself as she denounces: "Writing will confirm this separation. A French writer? A Maghrebin writer? Some will choose for me. Against my will. This will be another violence."[11]

In that sense, *Garçon manqué* denounces the violence of always being the other, but, at the same time, Nina is proud to point out that her name Bouraoui means in Algerian "son/daughter of the storyteller." The history of Algeria and France is continuously intermingled, as it is inevitably related to the history of her family, be it French or Algerian. This history is told obliquely through family stories such as the tales of her uncle Amar, who was a fighter for the independence of Algeria. Amar, the freedom fighter, reminds her of the Algerian war, "la guerre d'Algérie," which disturbs Yasmina because he has fought one part of herself and stresses the contradictions both families have had to assume and resolve. Nevertheless, she is proud of this "unmentioned" uncle within her French family. The act of writing makes her realize that the world is not Manichaean and that human relationships are surely complicated. She knows she is "in-between." The fight against "L'Algérie française" (2000, 32), a motto of the war for the French, becomes a contradiction, as she is a consequence of that complicated colonial history. Yasmina internalizes the conflict between the two peoples moving from negative to positive attitudes: "I am France and Algeria."[12] History becomes a burden for her because wherever she happens to be, she is on the wrong side. Her specific position makes her condemn the war, the killing of innocent people whatever side she takes, whatever argument she defends. The war is overly present, as it lingers throughout the story. The year in which Algeria became independent, 1962, is often referred to because of the actions of the Organisation de l'Armée Secrète (OAS) and its crimes against the Algerian population, against women, against the French soldiers who defended de Gaulle's political decisions and strategy.[13] Tragic events are inscribed

11. "Ecrire rapportera cette séparation. Auteur français? Auteur maghrébin? Certains choisiront pour moi. Contre moi. Ce sera encore une violence" (36).

12. "Je suis la France avec l'Algérie" (11).

13. The OAS was an armed group that did not accept the independence of Algeria and declared war on Général de Gaulle and the Algerians. The OAS declared that Algeria was a burnt land.

in the memories: "The complaint of Algerian women massacred by the OAS men" haunts her dreams.[14] The scene remains a recurrent image for Yasmina, who tries to understand. But the ghosts of the war are tragically present in the family flat in Algiers: "In the flat. Blood dating from 1962. My sister was born in 1962. At the time of crime. The year of the massacre of Algerian women in the apartment building. The year of the OAS massacre. Their last massacre. Their revenge spirit. The OAS men come back at every departure of my father. Three women alone in the apartment. Three memories. Three fragilities."[15] Yasmina wonders what her sin was, as she feels guilty about what happened during the war. Why must she think that she might be responsible for what the Front de Libération Nationale (FLN) did to the first couple assassinated on a road in the Aurès Mountains on November 1, 1954, the event that officially started the war against the French?[16] The victims were innocent teachers, so as a daughter of a mixed couple, Yasmina is constantly disturbed because deep down she wishes for more joyful memories, to be at ease with herself, within her two families: "What was the mistake then? Being the daughter of 1960 lovers. To transform time into an eternal one. Thanks to my presence, only . . . Through my identity only. To stir the knife in the scar. Insisting on this troublesome period. It was war time. The OAS. The FLN. The terrorist attacks."[17]

Garçon manqué constantly refers to history and to the relationship between the two countries, which did not end in 1962. Interestingly, a new wave of French people arrived in Algeria then: teachers and engineers who wanted to help the newly independent country wipe out the wounds of war. Yasmina is concerned about the generation of children born then, of mixed parents, like herself. That generation continues the strange human relationships between

14. "La plainte des femmes algériennes massacrées par les hommes de l'OAS" (63).

15. "Dans l'appartement. Du sang de 1962. Ma sœur naît en 1962. Au temps du crime. L'année du massacre des femmes algériennes de la Résidence. L'année du massacre de l'OAS. Leur dernier massacre. Leur esprit de vengeance . . . Les hommes de l'OAS reviennent à chaque départ de mon père. Trois femmes seules dans l'appartement. Trois mémoires. Trois fragilités" (62–66).

16. The FLN was Algeria's official liberation movement with the objective of removing the colonial power.

17. "Quelle faute alors? D'être la fille des amoureux de 1960. De rendre ce temps éternel. Par ma seule présence . . . Par ma seule identité. De remuer le couteau dans la plaie. D'insister sur cette mauvaise période. C'était la guerre. L'OAS. Le FLN. Les attentats" (128).

the two countries: "Who will know of the 1970s children? Who will hear of the independence marriages? Who will know the crazy desire to be loved? Two countries. Two solitudes."[18] The colonial period is present but not only as the postcolonial history between France and Algeria that continues to weave links. The development of historical events such as the integration of Algerians who have chosen the French nationality, deciding that France is their country, concerns Yasmina as a paradox of that love-hate relationship.

The book refers to the new war, that of the fundamentalists, and the recent tragic events that have destroyed Algeria. They hurt Yasmina, and she condemns them: "The massacres, the violence in Algeria."[19] She is troubled by postcolonial issues such as the concerns of the fundamentalists whose crimes against the democratic forces and the women who fight to be free are part of her wound and her revolt:

> Like all these bodies discovered after the massacre of the village of Children's bodies. Cut in two. Slashed women's bodies through and through like a zip. Men's bodies without heads and heads without bodies. Still with open eyes. With a look of blind people who have not seen anything coming, that night. Who haven't understood. Such a disorder. Such a rapidity. This moment of panic. Who haven't seen anything. Neither the attackers' faces, nor the blows of hatchets, nor the lights of torches. No. Nothing.[20]

Yasmina criticizes the silence that surrounds this new war. She is irritated by the recurrent journalistic sentence in the French news relating that another massacre has taken place in Algeria, again and again. Being in France, Yasmina cannot forget her other country that keeps suffering, as her French

18. "Qui saura les enfants de 1970? Qui saura les mariages de l'indépendance, Qui saura le désir fou d'être aimé? Deux pays. Deux solitudes" (36).

19. "Les massacres, les violences en Algérie" (89).

20. "Comme tous ces corps découverts après le massacre du village de B. Des corps d'enfants. Coupés en deux. Des corps de femmes tailladés sur la longueur. Comme une fermeture Éclair. Des corps d'hommes sans tête. Et des têtes sans corps. Avec des yeux encore ouverts. Avec ce regard d'aveugle. Qui n'a rien vu venir dans la nuit. Qui n'a pas saisi. Ce désordre. Cette rapidité. Cet affolement. Qui n'a rien vu. Ni les visages des assaillants. Ni les coups de hache. Ni le feu des torches. Non, rien" (158).

friends tell her: "With all what defines you. You know all those places. You know all those faces."[21] Colonial history and postcolonial history are present, as she is concerned by what happened and what is happening in both countries in terms of human relationships and possible exchanges.

The war of words is also denounced. The question of the rejection of the "Other" through language is obsessive in this autofiction. It is a significant part of Yasmina's psychological sickness. Her double identity makes her a privileged witness of racist attitudes. Her French friends use racist terms. When they remember her "dual being," they blame alcohol. They declare that words are meaningless: "It starts without noticing it. It is a mechanics of words. Integrated into the language."[22] But she feels the pain. With a great sense of irony, she shows the dangers of racism when the latter reaches an unconscious stage, maintaining differences, encouraging the survival of a colonial discourse. Her revolt echoes Fanon, who analyzes situations where Algerians are referred to as "Arabs" in the derogatory sense of the term and Africans as "Negros" (1952, 13–32).[23] Yasmina's Algerian collective memory recalls these racist terms with anger because they are addressed to her own father too: "Wog, yid, negro."[24] The whole novel is certainly a desperate call for tolerance.

Her introspective memory spans the time when her parents met during the "Algerian War" in Rennes. Their union was rejected without discussion by her mother's bourgeois family: "You will not marry an Algerian."[25] That rejection has become part of Yasmina's life, as she integrates the idea that her parents' love was perceived as a rape, a translation of racism that is not, as Fanon says, "a whole, but the most visible, the most daily, the rudest of a given structure" (1975, 33). Yasmina relives the experience her parents endured. She ponders the relation between sexuality and racism:

> The French won. The vicious one. Like those who go with the Blacks. Those faces. Those knives. Yes, this rejection is sexual. Yes, racism is an illness. A

21. "Avec ce qui te définit. Tu connais tous ces lieux. Tu connais tous ces visages" (159).

22. "Ça part tout seul. C'est une mécanique des mots. Intégrée au langage" (126).

23. In the February 1952 edition of the review *Esprit,* Fanon analyzed the consequences of racist attitudes toward Algerians in France in the paper "Le colonisé en question."

24. "Raton, youpin, négro" (126).

25. "Tu n'épouseras pas un Algérien" (33).

> vice. A shameful illness. It develops in the silence of homes. They murmur, then they close the windows. They shout during the family meals. Hating the other is imagining him against oneself. Feeling being possessed. Stolen. Penetrated. Racism is fantasmatic. It is imagining the smell of his skin, the tension of his body, the strength of sex. Racism is an illness. A leprosy. A necrosis. It is my mother's body against my father's body which was disturbing. Those two bodies. That relation. That rubbing. That red colour.[26]

Intimacy is sacred, untouchable. These lines recall Frantz Fanon, who argues in *Black Skin, White Masks* that the African represents unconsciously "a sexual instinct" for many white people (1986, 143). The autodiegetic character Yasmina progresses in her self-analysis, defending her mother's choice and liberty to go beyond prejudices to build her new life whatever the consequences, giving birth to Yasmina's sister in 1962, a symbolic date that indicates the end of seven years of war. The labor for a historical memory becomes an asset. Her mother's decision demonstrates her will to construct solid ground for herself and for her children.

As a child, Yasmina discovers that racism can also be felt on the other side of the Mediterranean, in Algeria, where racist rejections happen too. She remembers being called the "Roumia," "the daughter of the Frenchwoman," a situation that hurts her in exactly the same way and must be fought equally. All these recollections become part of a reconstruction. The past must not be ignored if a sound future, without hatred, is to be built.

The literary construct of Yasmina expresses a tormented dual personality through sexuality that symbolizes her whole story, written down in a specifically postcolonial context. Yasmina does not know whether she is a boy or a girl, as suggested in the very title, *Garçon manqué* (Tomboy). She writes

26. "La Française, la vicieuse. Comme celles qui fréquentent des Noirs. Ces visages. Ces couteaux. Oui ce rejet est sexuel. Oui le racisme est une maladie. Un vice. Une maladie honteuse. Qui se développe dans le silence des maisons. On murmure puis on ferme les fenêtres. On crie pendant les repas de famille. Haïr l'autre, c'est l'imaginer contre soi. C'est se sentir possédé. Volé. Pénétré. Le racisme est un fantasme. C'est imaginer l'odeur de sa peau, la tension de son corps, la force de son sexe. Le racisme est une maladie. Une lèpre. Une nécrose. C'est le corps de ma mère avec le corps de mon père qui dérangera. Ces deux chairs-là. Ce rapport-là. Ce frottement-là. Ce rouge-là" (153–54).

repeatedly of her despair, mixing sexuality and nationality: "I don't know who I am anymore . . . A girl? A boy? French? Algerian? Algerian-French?"[27] Yasmina reveals that she has always ignored the feminine part of her personality, that she has a "body without a name."[28] She disguises herself as a boy, a reaction to that history and to a social environment that always gives reason to the male: "I distort my family body. . . . I comb my hair backward. I wear a whistle around my neck. I have a mock gun. I open my shoulders. I open my legs apart."[29] The disturbance leads her to change her name. In a country where males hold power, she calls herself Ahmed: "I disappear. I join the country of men," strangely echoing the character Ahmed in Ben Jelloun's *La nuit sacrée* (1987) in which the main protagonist, Zahra, becomes Ahmed for a period of twenty years (see Lebdai 2002).[30]

This intertextuality reveals the sensitive question of gender in the literature of North Africa, where "sexuality is territorial," as Fatima Mernissi writes (1985, 137). Yasmina breaks down the boundaries between men and women through her body. The implicit fictional elements express deep scars reflecting the span of a "transitional" History. The protagonist clearly becomes a paradigm for the impact of History on human psychology. Yasmina's sexuality is certainly symbolic of her hybridity, as she bears a fractured identity. This quest for sexual identity strongly symbolizes her quest for a more peaceful history because she does not want to be in the wilderness ("dans l'errance" [35]). Despite her situation as a person "in-between," Yasmina bears hope for more peaceful relations between her two countries, as she succeeds in steadily constructing an authentic personality out of violent experiences. As a child of two worlds, she integrates into her deeper soul both the Algerian and the French worlds, through language and culture, through the telling of history, and by naming their tragedies. There is no doubt that Yasmina stands for the human link between the two countries that today face their common history, colonial and

27. "Je ne sais plus qui je suis . . . Une fille? Un garçon? . . . La Française? L'Algérienne? L'Algéro-Française?" (145).

28. "Un corps sans nom" (42).

29. "Je dénature mon corps féminin . . . Je plaque mes cheveux en arrière. Je porte un sifflet autour du cou. Je porte un faux revolver. J'ouvre mes épaules. J'ouvre mes jambs" (51).

30. "Je me fais disparaître. J'intègre le pays des hommes" (17).

postcolonial.[31] The way in which the character Yasmina is handled implies the way the future for both communities should be, according to the writer. Born out of violence, Yasmina finds her "way," which is accepting herself through better relations and understanding between the two countries:

> Who am I, honestly? Towards this sophisticated accent. Towards this French language. My mother's tongue. I speak in French. Only. I dream in French. Only. The Arabic language is a sound, a song, a voice which I remember, which I feel. But I don't know it. The Arabic language is an emotion. It is this "other" which I protect. Algeria is not in my language. It is in my body. Algeria is not in my words. It is inside me. Algeria is in what goes out. It is in what consumes. It is physical. It is in what I don't control. In my excesses. In my requirements. In my volunte. In my force. Algeria is in my desire to be loved.[32]

The colonial world was divided into two parts, economically and psychologically (see Fanon 1986, 7). We can see that such a duality is expressed through Yasmina's psyche. Her deep desire to combat that duality, to liberate herself from it, and to come to terms not only with *her*story but also with "History" is well rendered in terms of style and writing through the use of meaningful images and powerful metaphors, through a harrowing autofiction. This postcolonial writing explores the intimate self, the "I." Indeed, rejected on both sides of the Mediterranean, by those people who still carry hatred owing to the war, Yasmina embodies the positive bridge between the two coasts of the Mediterranean: "Algeria is too close to France. As if crossed through. Too close also."[33]

31. The reference is to the tragic war of Algeria; for example, torture.

32. "Qui suis-je vraiment? Vers cet accent pointu. Vers cette langue française. Ma langue maternelle. Je parle en français. Uniquement. Je rêve en français. Uniquement. J'écrirais en français. Uniquement. La langue arabe est un son, un chant, une voix. Que je retiens. Que je sens. Mais que je ne sais pas. La langue arabe est une émotion. C'est cet autre que j'abrite . . . L'Algérie n'est pas dans ma langue. Elle est dans mon corps. L'Algérie n'est pas dans mes mots. Elle est à l'intérieur de moi. L'Algérie n'est pas dans ce qui sort. Elle est dans ce qui dévore. Elle est physique. Dans ce que je ne contrôle pas. Dans mes excès. Dans mes exigences. Dans ma volonté. Dans ma force. L'Algérie est dans mon désir fou d'être aimée" (171).

33. "L'Algérie est trop proche de la France. Comme traversée. Trop liée aussi" (165).

She finds her way out of the chaos through love, expressing her personality through both the use of the French language, her mother tongue, and the Algerian culture and sensibility. She discovers herself as she reveals her inner self, which leads to the acceptance of her postcolonial hybridity assumed and expressed through this meaningful metaphor: "In our dreams. Through our force. In this joy of meeting. In this Algerian smell which comes back like a miracle in each French spring."[34] On a fictional level, a balance within her personality is found in the cultures she has acquired throughout the years moving from one camp to another, from one territory to the other, learning from mistakes, rejections, attractions, experiences, and love, which helps to absorb discrepancies and shortcomings. The character Yasmina reveals the long quest for a serene identity, without revenge, in complete understanding of all the issues at stake in order to move toward a peaceful normalcy, which happens to be Frantz Fanon's ultimate message on the relations between oppressed and oppressors: "There is no Black mission; there is no White burden. . . . It is through an effort of renewal and renouncement upon themselves, it is through a continuous tension on their liberty that men can create ideal conditions for the existence of a humane world. Why not simply try to reach the other, to smell the other, to reveal oneself to the other? Is my liberty not given to me to build up and put together the world of the 'you'?" (1986, 185–88).

The development of such a narrative autofiction, a consequence of the evolution of Yasmina's personality, shows the capacity of men and women to adapt to new worlds and to climb out of psychological ghettos. *Garçon manqué* is fully inscribed in a new postcolonial discourse, as it addresses the sensitive questions of hybridity, cultural affirmation, reconciliation, and the painful experience of the path toward understanding.[35] Like Hanif Kureishi's, Nina Bouraoui's autofiction belongs to those postcolonial texts that demonstrate they are "symptomatic of the centrifugal pull of history . . . believed to demonstrate the fragility of 'grand narratives,' the erosion of transcendent authority,

34. "Dans nos rêves. Dans notre force. Dans cette joie à retrouver. Dans cette odeur algérienne qui revient comme par miracle à chaque printemps français" (197).

35. It is quite significant to note that during the colonial period, hybrid characters always had a tragic end, such as *Le fils d'Agatha* by Francis Bebey, *A Few Nights and Days* by Sonne Mbella Diboko, or *The Edifice* by Kole Omotoso.

the collapse of imperialistic explanations of the world" (Boehmer 1995, 244). It is true in the sense that Nina Bouraoui's narrative demonstrates the power of the inner self that marks the positive march of "History." Bouraoui's powerful storytelling in this postcolonial history, subtly mixing realism, metaphors, and symbols, shows her capacity to "encapsulate the contradictory experiences of global development for some generations to come," in the sense that *Garçon manqué* communicates the vision of those individuals who are "in-between" and want to exist outside of colonial references (Head 1997, 160).

PART TWO

Autobiographical Writings and Transnationalism

We always embody in our multiple shifting consciousness a convergence of traditions, cultures, histories coming together in this time and this place and moving like rivers through us.

—Leila Ahmad, *A Border Passage: From Cairo to America—A Woman's Journey*

The true chameleons are the ones who straddle the two worlds, segueing smoothly from one to the other, adjusting language and body, calibrating the range of emotions displayed, treading the tightrope of mannerisms and mores. If it is done well, it can look deceptively effortless, but it is never without cost . . . for the chameleon, it is a matter of survival.

—Samia Serageldin, *The Cairo House*

4

Poetic Geographies

Interracial Insurgency in Arab American Autobiographical Spaces

KEITH FELDMAN

I was born a Black woman
and now
I am become a Palestinian
—June Jordan, "Moving Towards Home"

We are taking the Great White Way and making it yellow, brown, and red, and black, and all of the colors we represent.
—Suheir Hammad, *Democracy Now!* radio program, 2003

In the fall of 2001, Russell Simmons, the president and chief executive officer of the major hip-hop recording label Def Jam Records, first produced *Def Poetry Jam,* a thirty-minute televised special on the Home Box Office (HBO) network documenting the performance at the Supper Club in New York City of seven spoken-word poets.[1] A panoply of white, African American, Puerto Rican, Jamaican, and Palestinian American poets performed largely autobiographical pieces that documented the struggles and the structures of life on the margins of U.S. culture. The show has become a staple of HBO programming, running for the past five seasons, and, in 2003, *Def Poetry Jam on Broadway* took to the theatrical mainstream with an open-ended run at New York City's prestigious Longacre Theatre.[2] By 2003, there was enough national interest

1. *Russell Simmons Presents Def Poetry,* Home Box Office, 2001.

2. *Def Poetry Jam on Broadway,* directed by Stan Latham, Longacre Theatre, New York, April

to take the Broadway show on the road. Poet and activist Suheir Hammad, born in Jordan and raised in Brooklyn, and one of the performers and organizers for all three productions, described on *Democracy Now!* radio *Def Poetry Jam*'s critical cultural work contesting U.S. racial regimes: "We are taking the Great White Way and making it yellow, brown, and red, and black, and all of the colors we represent." *Def Poetry Jam,* as Hammad helps make clear, intervenes in the liberal multiculturalist space of U.S. mainstream popular culture by making legible the ways in which the effects of "minoritization" have been confronted through the performance of interracial solidarities that explicitly critique narrow conceptions of national belonging through dynamic autobiographical performance. This mode of confrontation we might think of as "interracial insurgency."

Def Poetry Jam emerged from a post–September 11, 2001, conception of cultural production that saw such autobiographical performance poetry as a means to struggle against current U.S. imperial-state projects. But we can trace such modes of interracial insurgency to earlier historical moments. The aim of this chapter is to explore the particular production of one form of this confrontation—an articulation of Arab American autobiographical poetry in the late 1980s and early 1990s by Etel Adnan and Suheir Hammad. These strategies, as I will show, imagine poetic geographies from which an interracial insurgency can be made legible, and do so by navigating the apparent contradiction of the simultaneous critique and transvaluation of the nation form. That is, following Etienne Balibar's work (1994) on the "paradoxes of universality" endemic to modern forms of nationalism, we can read for the ways Adnan and Hammad have confronted the structures of a U.S. racial regime that posits the possibility of a universal identification with the nation through the particular restriction of access to that universal both within and outside the nation's borders.

Reading practices that attend to these strategies have been amply developed across a range of scholarship on ethnic and minority literatures in the United States since at least the mid-1990s. For example, Lisa Lowe's *Immigrant Acts: On Asian American Cultural Politics* (1996) reconceptualizes

---

10, 2003. Subsequent print collections of these works have appeared as well. See Medina and Rivera 2001; and Simmons 2003.

the multiple strategies through which Asian migrant literature works within and against U.S. imperialist maneuvers in East Asia. These strategies, Lowe argues, clarify the material reality of an ethnicized minority in the United States. Lowe's interpretations of immigration law and the ways in which constructions of race and ethnicity by the state have been contingent on U.S. foreign policy interests have similarly been put under the microscope in the Arab American context, including by Steven Salaita (2006), Lisa Suhair Majaj (2000), Nadine Naber (2000), and Suad Joseph (1999). The rhetorical and poetic strategies employed in performances such as *Def Poetry Jam*—many of which oppose the marginalizing force of U.S. foreign policy for people of color through autobiographical narrative—take on a particular cast in an Arab American context. Peculiar to this articulation of an Arab American diaspora is a finely honed and long-standing counternational concern of many Arab American writers, activists, and intellectuals with the establishment of the State of Israel and the present-day deferral of statehood for Palestine. In other words, it is not solely the U.S. nation form that is taken to task; as I show in what follows, Adnan's and Hammad's poetic autobiographical works incisively critique a nation form composed of a system of closed borders meant to contain and secure a homogenous community—the very rationale for the establishment of Israel since at least the 1922 Mandate for Palestine. Not only does the State of Israel continually and radically limit the life choices of those communities who fall outside its borders, but the U.S. military and economic engagements in Afghanistan, Iraq, and beyond continually work to minoritize, subjugate, and marginalize individuals of Arab descent in ways that supplement Israeli policies of practical apartheid. In this way, the category "Arab" has become marked as a racialized oriental construct intimately linked to both U.S. foreign policy in the Middle East and the legal and military practices of Israeli exclusion. It shuttles between that which is akin to whiteness (unmarked, assimilated, successfully attaining the privileges of abstract citizenship) and that which is a separate racial or ethnic formation entirely, a category that bears the brunt of post-9/11 civil and human rights abuses in the United States, Iraq, and Israel; that is, considered a "threat" to the security of the United States and Israel; that is, continually profiled based simply on kinship and heritage; that is, in short, marked as a visible enemy of the nation within its own borders.[3] In this context, then, there is no stable instance of the modern nation form from which to speak.

In response to this set of racialized national constrictions, Adnan's and Hammad's autobiographical poetry conceptualize critical counternational notions of belonging that work through the logic of a shared interracial alliance. I read these strategies as a mode of revaluing "Arab" as a transnational category through which to forward specific literary projects that imagine the possibility of a Palestine built through transnational solidarities. Such work, as I show later, conceptualizes poetic autobiographical spaces for interracial insurgency that begin by understanding the linkage that enables U.S. and Israeli national exceptionalisms to have wholly unexceptional effects for those individuals minoritized by the nation form.

FRONTIER VIOLENCE AND FRONTIER ALLIANCE

In *Writing Degree Zero* (1953), Roland Barthes takes up a key argument put forward by Jean-Paul Sartre's work on the engagement of the writer with a reading public. Sartre, in *What Is Literature? and Other Essays* (1948), had defined a dualism in which the category "language" was conceived as a social concept defined by the context inhabited by the writer, whereas the category "style" was the collection of personal traits employed by the writer to shape an individual literary work. Barthes attempts to split Sartre's dualism by imagining a third term. If language is in essence a social concept and style a personal trait, then for Barthes occupying a middle position between the two is *écriture;* Barthes calls this space "the morality of form" (1953, 15). In stressing *écriture,* Barthes attempts to define the writer's own zone of freedom, albeit an ambiguous one. He writes, "On the one hand, it unquestionably arises from a confrontation of the writer with the society of his time; on the other hand, from this social finality, it refers the writer back, by a sort of tragic reversal, to the sources, that is to say, the instruments of creation" (16).

3. Suad Joseph (1999) amplifies the notion of Arab American identity kept incomplete by the dominant flexible strategies of minoritization. Louise Cainkar (2002) examines the manners in which Arabs and Muslims have been marginalized in the United States after September 11, 2001.

These "instruments of creation" emerge in two complementary ways in Etel Adnan's surrealist autobiographical poetry collection titled *The Indian Never Had a Horse, and Other Poems* (1985). First, *écriture* instantiates a transformation of physical setting, regardless of historical context; after works such as Adnan's critically acclaimed *Sitt Marie-Rose: A Novel* (1978), smothered in the concrete physicality of the city and the specific incidents of the Lebanese civil war, *The Indian Never Had a Horse* draws us to the topography of the U.S. frontier's mountains and rivers. Second, *écriture* instantiates a transformation of the manner in which one might read text itself. That is, *écriture* attempts to perform the mode of communication itself, language as a self-reflexive instrument of transaction. Modern poetic forms, which according to Barthes were shaped by one of Adnan's central influences, Arthur Rimbaud, privilege *écriture* over both language and style, seeing the practice of writing as process privileged against the relation between the social and the personal. Tellingly, *The Indian Never Had a Horse* (1985) closes with a return to the key question of writing: "I will bring the ink the key and the secret / on a future page" (103, ll. 17–18).

Using this Barthesian notion of poetic *écriture,* one can begin to comprehend the formal complexities apparent in much of Adnan's writing, particularly in *The Indian Never Had a Horse.* It allows us to trace the linkage of the astrologic with the geographic spaces that serve as the setting for Adnan's articulation of interracial alliance. The poetry continually evokes the cosmos, looking toward the universe, galaxies, and the moon. Adnan then links cosmos to the earthly setting and provides a geography infused with a particularized definition; the cosmic is the mirror of the Arab Islamic world: Beirut, the Mediterranean, Cyprus, Smyrna, Spain, Anatolia, Rabat-Salé, Egypt, and the "Arabian continent." Where much of the narrative action of these poems takes place is in the frontier spaces of the Americas, where intertwined are the violent histories of displaced Indian populations of the Southwest and Mexico, whose lives were destroyed first by the European conquest in the sixteenth century and then by the Manifest Destiny-driven U.S. continental expansion of the nineteenth century. These geographic edges of American empire are tirelessly referred to throughout the text: San Diego (3, l. 7), Mount Rainier (11, l. 5), Yosemite Falls (21, l. 6), Mount Tamalpais (53, ll. 8–9), Indian America (72, l. 9), and several dozen others all contain Adnan's surrealist poetics in the precise spaces of U.S. imperial conquest.

That Adnan explicitly locates much of *The Indian Never Had a Horse* in these western regions of the United States is not surprising considering she has resided in California for much of her life. Indeed, she is writing through the images of her own geographical location. But such a location serves not only to represent Adnan's own particular life experience. It also works as a setting for the movement between the destabilizing surrealism of the cosmos and a genealogy of interracial insurgency in the face of national exceptionalism and imperial violence. That is, for Adnan's poetry here, surrealistic forms of social space are where the material experiences of history can be properly thrown into relief, creating a site where interracial alliances can be viably forged and the effects of historical violence can be properly redressed. The American frontier becomes the site where the dwindling Indian population and the exiled Arab woman can come together. From the standpoint of an interracial insurgency, the violence running rampant in the Arab world can be confronted concurrently with localized American-based histories of racial violence.

There are three key moments in the collection that develop this notion of a genealogy of interracial insurgency between and across minoritized histories. The first comes midway through the poem that gives the collection its title, "The Indian Never Had a Horse," just after Adnan has described a group of cowboys in Arizona, rubbing

> each other's
> tales against their boots and throw[ing]
> their dead in the creek. (23, ll. 3–5)

In contrast to the violent Manifest Destiny conquerors celebrating their kill, Adnan writes of the space between histories of Indian and African American insurgency.

> I am between Smohalla
> and Malcolm X, sitting,
> having lunch on
> riverbanks,
> throwing stones . . .
> is the rainbow over us

glow-paint or a
visitation? (23, ll. 7–14)

Smohalla was chief of the Wanapun tribe in the Upper Columbia River Valley of the Pacific Northwest during the Indian Wars of the mid-nineteenth century and was considered a prophet by many of his followers, known as the Dreamers. Smohalla preached the importance of traditional modes of living to confront the growing penetration of industrialization in the American frontier. In 1870, Smohalla led a group of Dreamers in an action against Native resettlement.[4] Malcolm X similarly struggled against the forces of U.S. capitalism and racial nationalism through the articulation of a black internationalist movement against global white supremacy. The speaker here, an Arab American woman, occupies a mediating space between these two leaders of racial insurgency. The calm of sharing a meal is juxtaposed with "throwing stones," an act historically located in the violent responses of Indians, African Americans, and Arabs in Lebanon, Israel, Palestine, and the United States. And the natural setting, made surreal through the plural riverbanks and the rainbow, places this conjoining of multiple histories of racial insurgency in the context of an ethereal, dreamed frontier space.

The second moment more explicitly draws together counternational concerns into an interracial transnational framework. It comes at the end of "Love Poems," the only series of poems in *The Indian Never Had a Horse* that firmly delineates a single speaker and addressee in an extended passage:

from the persistent Mediterranean
to the persistent
Pacific
we cut roads with our feet
share baggage and
food
running always one second

4. For a history of Smohalla as dream-prophet and leader of the Wanapun, see Ruby and Viola 1989.

ahead of the running of
Time (65, ll. 17–25)

The Mediterranean Sea, one of the central bodies of water for Arab Islamic culture—and one Hammad will return us to—is throughout *The Indian Never Had a Horse* constructed as both a boundary containing localized violence within the Arab context and a passageway out of that violence to imagine possible modes of freedom. The Pacific Ocean is figured throughout Adnan's poetry as a provider of nourishment, both spiritual and nutritional. By linking both bodies of water, and utilizing both to enable forms of movement, displaced Indians and Arabs alike forge possible avenues to imagine other futures. Such a practice, Adnan implies in the last lines, keeps both Indians and Arabs one step ahead of the dominant national forms that write history.

A third moment foregrounds the oppositional experience of the American frontier itself and takes place at the beginning of "Spreading Clouds"—a poem dedicated to June Jordan, one of the most prolific African American women writers working on social justice for black women in the last third of the twentieth century. The stanzas read:

The new ancestors are lying
at the foot of other
mountains
and other graves:

Malcolm X Martin Luther King
Abdel Kader the sufi soldier
and all of you Indian Chiefs
whose tears are the great storms
of California. (68, ll. 12–20)

Brought together in the shared frontier space of California's natural landscape are prominent figures in African American, Arab, and Native American insurgent histories. Malcolm X's and King's strategies to articulate an anti-imperialist racial insurgency are both cited here, as is Ali Hasan Abdel Kader's work to contextualize Sufi theology in the scene of social upheaval. Adnan groups these three together with "all of you Indian chiefs" to imagine a space in which contemporary minoritized groups might locate counternational acts of alliance that confront the devastating effects of exile and displacement.

FROM THE FRONTIER TO THE GHETTO

The *écriture* that Adnan employs in *The Indian Never Had a Horse* is one strategy used by an Arab American woman to confront these realities. We now can turn to Suheir Hammad's work to see how one of the "new ancestors" of this complex history of opposition to U.S. minoritization and Palestinian occupation shapes an autobiographical space from which to forge interracial alliances. Whereas Adnan and her generation lived through the violent history of Palestinian displacement after 1967, in the contemporary context, social as well as textual strategies have been refashioned to confront U.S. policies of minoritization and infringement on civil and human rights. Although many of these statist policies were also employed during the early waves of post-1967 immigration, the tenor of the contemporary responses to U.S. minoritization has distinct differences. I turn to the early work of Suheir Hammad particularly because she is one of the most prominent figures of post-1967 Palestinian American literature. Like Adnan's, Hammad's work grapples with the diasporic Arab recontextualized in a nation in which Arabs are minoritized. Like Adnan's, it specifically articulates a feminist politics around notions of women's voice and representation, the privileging of a vital sexuality in the midst of mainstream subjugation, and the unequal power structure in relations between men and women. And like Adnan's, it specifically addresses the complex struggles in and around Palestine.

A key difference in their respective works, though, is the scene of interracial alliance. The border crossing that Adnan radicalizes through surrealist form in the American frontier space is refashioned by Hammad into a ghettoized cityscape and has been employed as a springboard for much of Hammad's autobiographical work. Whereas Adnan relocated several times in the course of her life (from Beirut to Paris to the United States, back to Beirut, before returning to the United States again), Hammad's own physical displacement occurred only once, when she was a young child, leaving a Jordanian refugee camp with her parents to settle in Brooklyn, New York. I do not mean to dwell extensively on this biographical difference between the two authors; however, the distinction proves useful to chart how Adnan's textual strategies are refashioned by Hammad. For example, a work like *The Indian Never Had a Horse* employs many of the rhetorical strategies that Adnan learned as a product of the French *mission civilisatrice* in Lebanon and the confrontation with the aesthetic interests of the American language—Rimbaudian symbolism, Beat-era language poetry, the idealization of the frontier, and so on. In contrast, much of Hammad's work employs strategies of contemporary avant-garde hip-hop by utilizing a vernacular form to bring together the multiple strains that situate the Arab American diaspora in the wider scene of transnational belonging.

Born Palestinian, Born Black (1996) is structured around the transformation and translation of individual experience. Hammad opens the "Author's Note" to the collection with an epigraph containing the last lines of June Jordan's poem "Moving Towards Home":

> I was born a Black woman
> and now
> I am become a Palestinian
> against the relentless laughter of evil
> there is less and less living room
> and where are my loved ones?
>
> It is time to make our way home (ix, ll. 1–7)

Here, the scene is set for a mode of transformation in the present tense, a translation from the naturally and biologically "born" to the historically contingent "am become." The becoming from "Black woman" to "Palestinian" compactly traces the strategy of racialized and gendered descriptors of the speaker in the first line to a context of politicized self-determination in the last. In ventriloquizing Jordan's shift, Hammad locates the possibility of resistance outside the context of social constructionist discourse. "[Jordan] dared speak of transformation," Hammad notes, "of re-birth, of a deep understanding of humanity. The essence of being Spirit, *something no label can touch*" (x; emphasis added). The move to the realm of the other-than-social in order to enact resistance bears resemblance to the symbolist textual strategies Adnan foregrounds in *The Indian Never Had a Horse,* in which the American frontier space facilitates the commingling of the spirits of displaced bodies.

Adnan's timelessness, though, is refashioned by Hammad. The striking focus on the present tense situates the setting from which such a transformation and translation might open up the possibility of a pluralized passage "home." It is imperative that the passage take place now.

But where is home located? From what space has the black Palestinian woman been exiled? As Hammad makes clear in *Drops of This Story* (her 1996 memoir), *Born Palestinian, Born Black* (1996), and her recent collection, *ZaatarDiva* (2006), there are two homes hailed through diaspora. The first is a self-determined Palestinian nation-state with contiguous geographic and political borders in which people displaced after 1948 and 1967 might construct a viable democratic state. The second is access to the rights of full citizenship in the United States—indeed, a revaluation of the terms of citizenship—for working-class colored women generally, and Arab American migrants specifically. Neither Jordan nor Hammad, though, conceptualizes home as a site to which one might *return;* it is a space, as Jordan emphasizes, that must be "made," constructed, represented anew. *Born Palestinian, Born Black* thus makes its way home.

I begin a reading of the poetry in *Born Palestinian, Born Black* (1996) by turning to a poem that formulates the specificity of the Arab diasporic experience in the United States. In "Argela Remembrance," Palestinian cultural memory moves between two interconnected scenes, concomitantly locating the present tense of the opening speaker with the familial cultural heritage of the past in the same temporal moment (ll. 33–34). The first scene is the physical location of the Hammad family apartment in Brooklyn, "living room politics and tobacco / stained teeth" (32, ll. 13–14). Here, the speaker is the present-tense daughter of a displaced heritage. She and her father pass the *argela* (hubble-bubble) between them, "exhaling mediterranean breezes / mid east sighs" (31, ll. 6–7). The stanzas in which the daughter speaks are left-justified. In the first stanza, she passes the pipe to her father, and he begins to speak. The second scene is the imagined location in which her father places the memories of a lost culture, a "people" standing "on the edge of the sea," and these stanzas are center-justified (ll. 9–10). In this space, the father speaks of what has been lost in the "departure" from the edge of the sea, of asking the sea to "kiss our toes goodnight" and instead "she kissed them good-bye" (ll. 11–12). The shared experience of displacement from the edge of the Mediterranean allows the father to claim a first-person plural "we" that signifies "a people" united in a common experience of diaspora:

> we . . .
> eat with upturned hands
> plant plastic potted plants
> in suffocating apartments
> tiny brooklyn style
> in memory of the soil once
> laid under our nails
> collect sea shells in
> honor of goodnight kisses (13, l. 9; 32, ll. 1–8)

The back-and-forth movement of the *argela* between daughter and father is textually charted in the alternation between left-justified and center-justified stanzas. "We" is infused with the shared cultural memory existing in the physical space of "mediterranean breezes," a space in which the topography itself shows affection for its inhabitants through kisses that connect each member experientially. For Hammad here, abjection in the diaspora is implicitly tied to the shuttling between the stories of an imagined location, an intangible and immaterial possibility figured through "yellow hibiscus kisses shadowing / our path good-bye" (31, ll. 15–16). The Palestine that the daughter and her father articulate in this poem is one of spirit, of the exhaled breath of conversation over the *argela,* constructed wholly through conversation, a community emerging not through material goods but through the spoken discourse of a remembered culture.

In several poems, this movement between a scene of cultural memory and the materiality of the diaspora is complicated greatly by the experience of abjection in the geographic ghettoized spaces of Palestine. "Taxi," for example, like "Argela Remembrance," shuttles between New York City and Palestine. But whereas in "Argela Remembrance" Palestine is figured as a spirit around which a common heritage can be constructed, "Taxi" amplifies the material reality of present-day Palestinians living through displacement in daily contact with the Israeli occupation. The poem is divided into three sections. The first addresses an "urban warrior" in a scene of U.S. cosmopolitanism, where the experience of racial minoritization and prejudice has been softened by the effects of a prosperous economy:

> urban warrior i think we're
> too used to bottled water and soft ass wipes
> street soldier not getting taxis and little white ladies
> claspin purses ain't all it's about (11, ll. 1–4)

The second section addresses "my father's city," Gaza, in which human conditions for its inhabitants are squalid, inhuman (l. 5). Six stanzas detail the horrid circumstances of the lives of Palestinians under military occupation: "140 miles of 850,000 souls . . . gaza . . . the most people in the tiniest place anywhere" (ll. 10, 13). The details of these representations come fast and precise; unlike the discourse of "Argela Remembrance," which works on the level of general metaphor, here the brutal material conditions of everyday life are foregrounded. Indeed, Hammad documents the violence against children, a sexualized violence, with uncompromising candor. The body of the Palestinian boy becomes the site for a gendered, sexualized, and national violence. So too does the Palestinian girl's. The poem then links such state-sanctioned violence to U.S. financial aid being utilized by the Israeli military: "least I didn't turn your insides to confetti / with a u.s. made machete" (12, ll. 11–12). And the final stanza of the section makes the connection even more overt, tying the national symbology of each state together:

> the israeli flag is red white and blue too
> this red drips from billy clubs and soldiers boots
> this red soaks the faces of mournin mothers
> losin more sons to american tax dollars (ll. 21–24)

By making these material connections, Hammad links bodily violence—committed against the reproductive possibilities of Palestinian children's bodies—to the economic and political practices of the United States. Not only, then, does the poem represent the concerns of maintaining Palestinian culture in the diaspora, but it also amplifies the ways in which the existence and production of Palestinian culture are contingent on the material well-being of those individuals affected by military occupation.

The third section of "Taxi" returns to the scene of the U.S. city street, calling on the "urban warrior" to grapple with this abjection. The strategy employed by Hammad is to contextualize the plight of the people living in Gaza to the localized concerns of ghettoized minorities in the United States:

> so when we're vibin on the pale
> evil of welfare and crack   know i'm
> across the street and across the sea   so when
> we're combatin cops and prisons   know there are prisons
> like ansar III   nazis woudn't touch   pigs wouldn't visit
> so when we read baraka and listen to malcolm
> let's read darwish and keep on
> listenin to Malcolm (13, ll. 13–20)

Rigorous political engagement, according to the text, must be not only focused on the localized concerns of the minoritized American but also directed toward wider transnational concerns of material well-being. Hammad is not merely celebrating the hybridized construction of a first-person plural cultural identity, of an abundance of different foods and musics and styles, of a liberal multiculturalism; rather, she is explicitly linking the cultural with the material, and doing so through the inscription of a genealogy of interracial insurgency that links Amiri Baraka, Malcolm X, and Mahmoud Darwish. She writes, "so when you call me sista / ask after our family" (ll. 21–22). If one is to incorporate the multiple fractures of identity politics into the composition of self, then one must also address the political concerns of those individuals living beyond the political borders of the United States from whence the cultural elements have originated, the multiple heritages that have imbued the urban site with its complex of cultural forms. In this way, the protagonist of the poem links ghetto with ghetto and forwards a political act both across the street of the urban metropolis and across the sea in the material locale of her national heritage.

Two poems in particular expand on this articulation of political act. The struggle for political representation among people minoritized in the United

States is elicited as a first-person plural act in both “Manifest destiny” and “Open poem to those who rather we not read . . . or breathe” (ll. 79–80, 81–83). Both poems

emphasize the conjoining of several strains of cultural heritage. “Open poem” uses this notion of a politicized first-person plural rooted in the construction of interracial solidarity to enter into more specific descriptions of the content of such a community. The opening stanza insists on the central importance of respect toward those transnational figures minoritized economically and politically:

we children of children exiled from homelands
descendants of immigrants denied jobs and toilets
carry continents in our eyes
survivors of the middle passage
we stand
and demand recognition of our humanity (81, ll. 4–9)

Whereas in “Taxi” the unifying principles that bring community together are politically oriented around shared cultural practices—and as will be seen later, “Manifest destiny” ties those principles to a refashioning of the concept of heritage and family—“Open poem” emphasizes the shared material history of displacement, of multiple migrations between a location abroad and one within U.S. national borders. The basis in common material history is then deployed as the groundwork for a central “we” constituted through both style and action. Forms of cultural hybridity that compose much of the minoritized community in the ghettoized spaces of New York City are here still quite relevant. Unlike the other poems, though, Hammad situates the figuration of this community within a particular embodied subject:

heads sport civilizations
hips velvet wrapped in music. . . .
we braid resistance through our hair
pierce justice through our ears
tattoo freedom onto our breasts
the bluesy soul of brown eyed girls

clash with blood on the pale hands of
governments of war . . .
our very breath is a threat (82, ll. 5–6, 15–20; 83, l. 11)

The embodied act of counternational resistance is here composed of hybrid cultural material from a variety of diasporic histories. Further, the body becomes the site for complex resignifications of color. If phenotypic attributes have been the hegemonic means of categorizing and disciplining U.S. citizen-subjects, then here Hammad calls for a disidentification of national community based solely on skin color. The commonality shared in this community is that not only are members using their bodies for explicitly political ends, but they are also attempting to compose themselves beyond the differences of hue: "you can see the earth running / right under our skin" (82, ll. 7–8).

"Manifest destiny" places four different individuals around a meal together, in which each character "*should have been* other people / with other people" (79, ll. 4–5; emphasis added). The poem celebrates the fact that although these four figures had coped with social pressures to pursue other life paths, the paths they choose for themselves are politically and ethically oriented.

One . . . was a lover of both men and women . . . girl of riot . . . and a poet
another . . . was a scholar of african glory . . . lover of knowledge . . . and a poet
the other . . . was a fighter for independence . . . lover of an island . . . and a poet
and me . . . me . . . searcher of truth . . . lover of humanity . . . and a poet.
(79, ll. 6, 9, 10, 13, 14, 17)

Three elements are in play in this construction of alliance. The first is the privileging of political consciousness, engaging the central material depravations of others who have struggled against the rigors of social pressure. Sexuality, cultural nationalism, politicized conceptions of freedom independence, and wide-ranging human rights concerns are all brought together within the scene of a shared meal. Second, each individual is described as someone who engages in the political not merely through rhetoric and activism but also through the aesthetic forms of poetry. The written representations of the political are of central importance to the composition of community. Last, the poem closes with this community refashioned as a new type of familial heritage:

> missing my family
> who couldn't understand
> we four all missing family who wouldn't understand
> creating a family
> we struggling to understand
> we were where we needed to be
> we are who we have to be (80, ll. 1–7)

The family unit is renarrated here to contend with the notion of family as the social receptacle of an identity based on genetic descent; rather, it is reconceived in the scene of cultural and political exchange. Heritage is a component of identity here that becomes malleable and contingent on the social construction of wider community, a community situated, in this case, within a transnational urban setting.

If "Manifest destiny" places the scene of diasporic heritage in U.S.-based metropolitan alliances, the final poem in *Born Palestinian, Born Black,* titled "Broken and Beirut," explicates a wider notion of return (see ll. 95–97). The return Hammad scripts is not simply a return to a stabilized nation form in which citizenship is freely granted based on heritage; indeed, for Hammad, as a Palestinian, there is no simple state-citizen relationship in her history to return to. Nor is the return only to the spiritual essence of "mediterranean breezes" and "mid east sighs" that Hammad describes in "Argela Remembrance"; such an imagined site, though perhaps providing the structuring metaphors for imagining a Palestine rooted in cultural heritage, does not in itself provide a sustained account of a specific material history of diaspora. "Broken and Beirut" amplifies this material history. This history bears witness to both those individuals who were forced to leave their homes only to become minoritized in the United States as well as the destruction of their private property, the public infrastructure such as roads and plumbing, and the political organs that could provide the organizational potential for a future Palestine.

The poem is broken into two sections, divided by a short parenthetical stanza. The first section addresses the carnage incurred "here," an unnamed locale in which war has ravaged the bodies of its inhabitants. In this section, violence is a return "to what we know," a locale in which the questions asked are over the mangling of the body:

> where is the head that goes with this 7-year-old shoulder
> shattered . . . this leg looks like it fits with this hip
> this dead with that dead . . . cause they wear twin rings
> on bloated purple hands (96, ll. 2–5)

Returning to the carnage of war becomes figured as a return to a seemingly endless cycle of violence, of "getting / over shit to prepare for more shit" (ll. 7–8). Such images resonate across *Born Palestinian, Born Black;* whereas in the bulk of the collection the images are used as a springboard for a critique of the Israeli or the U.S. nation form, here violence simply feeds into more violence, a "return . . . / all over again" (ll. 11–12).

The second section, in contrast, is infused with a desire to return to another kind of home. I read the ways in which Hammad constructs home here as a theory of counternational solidarity built through the transvaluation of national belonging. Home here is not "only to mama and baba," the home of a familial heritage (l. 17). Rather, it is a home "before me," a return to a remembrance of "what i've never lived" (ll. 18, 21). Home is thus conceived as a potentiality, a return to that which has yet to exist. It is a location represented not geographically on a political map, but rather in the bodily shared experience of a common heritage, "a home within me . . . within us" (l. 22). To "become Palestinian," in this formulation, is to carry a concept of belonging that is not solely overlaid by structures of nation or geography, but rather is composed of a shared culture and a cultural memory that has withstood exile, displacement, and minoritization. Home is "what we've forgotten / what hunger has faked," and a return to that site is a process of becoming, of social transformation: "touch it taste . . . name it and / come back to here" (97, ll. 5–6, 10–11).

In short, Palestinian cultural identity, existent within the circulation of political concerns forwarded in a ghettoized setting like the ones addressed in previous poems, serves in "Broken and Beirut" as the potentiality for the construction of a Palestinian nation form, a form that in itself is predicated on process, on becoming. Hammad makes this notion of process clear:

> make no mistake
> be precise *get back to work*
> shifting through the rubble mathematically
> building a new day
> with offerings of honey and memory (ll. 12–16; emphasis added)

Home is thus a site of potentiality, a form where the dynamics of social transformation are not limited by the structures of the Euro-American nation form, are not bounded by the strictures of the past. It is not simply a site of rebuilding, of renewal, of return in any simple circular sense; rather, here, Hammad locates home in the production of a future through the manifold resources of a culture forged in a transnational context and through transnational solidarities. As a community surviving displacement, exile, and diaspora, as Palestinian, as Arab, as Arab American, as a community forged through material, political, and cultural connections with others who survive the material effects of the diaspora, Hammad locates the potentiality for the building of a new home in which members of those "othered" communities—like herself—might speak their own life experiences, the "sweet honey / on the lips of survivors" (ll. 20–21).

EPILOGUE

Looking to Adnan's and Hammad's autobiographical poetry from the 1980s and 1990s should help us think through the spaces of possibility in the wake of September 11, 2001. After 9/11, the marginalization and minoritization of and violence against Arab American communities have grown more severe. There is no more important moment than the present to consider the ways in which Arab American autobiography can and should be mobilized. As Muneer Ahmad has written about the catalyzing force of racial violence after 9/11, "The opportunity is there for these communities to forge necessary coalitions now, that they might endure beyond the period of immediate self-interest, and begin to imagine a shared citizenship outside the bounds of subordination" (2002, 111–12).

Moving toward a homespace, getting back to work, imagining possibilities for the future: Hammad's call for a transnational mobilization of diasporic communities in ghettoized spaces is one critical approach. The wide circulation of Hammad's 2001 poem, "First writing since," describing the complex contradictions of Arab American identification in the wake of the Trade Tower attacks, is one sign that these strategies for transnational mobilization are gaining a foothold after 9/11.[5] Another is the open-ended run of Simmons's *Def Poetry Jam on Broadway* in New York City, in which Hammad—and many other members of diasporic communities—critiques the nation form through its connection to the logics of U.S. imperialism. They are indeed signs that transnational autobiographical identification—placing the autobiographical self in solidarity with a network of diasporic populations—has had the effect of carving out access to increasing publics. But just as U.S. foreign policy continues to deepen its military and economic engagement with the Arab world, just as "the nation question" for Palestine is answered through policies of otherness and exclusion, so too must the multiple contradictions in the nation form continue to be addressed, critiqued, and utilized as a basis for social transformation.

5. Hammad reads this poem in the series premiere for *Def Poetry Jam,* and it has been widely distributed via the Internet.

5

Postnational Ethics, Postcolonial Politics

Raimonda Tawil's *My Home, My Prison*

JAMIL KHADER

> How could I be free?
> I am a Palestinian living under occupation.
> I am a woman living in a male-dominated reactionary society.
> I am a wife in a society that has made men into gods and women into submissive dolls. My house arrest has ended. My enslavement persists. My battle for emancipation has only begun.
>
> —Raimonda Hawa Tawil, *My Home, My Prison*

The Palestinian journalist and writer Raimonda Tawil is a unique voice in contemporary Arab women's writings. Her moving and controversial autobiography, *My Home, My Prison* (1980), contests and problematizes the dominant thematics and tropes of Arab women's literary tradition. Evelyne Accad (1995) and Mona Fayad (1996) point out that despite the opportunistic displacement and "metaphorization" of gender in the metaphysics of national presence, Arab women writers have traditionally valorized the metanarratives of nationalism, resistance to colonialism, and the unified community over women's personal identity and freedom from oppressive patriarchal traditions. Like many other women around the third world, Arab women felt obliged to identify with national resistance to colonial powers, consequently subsuming women's struggle for independence under the banner of masculinist national identity (Kandiyoti 1994). Ultimately, any womanist, or feminist, critique of Arab patriarchal structures and its nationalist master narrative had to be suspended until a collective subjectivity and a national sovereignty were affirmed. Especially in Palestine, since the convention of the Arab Women's Congress of Palestine in 1929, Palestinian women have been expected to commit themselves to the project of nationalist mobilization *(al-a'amal al-watani)* at the expense of their struggle for social rights and gender equity. Julie Peteet, for one, notes that "Palestinian women perceived themselves as victims of Zionism not as women, a separate social category, but as Palestinians who felt their national identity and survival in their homes threatened by British occupation and a hardly disguised Zionist claim to their country" (1991, 42). Palestinian women, however, have paid a heavy price for prioritizing national struggle over gender concerns. By 1990, as Rima Hamami and Eileen Kuttab correctly argue, the Palestinian national movement depolicitized gender, marginalized women's social rights, and even went as far as considering "women's political activism not as a contribution to national liberation but as a threat to it" (1999, 4).[1]

Unlike many of her sisters, however, the outspoken Palestinian journalist Raimonda Tawil insists on narrating her struggle for women's autonomy and national self-determination simultaneously as a Palestinian woman living in a repressive Arab society under Israeli military occupation and Zionist settler colonialization of the West Bank and Gaza. Raimonda Hawa Tawil was born in Acre in 1940 to an urban, bourgeois, Christian family and reluctantly became, after the 1948 Catastrophe (al-Nakbah), a citizen of the Israeli state, "the home of the Jewish people." She experienced firsthand the trauma of dispossession, separation of families, "minoritization," and the daily negotiation of the alien language and culture of the Israeli occupiers. She continued to live in Israel, but moved to Nazareth, where she attended a convent school. After her mother divorced her father, an unprecedented act of gender rebellion in Arabic culture, the father sent Tawil to a new school in Haifa, in order to separate her from her mother. In 1957, Tawil revoked her "second-class" Israeli citizenship, crossing the Mandelbaum Gate (Gate of Tears) to settle in Amman, Jordan. In Amman, Tawil endured the repressive puritanical traditions of Arab patriarchy, which robbed her of any sense of economic independence and the freedom of movement. Unable to return to Israel, because the Law of

1. For more on this issue, see Abdo 1994; Glavanis-Grantham 1996; Gluck 1995; Jad 1995; and Sharoni 1995.

Return did not apply equally to the indigenous population of Palestine, Tawil had no option but to get married. Her marriage entrapped her in a "golden cage" under patriarchal custody. But in her quest for personal autonomy and emancipation, after reading none other than *The Second Sex* by Simone de Beauvoir, her marriage was troubled, as she continuously contested the image of a passive and docile wife.

Right after the 1967 Six-Day War (al-Naksah), she moved to the town of Nablus in the West Bank, where she witnessed once again the traumatic history of Palestinian dispossession and mass exodus. Tawil now began to participate actively in relief work for the refugees in the camps, using her knowledge of Hebrew to help alleviate the miserable conditions of the refugees. Tawil thus joined the General Union of Palestinian Women to protest the Israeli ruthless violation of Palestinian human rights, especially practices such as house demolitions, collective punishments, land expropriation, and deportation. Tawil then moved to Ramallah and began working as a correspondent for the foreign press; she would later establish the Palestine Press Service in Jerusalem, in order to help the Palestinians gain "the permission to narrate," to use the late Edward Said's words, and to reconstruct the abysmal Western and Israeli media representation of the Palestinians as primitive, irrational terrorists. Against all national dicta and Palestine Liberation Organization (PLO) policy at the time, moreover, Tawil fought for the Palestinian right of self-determination and independence in coalition with "dovish" Israelis and other cosmopolitan Jewish figures. Thus, she turned her Ramallah home into a salon, where the local Palestinian and Israeli as well as the international Jewish intelligentsia would meet to discuss the future of the Levant. She also traveled to the United States on a lecture tour to promote her two-state solution not in the name of inherently divine or natural rights over Palestine but in the name of global ethics and justice. These transnational connections, however, infuriated the Israeli military administration in the Occupied Territories, and she was placed under house arrest for fifty days, during which she wrote her provocative autobiography.

As this brief biographical sketch shows, Tawil situates her struggle, or what she refers to as her "double alienation," or double colonization, within the history of anticolonial struggle for national independence as well as against the established structures of Arab patriarchy in Palestine. Suha Sabbagh (1989, 6), therefore, frames her discussion of Tawil within Frederick Jameson's theory of "national allegory," mainly because this autobiographical act "combine[s] the political and the personal." But Sabbagh quickly dismisses Tawil's genuine national commitment, claiming that her interest in the national struggle is nothing but a ploy to protect her feminist agenda from patriarchal vengeance (5). Notwithstanding the problem of intention, Sabbagh glosses over those moments in the text when Tawil is adamant about not only refusing to conform to the PLO platform but also exposing the skewed sexual politics of national liberation movements. This defiance precludes any homological correspondence between Tawil's condition as a woman and the Palestinian nation, because the latter for her is predicated on the marginalization and silencing of the former. Instead of the prism of national allegory, I propose to read Tawil's autobiography within the discordances and tensions *between* the discourses of womanhood and nationalism, feminism and postcolonialism, through the prism of what is now referred to in literary circles as postnationalism.

Theories of postnationalism purport to resolve the ambiguous temporality of the notorious prefix *post* in postcolonialism, by encoding postnationalism as the time "after" the end of postcolonialism, and thus prematurely strike neocolonial formations out of international geopolitics.[2] Postnationalist theorists thus reread the colonial encounter as a transcultural event, or as a "cooperative venture," as Said writes (1993, 269). As such, they foreground the ambivalences and indeterminacies in colonial governmentalism and its discursive practices as well as anticolonial nationalism, as Homi Bhabha (1994) has shown after Frantz Fanon. Postnationalists also shift the grounds of the discussion from resistance and its Manichaean subtext of polarization to a recognition of colonizers and colonized as partners and collaborators against "institutionalized suffering," in Ashis Nandy's words (1989, 137). Colonialism, thus, turns out to be a mutually transformative process that celebrates the "mutual contagion and subtle intimacies" between oppressors and oppressed (Gandhi 1998, 129). It allows postnationalists to acknowledge not only that the oppressors are themselves victimized by their own "modes of oppression" but also that the

2. This same concern was articulated by Ella Shohat (1992), who contests the viability of postcolonialism to the question of Palestine, since the *post* as a temporal rupture with *colonialism* fails to register the continuous Israeli occupation of Palestinian territory.

colonized can act as "sometimes-collaborator, sometimes-competitor, with the oppressive system," in Leela Gandhi's words (138–39). Consequently, postnational discourse becomes a counterdiscursive site conducive to reimagining, as Edward Said writes, the "possibility of a more generous and pluralistic vision of the world," one that substitutes violence for collaboration (1993, 277).

For Tawil, the alternative language of possibility and transformation offered by postnationalism remains urgent for undoing the atavistic narratives of negation that imbue the conflict between Israelis and Palestinians, Arabs and Jews.[3] I would like to argue, however, that Tawil proffers a corrective reading of postnational discourse, one that rereads contemporary, and anachronistic, contexts of colonial hegemony such as Palestine not only with but also against postnationalism. Although she wholeheartedly believes in reconfiguring the contact zone in Israel/Palestine in terms of its intimacies, contiguities, and cooperation, Tawil does not simply lose sight of the asymmetrical power relations between Israelis and Palestinians within the international power structure of the cold war era. She cannot afford to ignore the daily humiliation and brutality her nation is subjected to at the hands of the Israelis. As such, she not only destabilizes the self/Other, colonizer/colonized binaries in a true postnational fashion but also recenters the history of resistance to the Israeli occupation and Zionist settler colonialism in the West Bank and Gaza Strip.

Tawil's autobiography, thus, illuminates the preconditions for the production of postnationalist discourse about which theories of postnationalism seem to be silent. These theories never spell out the conditions, contexts, or circumstances in which postnational identities and subjectivities can be articulated and performed in their singularities: Which postcolonial subjects are capable of becoming postnationals? Under what conditions? How? Tawil demonstrates that postnationalism can still be a viable strategy for outsider and cosmopolitan postcolonial subjects who can balance the ethical demands of hybridity with the political project of resistance and national liberation through solidarity politics.[4]

3. On this politics of negation in Palestine/Israel, see Abu-Lughod 1988.

4. In relating issues of postnationalism and hybridity to the Palestinian case, I am taking issue with Smadar Levie and Ted Swedenburg's contention that "hybridity . . . does not appear to be a viable strategy in the struggle for Palestine—a case of an exilic identity demanding to return

In what follows, therefore, I would like first to address the context and preconditions for the production of an insurgent postnational subjectivity in Tawil's autobiography. I will explore her reconstruction of an outsider, cosmopolitan subjectivity through a postcolonial reinterpretation of Simone de Beauvoir's *Second Sex*. I will also examine Tawil's critique of the sexual politics of the Palestinian national imaginary as she dissolves the boundaries between two major symbolic spaces of Palestinian resistance and regeneration, namely, the home and the prison to which she alludes in the title of her autobiography, and rewrites them into each other as uncanny sites of oppression, effacement, and unhomeliness. Second, I will show how her cosmopolitan outsiderness and her critique of Palestinian nationalism clear a space for the production as well as the interrogation of postnationalism: she destabilizes the Self/Other boundaries to promote a sense of intimacy and contiguity between Israelis and Palestinians while at the same time engaging in material and discursive forms of resistance to the occupation.

OUTSIDER, COSMOPOLITAN FEMINISM: A POSTCOLONIAL REINTERPRETATION OF SIMONE DE BEAUVOIR'S *SECOND SEX*

The precondition for the narration of Tawil's postnational politics is an affirmation of the multiplicity of the outsider identities that she inhabits throughout her life. Tawil engages the multiplicity of her subject positions and difference within the universal referent of womanhood as she reads Simone de Beauvoir's *Second Sex* (1980, 65). Thus, Tawil chooses not simply to valorize gender oppression and the Othering of woman as de Beauvoir does but rather to fashion a multiple subjectivity in a postcolonial context, or a postcolonial feminist subjectivity. Tawil does not blindly appropriate de Beauvoir's philosophical

---

to its historic territory" (1996, 12). Although Levie and Swedenburg are correct in claiming that because Palestinians' communal identity is "threatened with radical effacement" they "cannot not desire the basic privileges that accompany membership and citizenship in a community, group, nation," desiring a communal identity does not preclude the production of hybrid identities formed in the liberation struggle in solidarity with Israelis and reformed Zionists (12). Furthermore, Levie and Swedenburg's argument can be misinterpreted as saying that Palestinians are capable only of negating their negation, not transcending it in non-Manichaean forms.

discourse for an analysis of Palestinian women, as critics suggest.[5] She does, however, reconfigure de Beauvoir's valorization of gender oppression and the Othering of women across multiple identity narratives such as race, class, nation, religion, and education.

In her epochal work *The Second Sex* (1949), Simone de Beauvoir claims that patriarchy posits "Man" concretely through projects as a "continual transcendence toward other freedoms" while constructing "Woman" in opposition as the absolute immanent Other. Transcendence entails a superiority emanating from man's ability to master and annihilate the earth and the body, with which women have been associated by virtue of their reproductive capacity. Moreover, she espouses a belief in the essential unity of women based on their biological destiny, representing "Woman" as a universal category owing to the shared experience of gender oppression. De Beauvoir's homogenization of women's oppression poses two main problems for Tawil and other third world feminists. First, de Beauvoir's Eurocentric feminist narrative essentializes women as a universal category and elides differences in the experiences of women across various cultural spaces. Presupposing gender Manichaeism between the sexes in this universalistic discourse, de Beauvoir is unrelenting in suppressing other multiple, interlocking, and intersecting social determinants, between and across which the subject is constructed. Not until she coauthored with Gisele Halimi their book *Djamila Boupacha* (1962), on the young Algerian suicide bomber who was tortured and raped with a bottle by French interrogators, did de Beauvoir start to decenter her cultural identity and to examine her location along various yet discrepant cultural spaces.[6]

Tawil, however, manages to salvage an outsider, cosmopolitan feminist subjectivity from *The Second Sex* itself, remarking that de Beauvoir inflamed her "to resist oppression in all its forms" (1980, 170–71). Realizing very early in her intellectual development that patriarchal domination collaborates with colonial powers to suppress and erase her from the public space, Tawil articulates her multiple subjectivity between and across discrepant but overlapping

5. For instance, Elise Manganaro oversimplifies Tawil's dialogic construal of de Beauvoir to a naive assimilation of "Western outlook and a Western system of references" (1989, 131).

6. On de Beauvoir's Algerian writings and her departure from the existential intelligentsia's complicity with French colonialism, see Murphy 1995.

social determinants. Thus, her outsider, cosmopolitan subjectivity emerges in the interstices of dominant and emerging national, class, religious, gender, and linguistic identity narratives. In between and across these interstices, she articulates her politics of disidentification with the pedagogical narratives of Palestinian nationalism as a woman; with the colonial military hegemony as a colonized subject who is deprived of citizenship after the 1967 war; with the partisan Arab regimes as a Palestinian; with the Palestinian subaltern groups as a member of the elite bourgeoisie (255); with the predominantly Muslim society as a Christian (37, 81); with the conservative patriarchal culture as a feminist; with the monolingual Arab society as a fluent and competent speaker of multiple colonial languages—Hebrew, French, and English; and with the peasant and illiterate culture as Western educated and cosmopolitan.

The constant remaking and unmaking of this outsider, cosmopolitan subjectivity across and between various discrepant power discourses engenders a postnational condition of productive aporia. Tawil thus continues to problematize her location at any historical moment of her life to express her reluctance to belong to any identity narrative and ultimately to transcend these identities into an alternative condition with a radical language of possibility. The problematics of citizenship can provide a good example with which to illustrate Tawil's politics of disidentification. After the establishment of Israel, she decides to renounce her Israeli citizenship, despite the personal freedom she enjoyed, because "Israeliness" is predicated on an exclusive ethnoreligious identity narrative of "Jewishness."[7] But even when she reterritorializes in Amman, she realizes that she had to struggle not to forfeit her Palestinian identity under the Jordanian regime. Moreover, in the feudal, puritanical, patriarchal

7. As the "state of the Jewish people," Israel is based from its originary moment on the absence, or, better, the legal obliteration, of the Palestinian community that continued to reside in its lands after the Catastrophe. There still remains a disturbing confusion in Israel between nationality and citizenship regarding the Palestinian citizens of Israel. The writer Anton Shammas, who is a Palestinian citizen of Israel, points out that there is no nationality in Israel but rather "ethnic affiliation." To put it more bluntly, there are no Israelis in Israel but Jews, Arabs, or Druze. Both Tawil and Shammas, like the recent emergence of a post-Zionist discourse in Israel and in the Jewish diaspora, demand that Israel resolve the paradox of its foundational myth. In a post-Zionist era, Israeli law has to determine whether Israel is the state of the Jewish people or the state of its citizens. See, for example, Shammas 1995.

culture of Jordan, Tawil's personal freedom as a woman and an individual was restricted to the domestic space. At the interplay of privileged and oppressed positionalities in Israel and in Jordan along gender, national, ethnic, and citizenship discourses, Tawil contemplates her condition of aporia: "In Israel, I would belong to a despised minority and be treated as a second-class citizen. All the same, as a woman my personal lot would be much better than in Jordan. A difficult choice; humiliation as an Arab or repression as a woman—which is better?" (55). Yet Tawil decides to move to Nablus, in the West Bank, where she continues to defy easy classification in any comfortable cultural space. Tawil, in short, refuses to be fetishized in any slot of Otherness, by strategically articulating her location across shifting positions of both subordination and freedom, privilege and oppression, which undo the fiction of authenticity in the formation of identities and open up to an alternative postnational discourse.

UNHOMELINESS: THE UNCANNY CONTEXT OF POSTNATIONALISM

Not only does Tawil shed light on the preconditions for the production of postnationalist discourse in a colonial situation, but she also delineates the context for the production of such a discourse by engaging both the oppressive colonial occupation of Palestine by Israel and the sexual politics of the Palestinian national imaginary. She discloses not only the oppressive patriarchal traditions underpinning this nationalist imaginary but also the patriarchal complicity with Israeli colonial hegemony in suppressing Palestinian women. Tawil thus problematizes and deromanticizes the mythic representations of the home/land in the Palestinian national iconography, as she ruptures the phantasmagoric isomorphism between the home, the homeland, and women. Decentering the ideology of home, Tawil draws attention to the continuity of the terrain of terror and violence between the sphere of the Israeli prisons and the domestic sphere. Rather than dichotomize the prison and the home, Tawil suggests that the domestic sphere reproduces the oppressive economic and political technologies of Israeli occupation governmentalism and Zionist settler colonialism and encodes them as gender ideology.

Tawil's confinement within the claustrophobic space of home/prison provides not only the occasion of the production of *My Home, My Prison* but also its narrative frame and major structuring trope. The autobiography begins with a phone call, which replaces the "knock on the door" of traditional prison memoirs, from the military government bureau, summoning her to report to the military governor's office in Ramallah.[8] Without trial, the Israeli military authorities accuse her of threatening the security of the Jewish state by practicing false and inaccurate journalism. Consequently, they subject her to "special supervision," during which she has to "remain behind the doors of the house in which she resides in Ramallah, throughout all hours of the day and night" (6). Placed under this arbitrary house arrest, she realizes the implications of this sinister confinement on her mobility and freedom of thought and expression. In the meantime, Tawil decides to "record the story of all my prisons, all my walls," the national and patriarchal domination that collaborates on reducing the feminist subject to a docile body (9). Foregrounding the continuities between national and gender subjection, Tawil renders home as a prison and prison as a condition of unhomeliness. As she narrates her multiple incarcerations, Tawil recognizes the underlying condition of her detention: she is locked up in an existential imprisonment under which her "battle for emancipation has only begun" (257).

In Tawil's autobiography, the textual production of the home/prison configuration evolves into an uncanny space of displacement. Understanding this uncanny space, nonetheless, requires positioning the home/prison nexus in its cultural and political contexts. In particular, I shall examine how Tawil supplants the pleasures of the cultural discourses of Palestinian national formation with the tropes of deprivation, loss, and estrangement. These discourses are, first, the rhetoric of revolutionary regeneration in prison and, second, the familiarity of dwelling places. The radical nature of this strategy becomes even clearer when examined in the context of the political realities of arbitrary detention and house demolitions that Palestinians endured under the Israeli military occupation.[9]

Whereas Palestinian literary texts invoke the penitentiary as an imperialist topos, where Palestinian prisoners are dehumanized and Palestinian national identity is effaced, and home, in contrast, is seen as the space where women are

8. For more analysis of the conventions of prison writings, see Harlow 1989.

9. For a full discussion of the punitive measures undertaken by the Israeli military occupation, see Shehade 1988.

fetishized as the unadulterated image of cultural authenticity, Tawil deploys the trope of home in a way that projects the architectonics of the prison, turning both the prison and the home into embodiments of the condition of unhomeliness.[10] She reinterprets the topoi of home and prison by describing home in terms of objectification and oppression as well as of psychic disruption of the identification with the maternal body and voice. Thus, her condition of captivity entails first and foremost the unraveling of the obscenity of entrapment and persecution that are usually masked, rationalized, and neutralized in the familiar spaces of the homely. This unmasking constitutes an urgent project for Tawil, for whom Arab women in their denial of their gender oppression are pathologically schizophrenic (67). She exposes, thus, the space of domesticity as that ideological domain of the cult of femininity in which Arab women's autonomy and voice are subdued. Tawil writes: "My repression did not come from some amorphous and faceless 'society'; it was my own home and immediate social environment that imprisoned me" (64).

Moreover, she reconfigures the semantics of sanctity used to depict the motherland and the landscape of Palestine itself. Since the surplus feminine presence threatens to decenter the normative narration, discourses of national formation authorize the allegorical figuration of home and nation as mother.[11] This figurative displacement of women in official national discourse manages to suspend Palestinian women's agency in an ahistorical and apolitical realm. At stake here is the gender politics of revolutionary aesthetics that constructs the home in terms of the ideologies of the docile female body and its attendant discourse of virtuous female sexuality. Like home, the land becomes, in a metonymic economy, a part of her prison, "confining her to a stifling captivity" (68). The emotional investment in the rhetorical realms of home, homeland, and nation ends up reproducing the repressive allegiance to essentialist ideologies. Hence, Tawil asserts the ambivalence of her emotional attachment to an erogenous culture that devalues her as an erotic object of

10. A seminal literary analysis of Palestinian literature in terms of textualities of resistance can still be found in Kanafani 1987. See also Parmenter 1994 for a good study of place and identity in Palestinian literature.

11. For a discussion of the symbolic representation of women as mothers in the Palestinian national movement, see Antonius 1983, 67–68.

desire under conditions of spatial immobility. She remarks: "But as a woman, I could not feel that I belonged to this society that threatened to dehumanize me into a sex object. I felt like a stranger, persecuted and misunderstood. I did not want to remain a slave, a woman-child" (67). As such, the domestic space manipulates repressive masculinist technologies to efface, detain, constrain, surveil, discipline, confiscate, and dehumanize the body and agency of the feminist subject.

In short, Tawil correlates her imprisonment in the endogenous prison of patriarchal domination with her confinement in the colonial penitentiary. Home and prison, patriarchy and colonialism, then, function in an economy of synonymous substitution. Indeed, for Tawil the Israeli detention centers are not that different from the "prison called marriage," and her husband is not much different from her Israeli jailer and interrogator. Unsettling the carceral borders across and between the public space and the private terrain, therefore, Tawil is capable of envisioning a postnational language of ethics and possibility with the Other as same and different, intimate and hostile, at once, while insisting on the immanence of the language of resistance and national liberation in the name of the politics of solidarity.

POSTNATIONAL ETHICS, POSTCOLONIAL POLITICS

Disavowing the sacrosanct iconography of the Palestinian national master narrative, Tawil rewrites the traditional semantics of the Israeli-Palestinian colonial encounter with and against postnational discourse. She not only inscribes what Leela Gandhi calls the "unembarrassed—and potentially embarrassing—utopianism" of postnational reimagining of an alternative language of mutuality, intimacy, and solidarity between colonizers and colonized but also recenters the urgent language of resistance to the brutality of the Israeli occupation and Zionist settler colonialism (1998, 137). Like Edward Said's influential works on Palestine, Tawil warns against both fetishizing the production of a Manichaean colonial epistemology that posits not only the Self against its Other, Palestinians against Zionists, victims against oppressors, and conceptualizing their colonial encounter as a confrontation between antagonistic national narratives and identities (see Said 1993, 1994a, 2001). Tawil, thus, destabilizes the Self/Other boundaries by unraveling the indeterminacies and multiplicity in the construction of the Jewish Other in the Palestinian national imaginary and the Arab cultural unconsciousness. She also appropriates the traditional signifiers of Jewishness to uncover the Otherness, or Jewishness, of Palestinian identity. And finally, she works in dialogue and coalition with the Israeli peace camp and the international Jewish intelligentsia, turning this colonial encounter into a "collaborative venture," as Said says.

After the June war of 1967, Tawil immediately realizes that Levantine spaces, histories, and identities should be urgently reconfigured to accommodate the new realities of the Middle East. In that historical juncture, the Jew occupied a monolithic image in the Palestinian/Arab cultural and political discourses (Harkabi 1972). The Jew in the Palestinian national imaginary and Arab cultural unconsciousness was seen only as a Zionist Other whose existence was interpreted as the negation and erasure of Palestinian presence. In the ambience of fear and mistrust that dominated the Levant after 1967, the nationalists invoked Manichaean paradigms in which the Jew was always constructed as an oppressor, a fascist and even nazi persecutor, and an European imperialist. As such, Tawil was always reminded that "the Israeli with whom you want to make dialogue is in uniform and carrying a gun" (1980, 124) and that "they are all Zionists, they all serve in the army—therefore they cannot be trusted" (159). Even her young daughter Suha is understandably brainwashed by this boycott mentality. On one occasion, Suha tells her mother, "When they're in uniform, they can't disobey orders, can they? They are obliged to kill" (192).

Tawil defies this nazification of the Jews by splitting the image of the Jewish Other into colonial Zionists, on the one hand, and humanitarian Israelis, on the other. She emphasizes that it is necessary to engage a nonviolent struggle against the colonialist Zionists who believe in the dream of Eretz Israel, but it is equally imperative to fight in coalition with "dovish" and leftist Israelis. Underlying her unstable, slippery representation of the Israelis is her belief in the essential humanity of the Israelis and their Jewish ethics. Even the most racist, evil oppressor does not lack a conscience or sensitivity to distinguish between oppression and respect for Others. Tawil would constantly strive to reach out for and relate to the humanity of the Other: "As long as [the Israeli soldier] was in uniform, he was an enemy—but inside the uniform, he remained a man nonetheless. Time and time again, I encountered the same conflict—how to relate to an enemy as a human being? How to relate to a human being as an enemy?" (149). Therefore, she narrates how some Israeli soldiers did assist dispossessed Palestinians, despite the military prohibition against collaboration with the enemy. For example, the soldier Hanoch was honored by Nablus's mayor for his tremendous help to the refugees in the Nablus areas (14). In addition, she mentions how after the 1967 war, when the residents of Kalkilya were displaced from their town for the second time, an Israeli-Moroccan soldier defended those villagers against his troopers' sadistic humiliation of them. He angrily scolded them, saying, "You people don't have a heart! Don't you have a home, a family? Is this Judaism? You ought to remember Auschwitz!" (100). She also tells the story of Siah, a radical opposition group of dissident Israeli intellectuals who rallied in support of the residents of the small Palestinian village A'krabeh when the military government pressured them to sell their lands to Zionist settlers. By circulating these stories, Tawil shows both Palestinians and Israelis that there are Israeli Jews who "were prepared to clash with their own army, to risk beatings and imprisonment in order to express anger and disgust with their own government's treatment of a remote Palestinian village" (159).[12]

Besides splitting the monolithic representation of the Israelis, Tawil debunks the Jewish/Palestinian polarization by recognizing the Otherness of the Self. Tawil redefines the mythic codification of the Jewish diaspora by calling the Palestinians "the new Jews" (77). The mass exodus of the Palestinians in 1948 and 1967 led to an ironic reversal: "The place of the Jewish refugees was taken by the Palestinians" (111). Blurring the Arabs/Jews, oppressors/victims binaries ultimately transmits a sense of the atrocities and genocide that characterize Palestinian/Jewish histories. Tawil notes: "Any person of conscience—Jew or Christian—should acknowledge this injustice, whereby the persecuted survivors of Nazi concentration camps were given a home by making the Palestinians homeless. 'We are like you,' I told my Jewish listeners. 'We Palestinians are the Jews of the Arab world'" (201). This radical strategy problematizes dominant notions of identity, Self, and Otherness without offering absolution

12. Such stories of solidarity made it to the PLO's 1981 *Committee for the Occupied Homeland Report on Contact with Jews,* which praised the "positive role which the democratic and anti-Zionist forces play" in the conflict (Lukacs 1992, 357).

for the history of aggression and violence upon which the Jewish state is built. Refusing to subscribe to an originary authentic Self that validates the primacy of one cultural space, Tawil transvalues the national signifiers into the site of ontological ambiguity as it is caught in a network of differences. She uses those ontological slippages to suggest interconnections and mutuality between Israelis and Palestinians while preserving their difference.

Encoding "Palestinianness" by the traditional signifiers of Jewish identity, including diaspora and genocide, Tawil decenters the privileged location of Jewishness as synonymous with trauma and suffering in post-Holocaust Eurocentric culture. As such, the archetypal representation of the suffering Jew is transformed into the haunting image of the persecutor. Tawil's postnationalism is used to contest the Jewish monopoly of the industry of pain and suffering in Euro-America and to elicit sympathy for the Palestinian cause within a framework of justice. As Nubar Hovsepian correctly points out, the ideological "privatization of pain prevents the victims from imagining let alone comprehending that they are capable of heaping pain on another people" (1994, 53). Evoking this postnational interconnectedness, Tawil does not mean either to retrieve (like discourses of assimilation) or even subvert myths of origin, sameness, and purity. Instead, she endeavors to claim an *inauthentic* ontological origin that is marked always already by disjunctive hybridity. This inauthentic origin derives from processes of transcultural exchanges that do not render Otherness either antagonistic to sameness or identical to it. Rather, she postulates a constant slippage and recognition of the self in its heterogeneity and of Otherness in its diversity as she recognizes Otherness as the Self and the Self in Otherness.

This postnational reconfiguration of Israeli and Palestinian identities through intimacy, mutuality, and contiguity clears a space for a dialogic exchange and the politics of solidarity between Palestinians and Israelis. She thus becomes a worker for dialogue and solidarity between Israelis and Palestinians, as she struggles in coalition with "dovish" Israelis and other leftist cosmopolitan Jewish figures to promote channels of dialogue and to forge alternative relations between the two nations, for which other Palestinians accused her of treason and collaboration (1980, 122). Tawil turned her home into a salon where the local, regional, and international intelligentsia would meet to discuss ways of ending the Israeli occupation of the

West Bank and Gaza and guaranteeing the Palestinian people their legitimate rights for self-determination and national sovereignty. In the volatile context of the post-1967 period, Tawil's coalition politics can indeed be seen as radical. Tawil's political stand required a lot of courage and staunch belief in the possibilities inherent in dialogue and solidarity, for in the post-1967 context the few workers for dialogue and solidarity were jailed and interrogated by the Israelis, received death threats, or were even assassinated by Palestinian rejectionists.[13]

Although she calls upon both Palestinians and Israelis to rethink a century of relations rooted in antagonism, negation, and denial, through this ethics of postnationalism, by embracing dialogue and the politics of solidarity, Tawil does not gloss over the imperative of resistance to the Israeli occupation and Zionist settler colonialism. As previously stated, her postnational ethics is corrected by recentering the history of material and discursive resistance to colonial hegemony in the West Bank and Gaza. In her struggle against the oppressive military regime in the Occupied Territories, Tawil became committed to grassroots work and organization, which were capable of mobilizing most Palestinians around urgent issues of daily concerns for the lives of the refugees and dispossessed. She joined the General Union of Palestinian Women, which has been affiliated with the PLO since 1965, mobilizing women and organizing sit-in demonstrations, boycotts, protests, and strikes in the struggle for Palestinian rights, dignity, and humanity. Tawil also cooperated with other popular women's committees in the West Bank whose major goal was "to mobilize Palestinian women together in a joint struggle for defending their rights as Palestinian women and for improving

13. To put this situation in context, we need to remember the atmosphere of insecurity and fear during this nondialogic phase. As the Palestinian feminist peace activist and Beir Zeit University English professor Hanan Mikhail Ashrawi observes, "Nondialogue dominated Israeli-Palestinian discourse for a long time as an affirmation of conflict and the non-recognition by either side of the other in a mutually exclusive equation, whereby any direct verbal 'contact' was perceived as an implicit admission to existence, hence legitimacy" (1991, 103). Moreover, the assassinations of two leading Palestinian pioneers of Israeli-Palestinian dialogue, Sa'id Hammami in London in 1978 and Isam Sartawi in 1983, as well as the imprisonment of Uri Adiv of the Revolutionary Communist League in Israel serve as painful reminders of the extreme difficulties and the high price of speaking out for dialogue and peace in the 1970s and 1980s.

their socioeconomic position within the context of total national struggle" (Dajani 1995, 47). She would even contact the military governor to demand provisions for the expelled masses of refugees, bold acts that made others label her a "traitor" and "collaborator" (1980, 123). And to that Palestinian man, who was involved with other men, including her husband, in manly matters, ignoring the predicament of the throngs of refugees outside her place but labeling her a traitor, Tawil and her friend the Palestinian novelist Sahar Khalifa say, "We have suffered enough from slogans and ideologies . . . Ba'athism, Marxism, and all the rest. Now we have thousands of mouths to feed, hundreds of wounded to care for. We've talked enough! Let's go to work and save what we can of the Palestinian people" (98). To ensure the continuity of the Palestinian nation, Tawil and her comrades consent even to cooperate with the occupation forces: pragmatism rather than empty rhetoric. The irony here is that the Israeli occupation managed to foreground the crisis of traditional (androcentric) leadership structures in the West Bank and Gaza and put women in the forefront of movements and organizations that resist the occupation as well as provide human relief services to the victims of the occupation. Such work laid the grounds for the politicization of Palestinian women and for the emergence of civil society in Palestine.

Tawil's struggle against colonial hegemony can also be seen in her discursive resistance to the colonization of the mind that is all too familiar in colonial contexts, namely, her journalistic work, her re-presentation of the Palestinian freedom fighter *(fidayeen),* and her intervention in the debate over the curriculum. Her journalism became a major site for the practice of anticolonial politics; as a freelance reporter, Tawil leaked reports to the international press about the realities of Israel's "enlightened, democratic occupation" of the West Bank and Gaza. She was thus censored and arrested for security reasons and accused of "incitements to riots, taking photographs of Israeli troops mistreating demonstrators, contact with PLO leaders in Beirut, and contacts with terrorist cells in the West Bank" (259). In her career as a journalist, furthermore, she found herself defending the cause of the Palestinian freedom fighters. Her celebration of the guerrillas is not a glorification of violence and bloodshed but an attempt to force Western public opinion to reconsider the legitimacy of the Palestinian will to exist. Instead of the abysmal representation of the armed resistance as an act of savage terrorism, she interprets the textuality of the freedom fighter's body as a sign of agency and empowerment for the humiliated and defeated Arab and Palestinian peoples. She writes: "The fact that after the Arab defeat Palestinians had taken up arms restored our sense of dignity and self-respect" (125). This defense of the freedom fighters was a controversial issue throughout her travels in the United States to promote the two-state solution to the Israeli-Palestinian conflict. As Edward Said and Christopher Hitchens (1988) note, the distinction between terrorism and the universal right of "armed struggle" accorded to all nations under foreign occupation is deliberately blurred in the hype of U.S. media coverage of the Middle East. Moreover, the acquiescence of the U.S. media to represent the PLO only as a terrorist organization became, as the Israeli journalist Amnon Kapeliouk argues, a tactic "to delegitimize Palestinian nationalism in toto . . . , the better to be able to ignore its undeniable claims on Israel" (quoted in Said and Hitchens 1988, 153). Ultimately, as Said and Hitchens correctly point out, ascribing terrorism to them, the Palestinians, the Arabs, and the Muslims, turns every act of Israeli terrorism into an example of the "nobility and purity of the Judeo-Christian freedom fighters" (152).

Moreover, Tawil fights imperial domination as manifested through the struggle over the curriculum in the Occupied Territories. After the 1967 war, Israeli authorities were determined to impose the Israeli-Arab curriculum on Palestinian schools, which can be seen as a pedagogy of colonial interpellation. Tawil was very conscious that the ultimate agenda of this pedagogy was to enforce a traumatic split between Palestinian students and their culture, history, and literature. Under the threat of erasing Palestinian identity and interpellating students to gain their consent to the occupation, Palestinians refused to send their kids to school. However, only after the Israelis had agreed to allow schools to implement the Jordanian curriculum were the schools reopened. Notwithstanding, the decision to implement the Jordanian curriculum was equally ironic for Tawil. Education was still a site of fierce struggle over the production of identities, since the Hashemite regime was aiming at camouflaging Palestinian identity by Jordanian citizenship and passports (1980, 120).

In these peculiar times of post-alities, globalization, and neoimperialisms, attention to existing, yet by all means anachronistic, sites of colonial exploitation and oppression remains central to the utopian impetus of the postnational project. Raimonda Tawil's autobiography demonstrates the need to repoliticize postnational theory and to problematize it in more nuanced readings that examine the preconditions of its production and dissemination in colonial and neocolonial geopolitical configurations across the globe.[14]

14. The importance of reimagining new alliances or rereading the contact zone in terms of collaborations remains vital today, as Michael Hardt and Antonio Negri have shown in their recent work *Multitude: War and Democracy in the Age of Empire.* Imperialism, they argue, inadvertently produces its antithesis in the form of transnational alliances that can organize along "fluid matrices of resistance" (2004, back flap). And Tawil will look with pride at the proliferation of the local, regional, and international "multitudes" in Israel, Palestine, and the United States such as Women in Black, the Peace Quilt, Women for Women Political Prisoners, Shani (Israeli Women Against the Occupation), the Jerusalem Link, the Tikkun Community, and Seeds of Peace, all of which work in solidarity to bring about a lasting peace and social justice in the Middle East.

6

A Muslim Woman Writes Back

Leila Abouzeid's *Return to Childhood: The Memoir of a Modern Moroccan Woman*

PAULINE HOMSI VINSON

In her contribution to *Going Global: The Transnational Reception of Third World Women Writers,* Mohja Kahf isolates three Western stereotypes about Arab women and Islam: "One is that she [the Arab/Muslim woman] is a victim of gender oppression; the second portrays her as an escapee of her intrinsically oppressive culture; and the third represents her as the pawn of Arab male power" (2000, 149). According to Marnia Lazreg, whose article appears in the same edited collection as Kahf's, even academic feminism is guilty of similar charges: "At first glance, a shift seems to have occurred, from portraying Other women as victims to portraying them as individuals endowed with agency. However, the emphasis is still on what customs, traditions, religions *do* to women. Women's achievements are couched as struggles 'against' not 'for.' . . . What we need is the expression of reality by those who live it and on their terms" (2000, 38; emphasis in original).

In recent years, several women from the Arab world have written autobiographical works that are specifically directed toward Western audiences. They have done so "on their terms" and with the explicit aim of dispelling prevalent stereotypes against them. Leila Abouzeid's *Return to Childhood: The Memoir of a Modern Moroccan Woman,* published in English in 1998, is one such book.[1]

1. Along with Leila Abouzeid's memoirs, one thinks of fellow Moroccan Fatima Mernissi's *Dreams of Trespass: Tales of a Harem Girlhood* (1995), Egyptians Leila Ahmed's *Border Passage: From Cairo to America—a Woman's Journey* (1999) and Nawal el-Saadawi's *Daughter of Isis*

As Abouzeid tells her readers in the preface to the English translation of her memoirs, "The work was meant for a non-Moroccan audience, and I felt it would give me the opportunity to correct some American stereotypes about Muslim women" (iv). Abouzeid thus frames her memoirs as not so much a revelation of her inner self as a revision of an "Other's" presumed perception of her self. In so doing, she positions her work as a type of "writing back" in response to hegemonic discourses that misrepresent the reality of Muslim women's lives.

As Abouzeid's statement indicates, however, the "center" to which she writes back is not the unified center of empire referred to by Salman Rushdie, Bill Ashcroft, Gareth Griffiths, or Helen Tiffin; rather, Abouzeid seems to write back to what one might term a splintered center.[2] Her memoirs seem to respond not only to current American misconceptions of Arab women's lives but also to the legacy of French colonial rule in Morocco as well as to certain aspects of her own family and country. Significantly, she conducts her multiple critiques from within a particularly woman-centered Muslim framework.

In the preface to the English translation of her memoirs, Leila Abouzeid also points out that the notion of writing about herself was prompted by a request from her American academic friend Elizabeth Fernea, who asked her to compose "a piece of fifteen to thirty pages to be included in an anthology of childhood narratives from the Middle East" to be published in English in the United States (v). Indeed, Abouzeid seems to be suggesting that were it not for her American friend and the prevalence of American misconceptions, she would not have thought of writing her memoirs at all.

In offering her life as a counterexample to Western misconceptions of what it is like to be an Arab Muslim woman, Ahmed may be seen to be

---

(1999) and *Walking Through Fire* (2002), Algerian Assia Djebar's *Fantasia: An Algerian Cavalcade* (1993), and Palestinian/Lebanese Jean Said Makdisi's *Teta, Mother, and Me: An Arab Woman's Memoir* (2005).

2. In "The Empire Writes Back to and from the Centre," Chantal Zabus explains: "'The Empire Writes Back to the Centre'—is a phrase originally used by Salman Rushdie, as he was punning on "The Empire Strikes Back," the famous American T.V. show [*sic*]. Here, the Empire is the sum total of the colonies of the British Empire, which Britain lost with the coming to independence in the 1960s of nation-states from Africa to Sri Lanka" (2006, n.p.).

assuming a strategic stance that I have referred to in a different paper on the autobiographical works of the Egyptians Leila Ahmed and Nawal el-Saadawi.[3] This stance is what Uma Narayan has termed the "Authentic Insider Position." In *Dislocating Cultures: Identities, Traditions, and Third World Feminism,* Narayan remarks, "Part of the value attributed to 'insiderness' and of 'authenticity' seems to lie in the 'Authentic Insider's' capacity to produce accounts that are widely shared by those at 'home' and to produce an account that 'gives voice to' these shared accounts, thus conferring upon her the authoritative status of 'being a representative' of her community or nation" (1997, 147). As Narayan also asserts, however, "The 'Authentic Insider' position sets up a 'proprietary relationship' between Third-World individuals and the 'culture' of their nation or community, in ways that have the potential to function as a set-up" (143). According to Narayan, one way to avoid this "set-up" is to allow a multiplicity of voices to be heard so that there would emerge a "polyphonous richness, with internal divergences, with differences and tensions in evidence" (143).

A single autobiographical account would seem contrary to such an endeavor, as it highlights one person's reconstruction of an individual life. At the same time, however, the autobiographical form seems especially suited for attempts at offering counterexamples to Western misconceptions and generalizations about non-Western women. This idea is one that Nawar Al-Hassan Golley voices in the introduction to her book *Reading Arab Women's Autobiographies: Shahrazad Tells Her Story:* "One of the issues here involves cultural representations, especially the prevailing image in the west that women in Arab countries probably suffer more oppression than women anywhere else in the world. I, for one, should know that not all Syrian women are downtrodden. I have never suffered sexual discrimination within my own family; but I have seen bad forms of sexual discrimination in my society" (2003, xii).

Abouzeid seems aware of the pitfalls of addressing Western stereotypes in autobiographical form. In doing so, she risks not only being "set up" by her

3. I borrow Uma Narayan's term in my paper titled "Shahrazadian Gestures in Arab Women's Autobiographies: Political History, Personal Memory, and Matrilineal Oral Narratives in the Works of Nawal el-Saadawi and Leila Ahmed." This paper is forthcoming in the *National Women's Studies Association Journal.*

Western readership but also being discredited by her Arab environment. To ward off criticism, she is sure to establish her authenticity by her own community. As she tells her non-Moroccan readers, "Since the autobiography had been written for a foreign audience in a sharp tone and in total frankness, I was apprehensive about the reactions of many people, including particularly my family. . . . When [the manuscript] was finally published in Casablanca in 1993, my family did not only approve but were very enthusiastic. Moroccan readers and critics also received it with enthusiasm" (1998, v).

The issue of credibility seems particularly important to Abouzeid because, as she also tells her readers, she views autobiography as "an imported genre in modern Arabic literature" (iii).[4] The idea that autobiography is "imported" to the Arab world is becoming increasingly contested—and rightly so—by critics such as Nawar Al-Hassan Golley, who points out that "there is evidence . . . that the earliest autobiographical text [in Arabic] was written in the eleventh century" (2003, 75). Nonetheless, it is also true that autobiographical writing as such did not flourish (though it existed) in Arabic until the twentieth century.[5] Moreover, in spite of the prevalence of autobiographical works by Arab women in the latter half of the twentieth century, there is still a feeling of unease among Arab women writers who disclose aspects of their "private" lives in "public." As Leila Abouzeid remarks, "A Muslim's [male or female] life is considered an *'awra* (an intimate part of the body), and *sitr* (concealing it) is imperative" (1998, iii). Autobiographical writing for women thus becomes especially difficult, according to Abouzeid, because, as she puts it, "women in [her] culture do not speak in public, let alone speak about their private lives in public" (iv).[6]

As Abouzeid's own testimony reveals, however, this view of women's public speech seems to be outdated, or perhaps limited to the conservative elements of Muslim society. She herself, for example, is not only a respected

4. Among recent studies of Arabic autobiography are Faqir 1998; Fay 2002; Golley 2003; Ostle, de Moor, and Wild 1998; Reynolds 1997, 2001; and Rooke 1997. In Arabic, see Abbas 1956; and Hassan n.d.; among others.

5. For a historical discussion of the autobiographical tradition in Arabic literature, see Reynolds 2001.

6. For discussions of private and public spaces in Arab women's autobiographies, see Enderwitz 1998; Faqir 1998; al-'Id 1998; and Manisty 1998.

published author in her native country but also someone who has held public positions in the press and government ministries of Morocco. Moreover, although Abouzeid's account of her childhood may have been novel in Morocco at the time of its composition, it nonetheless falls within a growing body of autobiographical works by Muslim women from Arab countries. One thinks, for example, of the Egyptian feminist Huda Shaarawi and the Palestinian poet Fadwa Tuqan, both of whom wrote their autobiographies for Arab readerships several decades before Abouzeid. More recently, one thinks of fellow Moroccan Fatima Mernissi and Algerian Assia Djebar along with Egyptians Leila Ahmed and Nawal el-Saadawi. Interestingly, however, among the more recent women autobiographers, one finds echoes of Abouzeid's stated reasons for writing her memoirs as a response to Western stereotypes of Muslim women. Leila Ahmed, for instance, has remarked:

> Living now in America I found myself constantly encountering people who made assumptions, and usually wrong assumptions about Islam or about what it was like to grow up a Muslim girl and what society was like and so on. Besides saying "no that wasn't how it was," and making some general reply, I had no simple way of conveying what that world had in fact been like. And so in part this book was written out of the need to be able to say here, this was what it was like to grow up a Muslim girl, read this [her memoirs]. (1999b, n.p.)

Unlike Leila Ahmed or even Fatima Mernissi, both of whom composed their autobiographical works in English, and unlike Assia Djebar, who wrote hers in French, Abouzeid makes a point of having written her memoirs in her native Arabic in spite of her fluency in both French, the language of Morocco's former colonizers, and English, the language of her intended audience. She tells her readers, "I wrote *Ruju 'Ila* [*sic*] *Tufula (Return to Childhood)* in Arabic and did a rough translation of it into English" (1998, v). In so doing, Abouzeid specifically aligns herself with nationalist writers such as Ngugi wa Thiong'o who view their choice to write in their native languages as a form of national assertion.[7]

7. On questions of language, see Ashcroft, Griffiths, and Tifflin 1989; Thiong'o 1981; and Suleiman 2004.

By composing her memoirs in Arabic and publishing them in her native Morocco before their appearance in English, Abouzeid establishes her allegiance to her culture and community before exposing them to Western readers. By garnering the approval and backing of the group for her individual voice, she is able to utilize what she regards as "an imported genre" without seeming untrue to her local culture. At the same time, by gaining the stamp of authenticity from her community, she is able to speak to a transnational audience without fear of repercussions for her "sharp tone" and "total frankness" with regard not only to Western misconceptions of Muslim women but also to women, Moroccan nationalism, and Islam.

Significantly, Leila Abouzeid highlights the ways in which her autobiographical writing does not offer a story of an individualistic self, as might be expected from a great many Western autobiographies, but rather a portrait of a politicized life in which personal experiences are intimately connected to national politics and contested notions of collective identity.[8] This conception of the self is clearly evident in Abouzeid's declaration: "I wanted to say that, yes, I am a Muslim woman but I am perfectly capable of taking up the pen to present my own perspective about my country's reality" (iv). In Abouzeid's text, as in so many postcolonial Arab women's autobiographical works, the private lives of women are shown to be intimately linked both to the lives of other women around them and to the public events that shape national politics.[9]

Furthermore, by describing herself as "a modern Moroccan woman," Abouzeid seems not only to assert her individual self but also to highlight her position as an example of a non-Western, Muslim woman who lives comfortably in the modern world. In so doing, she allows her voice to join the voices of other postcolonial Muslim women whom miriam cooke calls "Muslim feminists" in *Women Claim Islam: Creating Islamic Feminism Through Literature* (2001). Although Abouzeid herself may not be comfortable with such a term,

8. For a discussion of the differences between Western and Arab conceptions of autobiography, see Reynolds 1997, 3. For a discussion of Arab women's views regarding individual and collective identity, see Golley 2003, 69–74.

9. For examples of Arab women's texts that make similar claims regarding the private lives of women, see among others Ahmed 1999a; and el-Saadawi 1999. For discussions of how similar phenomena appear in non-Arab postcolonial women's autobiographical writing, see Whitlock 2000.

it does help place Abouzeid among the growing number of Muslim women who argue that the principles for a just society that oppresses neither men nor women are already present within Islam. Throughout her memoirs, Abouzeid illustrates the ways in which Moroccan Muslim women have both participated fully in the nationalist resistance to French colonial rule and demonstrated their capacity to take active roles in shaping the direction of their country's ethical and political life. As Abouzeid insists, moreover, Muslim Moroccan women need not feel any conflict between their Muslim, nationalist, or modern identities.

Like so many other Muslim women autobiographical writers such as Leila Ahmed, Nawal el-Saadawi, Fatima Mernissi, and Assia Djebar, Leila Abouzeid celebrates the value of female oral narratives as a shaping force in her life. To that end, she includes the voices of other women within her narrative, especially her mother's and grandmother's. In so doing, she endows her text with a "polyphonous richness, with internal divergences, with differences and tensions in evidence." In fact, the inclusion of other women's voices within the text illustrates how the author's sense of herself is interconnected to the voices of others around her, even if they are reconstructed and embellished through her selective memory and retrospective stance. The numerous embedded quotations and narrations place Abouzeid's written memoirs within a larger narrative of primarily oral female speech and transform her memoirs from an individual's chronological review of her childhood into a series of multiauthored interconnected, episodic stories. In thus adapting the "imported genre" of autobiography, Abouzeid seems to be offering an alternative history of her country, one that recognizes the unsung efforts of Moroccan women in sustaining not only the domestic sphere but also the nationalist movement and the building of Moroccan society after independence.

Speaking of the importance of female oral narratives in Algeria, Marnia Lazreg remarks in *The Eloquence of Silence:*

> The oral tradition established by women through the manipulation of speech is exceptionally rich. Throughout the colonial era and before the advent of television, storytelling was the quasimonopoly of women. They told stories about colonial invasion, relationships between husbands and wives, parents and children, brothers and sisters, stepmothers and stepdaughters,

> about orphaned children, marital infidelity, unknowing incest and the anguish of living on the margin of power centers. All these themes were drawn from real life, and often rang true to those who heard them, although protagonists included fairies, jinns, ogres and ogresses. Generations of boys and girls were reared on these tales. (1994, 108)

Although Lazreg is speaking about the Algerian experience in particular, her comments also ring true in connection to Abouzeid's Moroccan experience, as well as the experiences of many other women, both literate and illiterate, Muslim and non-Muslim, living in a variety of Arabic-speaking countries.[10] Indeed, the number of books that both record as well as translate Arab women's oral narratives is growing rapidly, partly, one may guess, in response to the increasing number of Arab women writers like Leila Abouzeid herself whose works disclose the richness and value of such forms of storytelling.[11]

The importance of women's oral narratives is emphasized repeatedly in Abouzeid's memoirs. Not only are her memories of childhood filtered through her mother's recollections of events and conversations, but they are also shaped by both the stories that her grandmother skillfully tells and the colorful conversations of other adult women. As Abouzeid puts it, "My grandmother knew how to exaggerate and embellish her narrations, how to fascinate and mesmerize the women of her audience. She would invite them to encourage her to continue by pausing from time to time, so that they would call out, 'And then?' 'Go on!' When we lived in El Ksiba I had always looked forward to her visits because of the wonderful stories she told and the fascinating way she told them" (1998, 43).

Following in her grandmother's footsteps, Abouzeid begins to develop her storytelling skills at a young age. Recalling her days at boarding school, Abouzeid remarks, "I was hungry for books and I read eagerly and widely, always in Arabic. This led me to become the boarding school's storyteller. On

10. Certainly, this view of female oral tradition is also true in my case, growing up in a literate environment in Lebanon in the 1960s and 1970s.

11. See, for example, Ahmed 1999a; Djebar 1993; and Mernissi 1995. Ahmed even connects women's oral history with a different, more "gentle, pacifist, inclusive, somewhat mystical" Islam (121). See also Atiya 1982; Mernissi 1988; and Shaaban 1988.

Sundays, if the weather was bad, the matron, a young Algerian woman called Badra, would take us all to the classroom, not to study but so that I could tell stories to the class" (81). Claiming a matrilineal heritage for her skill at oral storytelling, Abouzeid is also sure to lay claim to a written heritage of Arabic literature that she acquired at school.

Repeatedly, Abouzeid insists on the important role that stories and storytelling have played in both her upbringing and her education. For example, she tells us that whereas her father insisted that she and her sisters go to school to learn reading and writing in both French and Arabic, her mother made sure that her daughters acquired a practical trade that might later provide them with some form of income. Although the mother may have desired to teach her girls the skill of making caftan buttons, it seems that she also gave them the opportunity to learn the art of women's oral storytelling. Listening to the stories that the women told as they made the buttons and gossiped about the people they knew, the young Leila learned to appreciate the social as well as the linguistic value of such speech. As Abouzeid describes it, the button mistress Fatma and her family "would receive the neighborhood women in their courtyard, where they would gather and talk while working. They brought floor cushions along with their little work trays, and their silk thread. One of them would start the gossip and everyone would add a comment" (44). This "gossip" educated the young Abouzeid in the mores and attitudes of the time. The reproduction of such "gossip" in her memoir allows the reader a glimpse of an intimate social scene, where the women discuss and analyze marriage relationships, divorces, births, deaths, and other social issues and happenings.

For Abouzeid, then, as for so many other Arab women who write about their childhoods, women's oral narratives are a valuable component of their social upbringing and not simply a frivolous endeavor. By tracing her own penchant for storytelling back to her grandmother and the larger community of women from her childhood, Abouzeid seems to be insisting on the value of this tradition in constructing individual and social identity.

Not surprisingly, the stories that Abouzeid and her mother tell of Abouzeid's childhood often revolve around the political situation in Morocco and her father's repeated imprisonments, first for his nationalist activities and later for his opposition to the newly independent Moroccan government.

Significantly, the text opens with a scene that locates the young Abouzeid, along with her mother and sisters, at a crossroad. Literally, the family was at the time changing buses to return home from their visit to the mother's family. Figuratively, however, the crossroad signals a momentous change in the young Abouzeid's life, for it is there upon that road that the family learns of her father's imprisonment by the French for his nationalist activities. The young Abouzeid's understanding of the situation is filtered through her mother's reaction: "Then my mother told us, 'The Nasara [Christians, that is, French] have put your father in prison. Not because he did anything bad, but because he is a nationalist. 'Nationalist' means someone who wants the Nasara to get out of our country, and that's honorable.' But her moaning disturbed me much more than the news" (3). "That day," Abouzeid explains, "marked the beginning of our troubles" (4). The family soon discovers not only that the father has been imprisoned but also that the father's father and brother have taken possession of all their household belongings, leaving them with nothing but "a brass candlestick" (3).

The family dispute that ensues from the actions that the family of Abouzeid's father takes against her mother highlights the ways in which the political events taking place in Morocco at the time directly affected the intimate world of her domestic life and personal relationships. Through a novelistic approach that incorporates dialogue within dramatic scenes, Abouzeid reveals both the particulars of her family dynamic and the ways in which political events color familiar interactions. Refusing to visit his son in jail, Abouzeid's paternal grandfather declares, "He's my son, but he left me nothing when he decided to go to prison. Why should I visit him? He doesn't care about his duty to me. And what harm have the Nasara done to us anyway? It is in their time that we came to have running water and electricity and clean streets" (19). It seems, then, that the reason for the grandfather's displeasure with his son's nationalist activities is financial. As he tells the judge who hears his daughter-in-law's case against him, "My son supported us and now he is in prison for his nationalist activities. I'm old and I have to start selling his furniture to support us" (25).

In contrast to her paternal grandfather, who feels that the nationalist cause has displaced his son's allegiance to it from himself, Abouzeid's mother's dedication to her husband, who Abouzeid tells us has on more than one occasion been unfaithful to his wife, seems motivated by her own dedication to the nationalist cause. We learn that the reason she was not with her husband at the time of his arrest is because she was on her way back from getting her inheritance money in order to donate it to the nationalists. Abouzeid's father, however, though unfaithful to his wife in marital affairs, nonetheless stands up for her in recognition of her efforts for the nationalist cause. For instance, when he is questioned from his prison cell by a court official as to whether he "wrote the letter to [his] father telling him to give [his] wife [his] car and her belongings," he defends his wife against the accusations of his father and brother, replying, "If she says that a nail in the wall is hers, then it is. I don't own a needle of that dowry. Everything belongs to her" (28).

The various levels of allegiance and betrayal present in Abouzeid's family serve as a microcosm of Moroccan society at large. Each group within the family finds its supporters and detractors outside it. For example, Abouzeid narrates her mother's recollection of the actions of Kabboura, the sister of Abouzeid's paternal uncle's wife: "She and her husband had been in Casablanca to attend a celebration of the birth of a son of that same Moroccan police officer who called your father a bastard and who collaborated with the Nasara" (23).

Whereas Abouzeid's paternal aunt is willing to associate with those individuals who collaborated with the French, her maternal aunt and her husband wish to dissociate from the nationalists for fear of repercussions against them. As Abouzeid recalls her mother's words: "I was a fool, I think. I had no common sense. I said to Zhor's [her other daughter's] husband, 'Please, Omar, read this letter [from her husband] to me.' He took it and started shaking all over, then gave it back to me and said, 'Leave me alone.' He was afraid to come near anything related with the nationalists because he worked for the Nasara" (34).

Indeed, the father's nationalist activities and ensuing arrest seem to occasion a realignment in family relationships as well as a larger shift in social relationships. For example, the judge who arbitrates the dispute between Abouzeid's mother and paternal grandfather tells the grandfather, "I swear, if that man in prison had not been struggling for our nation, I'd have had to send his wife with the other beggars until this is settled" (26). Abouzeid's mother receives preferential treatment not only from the upper levels of society because of her husband's nationalist activities, as in the case of the judge, but also from everyday people and workers. For instance, the porters who finally transport the household furniture out of Abouzeid's paternal grandfather's house back to her mother's refuse to take payment from Abouzeid's mother for their labor. As the head porter tells her, the porters "'have done this job with pleasure and prayed to God for Si Hmed [Abouzeid's father]. And you talk of paying them! Don't be silly. He is no common prisoner. He's a nationalist'" (29).

Thus, the family's situation rises and falls in accordance with the successes and failures of the father's position as a nationalist. During the father's imprisonment, the family's fortune deteriorates, but when he is released after independence, their fortunes improve, as he is elected mayor of Beni Mellal and they are allowed to move into the former French colonizer's mansion. As Abouzeid reminds her readers, however, although the family fortune ebbed and flowed according to the father's fate as a nationalist, the father's fate and the nationalist cause were also directly linked to the integral role that women played both within the family and within the resistance movement.

According to Abouzeid, her father, who never ate with the family even when he was out of prison (17), became even more removed from the daily life of his family after his imprisonment. As she puts it, after his arrest "I hardly saw him at all" (17). Indeed, the father's nationalist involvement and subsequent imprisonment remove him from the family's domestic sphere at the same time that they force him to rely on his wife's freedom of movement for passing messages and conducting nationalist activities on his behalf. As many who come from the Maghreb countries have attested, women were actively involved in the nationalist resistance to French colonial rule. Though only relatively few participated in active fighting, many others protected fugitives, sustained prisoners, passed messages, and transported arms.[12] These activities are the types of actions that Abouzeid's mother engages in. She waits endlessly in line at the courthouse and prison gates to deliver food to her husband, and she passes messages back and forth between him and the nationalists. Early in the memoir, Abouzeid quotes her mother: "Your father said . . . 'The house you own in Sefrou . . . Some people want to rent it and want to get in touch with you.' (He meant the nationalists. I didn't own any house. The nationalists wanted to send

12. A thorough discussion of Algerian women's participation in the movement of decolonization from French rule may be found in Lazreg 1994 (118–41). Leila Abouzeid herself discusses the involvement of Moroccan women in nationalist resistance to French rule in her fictionalized novella, *The Year of the Elephant: A Moroccan Woman's Journey Toward Independence* (1989).

me money and your father was using this way of telling me because he knew that the [prison] guard wouldn't understand)" (23). Later, Abouzeid records her mother's account of how she transported weapons to the nationalists: "We went home and [the father] gave me the guns, the same ones that were in the cupboard [at home]. He tied them to me as he did before" (75).

By incorporating her mother's recollections of her involvement in nationalist activities, Abouzeid reveals how the political events taking place in Morocco at the time at once made use of and blurred the distinctions between spatial and gender boundaries. Stashed at home and transported by Abouzeid's mother, the weapons that the nationalists used against the French symbolize the ways in which political events affected intimate life. On the one hand, the traditional views of women as secluded and separate from men gave them greater protection against searches by French soldiers and so granted them greater freedom of movement than men. On the other hand, the use of homes as hideouts for both the nationalists and their weapons resulted in the incursion of the French soldiers into the domestic sphere. As Abouzeid's mother tells her, it was during a raid of their house by the French police that she "miscarried the twin boys" (75).

As Abouzeid's mother's recollections repeatedly testify, Muslim Moroccan women took active roles alongside the men in the fight against colonialism. Moreover, as Abouzeid illustrates, though many Moroccan women at the time were illiterate, they were fully capable of analyzing their own and their country's predicaments. For example, although Abouzeid's mother persists in believing in witchcraft, ignoring her daughter's remark, "When will God rid Morocco of witchcraft?" (78), she understands the meaning of her adult daughter's politicized rhetoric. In response to Abouzeid's comment regarding "self-interest" as a justification for the "right to colonize and exploit," her mother responds, "You mean if we said, 'We have to insure access to your wheat,' for instance? Self-interest, eh? May Allah the Almighty grant us all equity in this unfair world" (79).

As this example illustrates, the mature Abouzeid's "perspective about [her] country's reality" is one that recognizes the multifaceted aspects of Moroccan society. Just as she regrets her mother's belief in witchcraft at the same time that she recognizes her intellectual acumen when it comes to questions of political exploitation and economic justice, so too she acknowledges her father's nationalist political views while criticizing his personal moral conduct. For instance, she recounts her mother's account of how Abouzeid's father defended her mother in recognition of her work for the nationalist cause. When, after his release from prison, a judge in the town of Beni Mellal offers him one of his daughters as a second wife "to reward him for what he did for the nation," Abouzeid's father asks the messenger to tell the judge, "Go back and ask him what about my wife? Didn't *she* do something for the nation as well? Is that how he wants to reward her?" (79). For Abouzeid, however, this type of loyalty is difficult to reconcile with her father's marital infidelities. As she notes, after reaching adulthood, she "would get into heated debates with [her father], always about politics, and suggested that his behavior and that of some of his fellows in their private lives had shaken [her] confidence in the party as a whole" (93).

Thus, it seems that just as Abouzeid illustrates the ways in which political life affects the private, domestic sphere, so too she insists that one's domestic conduct should be consistent with his or her political ideals. As she puts it, "For me, activists who do not care about morality are no different from their opponents. How can a person fight the state to establish what is right when one does not respect this concept in one's own family?" (92).

Abouzeid does not flinch from publicly criticizing her father for his moral failings with regard to his private life. Similarly, she does not shy away from openly criticizing both the newly independent Moroccan state for its abuses of power and the opposition party to which her father belonged after independence. Speaking of the aggressive and rude behavior of the postindependence Moroccan police toward her when she went to see her father at court, she says, "I had never been treated with such vulgar hostility by the police of France. Could this be our Moroccan police?" (91).

More tellingly, Abouzeid contrasts the ways in which her father was treated by the French with the ways in which he was treated by his fellow Moroccans. Noting how fearful of authority her father had become after his release from the postindependence Moroccan prison, she remarks, "I realized . . . the extent of the torture he must have suffered in police stations when he was arrested again after Independence this time by his own countrymen and accused of conspiracy against the monarchy" (70). Later she adds, "How had he been able to stand up to the French police under torture, I wondered, only to fear now one of his own countrymen wearing a uniform of authority?" (87). Unflinching in her critique of injustice, Abouzeid is willing to point it out wherever she sees it, whether at the colonial, national, or familial level.

According to Abouzeid, even the Moroccan opposition party to which her father belonged after independence "looked for mistakes in the Moroccan system and inflated the significance of those mistakes" (89). In a telling remark, she notes, "I am amazed that my father has supported ideas such as those of the opposition. How could an intellectual, modern Muslim like my father have deserted eternal principles that emanate from his nature, his roots, his culture, and his identity, principles that were formulated by God? How could he have adopted the secular principles imported from the West?" (93). Though Abouzeid seems willing to adopt and adapt what she perceives as the "imported genre" of autobiography in her memoirs, she faults her father for adopting Western "secular principles" in his political life.

The reasons for Abouzeid's bewilderment at her father's actions as well as her willingness to openly criticize the Moroccan government's treatment of its prisoners seem to lie in her conviction that "the eternal principles" that should govern individual and political life in Morocco are rooted in the Arabic language and the Muslim religion. As she reminds her readers, obtaining a formal education in Arabic and practicing Islam were considered nationalist endeavors under colonialism. As she puts it, "The Knowledge School was one of the Moroccan schools that had sprung up during those years in reaction to the French administration's attempt to do away with the Arabic language and replace it with French throughout the country's formal school system" (64). Speaking of this school, she continues, "It was in that school that I learned the principles of Arabic, as pure as water from a spring, from teachers who loved the language and believed that to instill its principles in us was a religious and national duty" (64).

It seems that for Abouzeid, to be Moroccan is to speak Arabic and practice Islam. For instance, she tells us that at the same school where she enjoyed telling stories, she also insisted on fasting during Ramadan, the month when Muslims refrain from eating and drinking during daylight hours. When her teacher tries to force her to eat because she thinks that a growing child should not fast, Abouzeid responds, "'Christian logic,' I thought. God knows better. If it were harmful for a child who has reached puberty He wouldn't have required it. She is a Muslim but she thinks with a Christian mind. I was determined to resist and defend my faith no matter what, and I did so. Had not the Christian rule been done away with?" (81–82). As these quotes illustrate, for Abouzeid, the Christian religion and the French language are both linked in her mind to French colonial rule in Morocco. Resisting them, for her, seems to become at once a form of self-assertion and a means for national independence and pride.

It might be tempting to regard Abouzeid's views on language and religion as either a mere reaction to Western colonialism or a type of national and religious chauvinism. However, as Abouzeid insists, Islam, for her, is directly linked to the concept of justice: "According to the Qur'an, 'Those who do not rule with the law of God are indeed the unjust'" (92). Not only are the principles of Islam a basis for social justice, in Abouzeid's view, but they are also perfectly compatible with a modern, democratic society that respects the rights of its citizens, both male and female, to participate in various aspects of social and political life. This idea is clearly evident in the way Abouzeid defends her willingness to work for the same government that had sanctioned the torture of her father. As Abouzeid puts it, "I am Moroccan and have the right to work in any Moroccan organization if I am qualified for the position. Isn't that the true spirit of democracy?" (93).

In her association of Islam with justice, Leila Abouzeid echoes the views put forward by Leila Ahmed in *Women and Gender in Islam* (1992, 88). However, unlike Ahmed, who distinguishes between a "woman's Islam" and a "man's Islam" as well as between the ideals of Islam and chauvinist interpretations of Islam (1999a, 120–21), Abouzeid views Islam as an ethical basis for moral conduct, in both the domestic and the political spheres without addressing the ways in which such an approach to religion and nationalism would be implemented within the country's legal system.

In her search for an authentic and indigenous form of personal and national identity, Abouzeid seems to overlook the ways in which the very nature of those forms may be contested from within the group. For instance, although Abouzeid tells us that her father's mother was Berber, she does not directly address the question of the Berber language or cultural identity in Morocco. Furthermore, she acknowledges the Jewish presence in Morocco, noting that after their expulsion from Andalusia along with the Muslims by the Spanish

Christians in the fifteenth century, "Jews lived in our community, as in every Moroccan community, not greatly loved but tolerated" (42), but she does not address the idea that minority groups—Jews or otherwise—might demand more than tolerance from their government. Nor does Abouzeid address the question of religious fundamentalism and how that phenomenon opens up the idea of contested notions of what it means to be Muslim or even Arab. Indeed, in labeling secularism, as others have labeled feminism, as an "imported Western concept," Abouzeid adopts a type of rhetoric that is uncomfortably close to a type of discourse that ironically serves the interests of both Western hegemony and Muslim fundamentalism. Such discourses depict Arab Muslim societies as closed and static while claiming cultural purity for such ideas as secularism, feminism, or even democracy.

In spite of the many questions that the memoirs raise about the nature of identity, the question of authenticity, and the role of religion in modern society, they nonetheless present a powerful counterimage to Western stereotypes of Moroccan Muslim women and culture. The society that we see through Abouzeid's memoirs is one that, contrary to the rhetoric she adopts in her rejection of secularism, is in fact very much in flux. The type of country that emerges from the memoirs is neither like the "Morocco of Paul Bowles, meaning the underground Morocco of hashish addicts and outcasts" (Abouzeid 1998, v) nor like the Morocco of orientalist imagination, of sensual women secluded in harems as sex slaves for the pleasure of oppressive men.[13] Rather, Abouzeid presents us with an image of a dynamic society whose members hold opposing views and ideologies, attain mixed successes and failures, and exhibit "internal divergences . . . differences and tensions."

In addition, the memoirs present an image of Abouzeid herself as a Moroccan woman who insists on the harmony between such terms as *modern* and *Muslim* while evidencing tension regarding her feelings about her father and "Western importations." Most important, however, Abouzeid speaks of her childhood, her religion, and her country in her memoirs on her own terms and without apology. In so doing, she suggests that the solutions to her country's problems are to be worked out by Moroccans on their own terms and

13. On orientalism, see Said 1978; for orientalist images of Arab women, see Graham-Brown 1988.

through their own means, not by the imposition of Western ideology on an unwilling populace.

Last, by incorporating the matrilineal oral narratives that have been handed down to her through the generations within her own remembrances of her childhood, Abouzeid records the richness and polyphony of Moroccan women's voices. In so doing, she does indeed provide a counterexample to prevailing Western misconceptions about Arab Muslim women in general and Moroccan society in particular.

PART THREE

Autobiographical Writings and Communal Identity

Language, for the individual consciousness, lies on the borderline between oneself and the other. The word in language is half someone else's. It becomes "one's own" only when the speaker populates it with his own intention, his own accent, when he appropriates the word, adapting it to his own semantic and expressive intention.

—Mikhail Bakhtin, *The Dialogic Imagination: Four Essays*

7

Voices Across the Frontier

Fatima Mernissi's *Dreams of Trespass: Tales of a Harem Girlhood*

FILIZ TURHAN-SWENSON

Western writers have been intrigued by the harem and veil for centuries—repeatedly attempting to penetrate their mysteries and represent the Muslim woman in a variety of fictional genres.[1] From the so-called *Turkish Tales* of Lord Byron to Disney's *Princess Jasmine,* the Eastern woman is entombed in the harem and desperate for escape; she is an otherworldly creature, the oppressed victim of Islam either as a religion or as a political movement. Many artists envision an even more radical scene behind the *hijab:* fantasies of languid sexual excess abound, and all is rendered with documentary precision by artists such as Jean-Leon Gerome or with impressionistic finesse by artists such as Eugène Delacroix.

However, it is within the past century that Muslim women have taken to representing their own experiences in a stunning array of autobiographical works. Contemporary Muslim women writers hail from a variety of countries, from Afghanistan to Morocco, and from a variety of class positions, from royalty to the very poorest.[2] As diverse as these writers and their experiences are, they characteristically not only present their own individual experiences but also very keenly contextualize their personal development within the social constraints of their time. Chief among their concerns is a description of their daily lives and particularly how they are affected by critical public events. They

1. The scholarly work on this topic covers many centuries. See, for instance, Metlitzki 1997; Pike 1908; and Turhan 2003.

2. For example, Leila Ahmed, Azar Nafisi, Assia Djebar, and Queen Noor of Jordan.

actively define and cope with their domestic experiences and identities in the midst of enormous social and political changes, even including armed combat. In many of these texts, bearing witness, offering testimony, explaining and clarifying how their personal lives take shape within a particular social atmosphere are both deliberate and overt. For many of these writers, this project entails a description of some kind of circumscribed female existence, whether bound by a traditional harem (as a domestic space dedicated to women), by the veil in its various forms, or by unfavorable social customs and laws. In doing so, they succeed in debunking the Western stereotypes of Muslim women that have prevailed over the centuries; they are neither quiet, willing victims, nor are they lascivious odalisques, but thinking individuals. In their books they critique a variety of political and cultural forces, both imperial and domestic, that continue to shape the world in which they live yet simultaneously show the passionate resilience and dedication of women as they seek to live life on their own terms, whether traditional or modern.[3]

To illustrate these observations, this chapter focuses on Fatima Mernissi's *Dreams of Trespass: Tales of a Harem Girlhood* (1995), which recounts the author's early experiences in the family harem in 1940s Morocco, a period of intense political and cultural change. Trained as a sociologist, Mernissi teaches at Mohammed V University in Rabat and writes extensively on issues pertaining to women and Islam. Her work is characterized by its indefatigable support of women's literacy, education, and health, and it clearly expresses a fierce cultural pride in the face of a seemingly overwhelming onslaught of Western-generated media images. Mernissi's books range from the scholarly to the popular, blending stylistic elements to achieve a good deal of success in both

3. Many writers stage an all-out argument against the custom, narrating in crushing detail not only the insidious effects of constantly staying indoors but also scathing tales of state-sanctioned injustices often perpetrated against women by their own family members. The theoretical foundation that underpins arguments against women's oppressive living conditions comes in two main varieties. Some argue that Islam needs to be reformed to fall in line with the developments of other modern nations, whereas others claim that the veil is actually a corruption of an authentic Islam and that its abolition would be a return to the truly egalitarian ideal of the Prophet. In fact, it has been the focal point for narratives of modernization for Westerners and for Middle Easterners alike. For detailed explorations of these issues, see Fatima Mernissi's *The Veil and the Male Elite* (1991) and Leila Ahmed's *Women and Gender in Islam* (1992).

realms. *Dreams of Trespass* contrasts with orientalist fiction that envisions the harem as a space redolent of numerous sexy, reclining odalisques; instead, the Mernissi harem is an example of an upper-class domestic harem, a space that encompasses the private living quarters of the family, from which its female inhabitants can travel only with a male escort.[4] The memoir therefore corrects the common misunderstanding of what a harem is physically, as well as the image of the people living in it. It depicts the joys and camaraderie among the women of the Mernissi harem, but also shows its stifling effects on their minds and spirits. Mernissi describes how they must negotiate among the oft-warring influences of religious practice, family tradition, and political realities in order to achieve their personal goals.

The book shows through a child's eyes the personal experiences and influences that lay the groundwork for Mernissi's own feminism and that eventually made her sociological and theological arguments in favor of feminism and Islam possible. While describing the path to her own modern, academically inflected feminism, Mernissi also shows the feminist aspirations of many of the older women of the harem, specifically disputing the notion that such movements are only Western imports. As Inge C. Boer (1995, 13–16) has described it, Western feminism had the "implicit idea" that there was no feminism in the third world: "Western feminism set the agenda, presupposing from what might be called a (neo)colonialist perspective that the Third World was a *tabula rasa* as far as feminist activism was concerned" (111). Along these same lines, Mernissi points out the ironic connection between male fundamentalist Muslims and Western feminists who erroneously believe that women either love or are unaware of their deprivations under such a system. In contrast, *Dreams of Trespass* presents the powerful feminist perspectives even among supposedly traditional, older, illiterate women of the harem. Unfortunately, for many of these women, their hopes for increased access to education, travel, and employment are reserved not for themselves but for the younger generation, namely, Mernissi herself.

The author employs different voices to express the words, thoughts, and hopes of many of the older women in the harem; the analysis that follows shows how Mernissi breaks the silence of the harem by giving a louder voice

4. For more on the distinctions between imperial and domestic harems, see Peirce 1993.

to its various inhabitants, depicting them not solely as victims or odalisques but as complex human beings. She thus claims a public position and record for these previously silenced individuals and illustrates alternative forms of feminist activity at work in non-Western contexts. *Dreams of Trespass* demonstrates the kind of communal ideal possible within the harem, which ironically sows the seeds of its own demise: the solidarity and dedication borne of the adversity experienced by its inhabitants give them the tools necessary to transform it into a new kind of existence outside the walls.

THE POLYPHONIC VOICE OF *DREAMS OF TRESPASS*

One of the hallmarks of Fatima Mernissi's writing, which likely accounts for her appeal both to mass audiences and to scholars, is the compelling voice with which she writes; in fact, she frequently incorporates the personal voice into her highly researched scholarly texts. For example, in the introduction to the new edition of *Beyond the Veil,* Mernissi interrupts her own description of the salient features that connect fundamentalist recruits and nonfundamentalist unveiled women to "share with you some of the unpretentious mumblings of my illiterate Aunt Hatchouma" (1987, xi). Anyone unfamiliar with Mernissi's work might well be surprised at such a rhetorical turn. Not only does the personal anecdote intervene in the standard academic polemic, but it is also characterized as the sort of talk least valued in such discourse: being both the talk of an illiterate woman and her "unpretentious mumblings," which are hardly considered worth listening to. Yet Mernissi's presentation of Aunt Hatchouma's wisdom clearly suggests that a strong feminist message can come in a variety of vocal registers. In another of her books, *Scheherazade Goes West* (2001), Mernissi explores the way in which the powerful image of Scheherazade from *A Thousand and One Arabian Nights* has been transformed in Western culture into a weak, oppressed victim of the sultan. Although the book is scholarly and documented, its narrative style is personal and anecdotal.

Similarly, her personal writing merges a variety of stylistics and tones to present her early experiences and inquiries into the nature of harem life. The narrative voice of the memoir modulates to accommodate a number of different perspectives simultaneously. Anne Donadey's reference to the book as a bildungsroman notwithstanding (2000, 100), *Dreams of Trespass* does not quite conform to the standard expectations of a teleologically structured autobiography. Although she does describe her birth in 1940, to learn that Mernissi is an internationally famous sociologist, scholar, writer, and university professor, one would have to look elsewhere. Instead, the influential women in her early life are the lead actors of the memoir, and the long-term effects of their lessons on Mernissi herself are unnarrated. Each of these women maintains a distinct position within the harem hierarchy, and despite the fact that they are all "stuck in the harem," Mernissi communicates their powerful qualities of dignity and hope. They include her mother, desperate for reform and modernity; Yasmina, her maternal grandmother who lives in a farm harem with neither doors nor walls; Aunt Habiba, a divorced aunt whose powerlessness and need to please make her a figure of great pathos and admiration; and Mina, an Ethiopian former slave. Mernissi's account of her early years in the harem is thus marked by the strong presence of a variety of women who give her the tools through speech, stories, and role-playing to answer her questions, to situate her in the space of the harem, and to encourage her ambitions. Despite the oppression felt within the harem, the community of women living in it succeeds in establishing an atmosphere of nurturing guidance, thus exercising a kind of power in defiance of their seeming powerlessness. This environment is an ironic benefit of the female communal life explored in a variety of texts, including other works by Mernissi, Leila Ahmed (1982), and Nawal el-Saadawi (1986).

In addition to the various female voices mentioned earlier, Mernissi's own voice registers on three different levels within this polyphonic text. Predominant in the memoir is her position as a confused child asking questions of her elders, struggling to understand the world in which she lives. Very notably, however, this childish tone modulates into the voice of a mature poetic response to the life lessons of her elders. Finally, these two voices coexist along with the voice of the scholar and sociologist who intervenes at times with footnotes on political history and Islamic customs. By including these varied voices, Mernissi succeeds in *showing* us whom she has become rather than simply narrating the events of her life leading from birth to the moment of composition.

Mernissi's stylistic strategy of describing herself through a focus on others has noteworthy connections to autobiographical, feminist, and postcolonial theories of discourse. It is particularly interesting when one takes into account the ways that such "speaking for/through the Other" is inflected by powerful factors typically at play in a postcolonial context. Edward Said's *Orientalism* (1978) demonstrates how Western writers utilized the Eastern Other as a model against which they could define a self-image as both morally and intellectually superior and how their study of the East was then deployed in the work of empire building. However, because *Orientalism* focuses almost exclusively on the textual production of male Western writers, many scholars have responded to Said's thesis by pointing out the variety of voices within the spectrum of colonial and postcolonial discourse. This assortment includes strong revisionist works, particularly the ones that have sought to explore in greater detail the ways in which Western women writers engaged in the colonial project and how colonial subjects responded to it.[5]

We see very similar issues at work in examples of Muslim women's autobiographies because they frequently entail the rhetorical representation of other women as a way of telling their own stories. The writing subject does tend to self-define in sympathetic relation to others, as is true, for example, of Mernissi, Bouthaina Shaaban, and Assia Djebar. And because many of the writers are working from a place of distance, the problem of "authentic" representation without subjugation or co-optation of the Other's voice is real and imperative.[6] Even among these Muslim women writers, the distance between writer and subject comes in many forms: generational (many of them narrate stories of

5. For example, in *Critical Terrains: British and French Orientalism,* Lisa Lowe offers a revised reading of orientalist discourse by focusing on works produced by women travel writers throughout the eighteenth and nineteenth centuries. For instance, in the work of Lady Mary Wortley Montagu, Lowe isolates an entirely different kind of rhetoric at work, "an emergent feminist discourse that speaks of common experiences among women of different societies" (1991, 32).

6. The issue of authenticity is addressed by Nawar Al-Hassan Golley in her discussion of el-Saadawi's *Memoirs of a Woman Doctor:* "It is not factual truth that I am tracing in my study of women's autobiographical writings but the strategies that women adopt when talking or writing about the self and the issues that are of most importance to them" (2003, 147). Furthermore, issues of representation and authenticity have been the area of not only postcolonial studies but also autobiographical studies; for instance, several essays in the collection *Feminism and Autobiography: Texts, Theories, and Methods* deal with the question of mother-daughter relations and the possibility of re-creating the voice of the mother (Cosslett, Lury, and Summerfield 2000).

multiple generations); educational (many are very highly educated and speak for illiterate women); linguistic (many work in a variety of languages different from the language of their subjects, such as Berber, Arabic, French, and English); and geographical (many now reside in areas far removed from ancestral lands or have traveled widely). Thus, the challenges of truly re-creating the voice of the Other are intense, whether she is illiterate grandmother, aunt, or former slave. Happily, many of these writers actively question and even investigate the challenges and implications of precisely this project. For instance, in her novels, Assia Djebar explores the hybrid postcolonial condition with a distinct focus on the linguistic identity of individuals and the distance created between them as a result of linguistic differences.

For Mernissi, listening to the voices of these women and aiding in their acknowledgment and wider dissemination have been commitments fulfilled in several of her texts. As I have been pointing out, *Dreams of Trespass* operates on this premise; in addition, *Doing Daily Battle* (1988) presents direct interviews of such women, and *Women's Rebellion and Islamic Memory* (1996) asserts the theoretical underpinning that justifies the value of this practice. According to the latter, feminists must "grasp and decode illiterate women's rebellion, whether voiced in oral culture or in specifically dissenting practices considered marginal, criminal, or erratic" (16). This writing strategy succeeds overall in Mernissi's works because of the genuine care and humanity she demonstrates in recording her own experience of interacting with a variety of other women.[7]

WHAT IS A HAREM, ANYWAY?

By its very title, *Dreams of Trespass: Tales of a Harem Girlhood* clues us in to the fact that the memoir focuses on the harem as a space in which one dreams of some kind of trespass, whether physical or mental. The book features photographs by Ruth V. Ward that reinforce a notion of the solemn, stately nature

7. In *Reading Arab Women's Autobiographies: Shahrazad Tells Her Story*, Golley (2003, 87–113) discusses the issue of speaking for the Other as it pertains to anthologies of interviews with Arab women published by Nayra Atiya, Shaaban, and Mernissi. I am in particular agreement with her assessment of Mernissi's work (94–95).

of this upper-class domestic harem. However, even as Mernissi describes the beauty, calm, and order of the harem, the very walls, doors, and wrought iron of the photos suggest to us that "trespass" is but a "dream." Furthermore, the book's British title, *The Harem Within*, lets us know that its exploration is not limited to mere architecture but extends to the ways in which such processes are internalized. Indeed, we may say that within the book there are three distinct types of harems: in the countryside, in the city, and in the heart. Perhaps surprising to Western readers is the fact that much of Mernissi's youth was spent investigating the nature of the harem: she asks what a harem is and how one goes about living in such a place. This need to define the harem exists because in effect there is no such thing as "the harem," but rather "harems," both physical and mental, all of which come in different shapes and sizes. Not only is the space and image of a harem variable, but attitudes toward it by those women living in it vary markedly as well. Moreover, discussion of such things was anything but overt, especially so given that the political and traditional situation was in flux. She asserts, "'What exactly is a harem' was not the kind of question grownups volunteered to answer" (1995, 39). Mernissi acknowledges that the word *harem* introduced into any seemingly innocent conversation could elicit very passionate responses. Most notably, the women of the harem were struggling to cope with the life inside a traditional harem at a time when such practices were rapidly changing. As Donadey has noted, the period of her childhood that Mernissi covers in the memoir not only encompasses the end of the Second World War but also sees the end of Morocco's guerrilla resistance to French rule and the rise of political nationalism. King Mohammed V's Istiqlal (Independence) Party made its "formal demand for Morocco's independence from the French Protectorate" in 1944, when Mernissi was four years old (Donadey 2000, 86). The tension between cultural change and family tradition in the Mernissi harem created a strangely exciting and fragile atmosphere of progress and regression simultaneously; it is noteworthy that, among the harem women themselves, some were aching for reform, whereas others were among the most virulent reactionaries. For the children, learning their position in this rapidly changing world was especially challenging, and it is the pivotal figure of Mernissi's maternal grandmother, Yasmina, who embodies the notion that the progress made within the mind and spirit can go a long way toward bringing down the walls. She expresses the kind of protofeminism whose strength lies in its understanding and coping with a circumscribed life, while inspiring the hopes and ambitions of the future generations.

Since Yasmina lives in the countryside and does not appear to the young Mernissi to be locked in a harem at all, she innocently asks her grandmother to explain how such a life could be considered a harem. The fact that her grandmother gives several different answers to the question only confuses Mernissi more, but lets her know early on that, indeed, this situation is not clear-cut. The first part of the answer is that in a harem women have "lost the power of movement," and the second is that women in a harem may have the "misfortune of sharing their husbands with others." On her farm, Yasmina is one of eight cowives. It is noteworthy that despite being a traditional, illiterate woman, she yet hungers for a different future to be achieved through local, native means. She expresses faith in the promises made by the nationalists: women's right to education and the banning of polygamy and slavery (which disproportionately affects women). She punctuates this hope triumphantly: "Morocco has changed quickly little girl . . . and it will keep on doing so" (1995, 37). Throughout the text, the grandmother and mother will repeat the assertion and the hope that Mernissi and the girls of her generation will benefit from these changes and that their lives will thus be substantially different from their own.

This section nicely illustrates the book's polyphonic voice: Yasmina's idiosyncratic voice is rendered in detail and coexists with Mernissi's childhood perspective as she is instructed by her grandmother about the past, present, and hoped-for future of women in Morocco. In addition, Mernissi blends in her adult scholarly voice by including two lengthy footnotes defining and distinguishing between domestic and imperial harems and explaining the status of polygamy laws in Islam generally, and in Morocco specifically. The scholarly voice that narrates the history of Islam as well as the political history of Morocco shows both how things *have* changed for women (after all, she is a multilingual sociologist and professor, whereas her grandmother was illiterate) and how things *have not* changed (the footnote points out that "today, almost half a century later, Muslim women still are fighting to have polygamy banned. But legislators, all men, say it is *shari'a* law, religious law, and cannot be changed" (37n 4). Whereas Yasmina had to eke out her "little bit of happiness" in this world, sharing her husband with eight cowives, Mernissi herself becomes an internationally recognized voice on the very subject of women's legal position in the new nation. The immediate juxtaposition of Yasmina's energetic yet relatively powerless voice and Mernissi's professional one shows how a native feminism of an older generation could take seed and blossom in future ones.

Indeed, we may pause here to emphasize that the issue introduced by Grandmother Yasmina was critical to Morocco and throughout the Muslim Middle East and North Africa. As these regions emerged from colonial rule, women were employed in various ways to facilitate the forging of new national identities. Women's education, public dress, and health services were frequently cited as areas for reform and hallmarks of modernization. Nevertheless, it is sad that for many women, narrating the story of the establishment of their nation frequently entails a description of how they were abandoned or betrayed by the nationalists. As Deniz Kandiyoti has pointed out, all too often women are used in the early stages only to be relegated to the domestic sphere after the dust of nation building settles (1994, 376–90). In Islamic nations, this fact is frequently accompanied by a return to veiling and sequestering and the establishment of unfavorable family laws that negatively affect women, as Mernissi shows in Morocco's civil code in *Women's Rebellion.* Women find themselves caught among the seemingly irreconcilable forces of socialism, Western-style capitalism, and Islamic tradition expressed as sharia law. Just as a change in their lot would seem to herald progress, a return to prior customs identified with "authentic Islam" helps to maintain some semblance of identity in the face of a rapidly changing world. In *Beyond the Veil,* she explains this obstinate insistence on women's fundamental resistance to change as both psychological and political. It fulfills "a psychological need to maintain a minimal sense of identity in a confusing and shifting reality" (1987, xiii), and without a guiding ideology, Islam is "the only coherent ideology that masses and rulers could refer to" (23–24). Moreover, according to Mernissi, the effort to drive out the colonizers never went far enough to truly change society, which is why the so-called nationalists look to Islam as the ideology to legislate family issues.

The unequal burden placed on women in maintaining cultural identity is strongly felt among Mernissi's female relatives, especially her mother and seventeen-year-old cousin, Chama, who specifically challenges this double standard for women. For instance, when Chama discusses with Mernissi's father the issue of men and women adopting Western-style dress, the father states that "if Arab women started imitating European ones by dressing provocatively, smoking cigarettes, and running around with their hair uncovered, there would be only one culture left. Ours would be dead. 'If that is so,' argued Chama, 'then why can my male cousins run around dressed like so many imitation Rudolph Valentinos and cut their hair like French soldiers, with no one screaming at them that our culture is about to disappear?' Father did not answer that question" (1995, 181). Mernissi's father's insistence that culture itself is dependent on women's behavior is an amazingly prevalent trend, from Afghanistan to Morocco, from 1940 to the present: Islamic cultures must retreat to a strong tradition of female separation precisely because the country is assailed by foreign armies, and concomitant forms of cultural imperialism, and by doing so, they are resisting political and cultural invasion in one of the only ways available to them.

It is noteworthy that some women share Mernissi's father's attitude about women's role in protecting such traditions; some of the women in the book are not keen on changing traditions pertaining to veiling and sequestering. The promises of modernization and reform were especially controversial among the women of the Mernissi harem in the city of Fez. Although Mernissi and her cousins sought explanation and clarification of the harem from them, these urban women had no distinct answer either: "But whenever I tried to find out more about the word 'harem,' bitter arguments ensued" (40). Indeed, the women of the Fez harem fell into two camps with opposing views—leaving the children in a quandary. The debates for and against harems proceed logically on both sides until Chama explains her theory about how harems first got started. The story is enacted with a dramatic flair and is retold by Mernissi with a humorous tone that nearly belies the tragic undertone of the whole scenario: "Once upon a time," Chama would begin, men were violent and unrestrained; they decided to appoint a sultan to exercise authority and control. But who should be the sultan? They determined that whoever could catch and lock up the greatest number of women would be the sultan. Given that the women of the time were active and fearless warriors, the difficulty of the task was sure to be great.

Chama announces that the Byzantines won the first round: "The Emperor of the Byzantines conquered the world, caught a huge number of women, and put them in his harem to prove that he was the chief. East and West bowed to him. East and West were scared of him" (44). Then Arabs, she adds, improved their techniques until "they became very good at it and dreamt of conquering the Byzantines. Finally, Caliph Harun al-Rashid had that privilege. He defeated the Roman Emperor in the Muslim year 181 (A.D. 798) and then went on to conquer other parts of the world. When he had gathered 100 *jarya*, or slave girls, in his harem, he built a big palace in Baghdad, and put them in it, so no one would doubt he was sultan. . . . Everyone was very impressed after that—the Arabs gave orders, the Romans bowed" (44). In time, however, the Romans and the other Christians came together and changed the rules: the sultan would no longer be the one with the most women; instead, the winner would be he who builds the most weapons, machines, and ships. After hundreds of years of sleepy ignorance, the Arabs suddenly find that the man who rules us is "President de la Republic Française. He has a huge palace in Paris called Elysée and he has, oh surprise, only one wife! No harem in sight. And that single wife spends her time running in the streets, with a short skirt, and a low neckline. Everybody can stare at her ass and bosom, but no one doubts for a moment that the president of the French republic is the most powerful man in the country" (45).

Among the harem inhabitants, reactions to Chama's tale range from delighted agreement to outrage over the "ridicule of our customs," the latter attitude expressed most vehemently by Mernissi's paternal grandmother. Contrasted with the country grandmother, Mernissi's paternal grandmother is grand, urbane, and infinitely conservative, choosing to support the perpetuation of the harem system. Nevertheless, Chama's story certainly appeals to Mernissi's imagination and seems wholly plausible to her, for the following summer she reiterates the story as pure history to Grandmother Yasmina. The ensuing conversation balances very serious issues with a lightheartedness that characterizes her grandmother's wisdom. After explaining the word *harem* and its connection to *haram* (that is, that which is pure and holy), Yasmina clarifies the way the farm works as a harem by saying that the *hudud*, or "frontiers," are not physical but in the head; any space, she continues, has invisible rules that you must ascertain and follow. Unfortunately, there is not always much guidance in ferreting out these rules, until you are punished for breaking them: "the violence [that one experiences] after the fact" (63). Although this concept is alarming to Mernissi, Grandmother assures her that she need not "look for walls to bang your head on" (64). The hope is clear: "You will be a modern, educated lady. . . . Remember that even I, as illiterate and bound by tradition as I am, have managed to squeeze some happiness out of this damned life" (64).

The portraits of the Fez and farm harems complement the message of Chama's story that, although ridiculous, bears an uncomfortable note of reality to it. Reduced to such terms, the fight between East and West is seen to be waged on the backs of Eastern women. In the beginning, woman is a warrior, according to Chama, fierce and difficult to catch, but, in time, the warrior woman is rendered to be nothing but a *jarya,* a slave to the Muslim man, and, in turn, the Eastern Muslim man a dupe of the West. Everyone is used and exploited, and the fundamental insanity of the entire enterprise is satirized. As an allegory of gender relations and cultural contact, the story would be twice as funny if it were not half so true.

What is glaringly absent from Mernissi's harem is the sexual extravaganza of many orientalist images and texts. This is not to say that she totally omits issues of female sexuality, the body, or romance; indeed, these realms are all distinct elements of the narrative. However, its substance and style are of a completely different variety. For example, instead of showing the Arab woman as the sensual, perfumed femme fatale of Hollywood, such as Elizabeth Taylor's Cleopatra (1963), she not only describes in detail her mother's beauty rituals but also includes the very recipes for her homemade cosmetics. Mernissi presents her mother on beauty day as "running around with henna on her hair and a chick-pea-and-melon mask smeared on her face from one ear to the other ear" (231). Instead of intoxicating her husband with her irresistible sexuality, this getup of course induces him to "sneak out of the house as early as he could" (232). Furthermore, although Mernissi does take us on a trip to the *hamam* (public bath), the imagery there shares little with Jean Ingres's famous painting *The Turkish Bath* (1862), which features dozens of luminous naked women, enjoying each other with Sapphic delight. Instead, here we have the humorously detailed documentation of the "nightmare" of the hottest third chamber of the *hamam,* in which children are soaked in too cold or too hot water, scrubbed mercilessly, and made to wait in interminable lines while the adults perform their final ablutions. And finally, when the preadolescent Mernissi herself begins to take an interest in love chants and amulets, it causes a rift between her and her much-loved cousin Samir. His challenge for her to give up all the love "nonsense" and return to their childish games contrasts well with the young man who falls in love with his cousin in Byron's famous poem "The Bride of Abydos" (1813).

Mernissi shows that harem life for women in her part of the world was indeed very different from that image circulated in Western paintings, poems, and films. In its quotidian details, it was perhaps rather banal and certainly less titillating, but also far more compelling. As we have seen, learning to chart and navigate harem life was anything but easy, especially in a time of social change and modernization, yet the notion that such change was within sight made for very thrilling hopes. It is important for us to take note of the ways in which these strong women coped with their limitations and for us to acknowledge how they succeeded in passing on the desire and expectation for an increase in women's access to education, travel, and self-determination. The section that follows presents one of the primary ways it was achieved.

THE PLAY'S THE THING

Mernissi explains that the household compound is guarded by an ancient gatekeeper whose job is to ensure that the Mernissi women will not seek to leave the premises without a male escort. Since casual daily outings are not much of a possibility, life within the harem is passed and enriched by the women's staging their own plays and telling stories to each other. Cousin Chama, Aunt Habiba, and the elderly Ethiopian slave Mina are chief among the most thrilling "performers" in the place. Mernissi devotes several chapters of the memoir to redramatizing these plays and stories as a way to illustrate not only a coping mechanism but also a teaching tool. The entertainment on the terrace usually focuses on the lives of important women but ranges in mood and style from the very popular to the very serious. They love to dramatize the true story of Asmahan, the beautiful young Lebanese singer and actress whose shocking and amazing experiences give ample opportunity to blend songs and dances into the performance. Although popular, her life of breaking boundaries and forging new roles and identities for Arab women is a sublime and ironic model for the younger girls: whereas Asmahan actually lives adventures in her life, the women of the Fez harem are not even allowed to turn on the radio without male supervision. Another story that lends itself well to enactment is the tale of Princess Budur from *A Thousand and One Arabian Nights.* In this story, the princess masquerades as her husband, the sultan, after he mysteriously disappears one day; her story not only provides great entertainment but clearly illustrates the active life of which a woman is capable as well. On a more serious note, the terrace actors also stage the lives of real women feminists such as Aisha Taymour. In this way, they pass the time in the harem creatively, and the younger generation is educated to see the possibilities beyond their own limited experiences.

The dual role of art to please and instruct is reinforced by Aunt Habiba, who insists that stories are a form of magic that could help to change the world because, as she says, "liberation starts with images dancing in your little head, and you can translate those images in words. And words cost nothing!" (114). Aunt Habiba's position as a divorced woman living in her kinsmen's house renders her powerless, yet her thoughtful reflections on this fact help to cultivate the ambitions of her younger relatives. Habiba emphatically insists that the children are making a new future with their own inner power, and so this lesson is "hammered" into them. Mernissi's poetic response speaks to Aunt Habiba across the boundaries of time, space, and culture:

> It all seems easy, Aunt Habiba, with you and Chama going in and out of
> the fragile draped theater,
> So frail in the late night, of that remote terrace.
> But so vital, so nourishing, so wonderful.
> I will become a magician.
> I will chisel words to share the dream and render the frontiers useless. (114)

Mernissi's verse here simultaneously expresses a nostalgic longing for the "remote terrace" as well as a promise to break the *hudud* and translate Aunt Habiba's evanescent "images in your little head" into solidly "chiseled words." This response clearly encapsulates the dual nature of the harem as dramatized by Mernissi in *Dreams of Trespass.* Although nourishing as a community of women, the harem is also a restrictive and oppressive space: Habiba's tenuous social position is a clear signifier of this fact. Although guaranteed a home, she is nevertheless rendered wholly reliant on the good graces of her relatives and must play the politics of the harem carefully, inspiring the younger generation without offending the sensibilities of the conservatives in their midst.

A similar role is played by the only person in the household with even less overt power than Habiba: the Ethiopian former slave Mina, whose experience of kidnapping and resistance inspires the children to always hope and dream for a better future.

Mernissi's presentation of Mina's own rendition of her history as well as Mernissi's childhood and adult responses ideally represent the merging of different vocal registers in *Dreams of Trespass*. Mina repeatedly tells the story of her abduction to the children. Hers is a story they fear but love to hear: Mina, along with others, had been kidnapped by dark-skinned men, and the group of children was moved by day through a familiar forest, until they reached the Sahara desert region and were transferred to light-skinned men. After more travel, they approached another forest. Mina and another little girl thought perhaps it was the forest of their childhood, so they decided to run away but were caught a few hours later. As punishment, Mina was lowered into a well, hanging onto a rope. The men told her that she must hang on and concentrate if she wanted to live. So Mina managed to suppress her fear, dissociate herself from the other little girl, and concentrate on the rope. As she tells the story, all the children cry and commiserate with her situation but also enjoy her ironic victory over her captors. The moral of the story for the children is that "you always had a choice, when stuck in a pit, between pleasing the monster by looking down and screaming or surprising him by looking up. . . . If, on the other hand, you wished to astonish the monster, you fixed your eyes up high on that little drop of sky and avoided uttering a sound. Then, the torturer who was watching you from above would see your eyes and get scared" (171). The powerful effect of her story is certainly heightened by the irony of the slave's triumph over the slave owner. Although Mina's voice and presence are most prominent here, Mernissi's response is fascinatingly complex: she is the confused child listening to a life lesson, a learned scholar composing a simultaneous footnote on the slave trade, and a poet responding to Mina's story (165–70).

The lessons of Aunt Habiba and Mina point strongly to the idealistic notion that life for women will be improved by dreams that give the powerless wings and therefore liberty. In contrast, her mother's example focuses more on the practical. She insists on education for her children and emphatically opposes Mernissi's taking the veil, probably because she, more than the other women, is closer to actual improvements in her own status than they are. The ongoing exchange between Mernissi's parents about the harem is very telling. As her mother attempts to break with the communal living style of the harem, her father feels obliged and willing to make small concessions to her desires. Nevertheless, he insists that they cannot break away from the harem because "tradition would vanish: 'We live in difficult times, the country is occupied by foreign armies, our culture is threatened. All we have left is these traditions'" (78).

Despite the frustrations they experience, the Mernissi women manage to cope with the restrictions of the harem by utilizing the powerful tools of speech, stories, and role-playing. Each one promises in her own way that the nationalists will liberate the country from the colonial yoke and modernize its Islamic heritage. The previous quotation from her father indicates in what way that issue proves to be a difficult problem for many Muslim nations. As the dreams and methods of the nationalists fail to pay off, much of the population turns to the promises of the fundamentalists who believe that a return to the traditions of the East, in contradistinction to the culture of the West, will help them achieve both self-respect and economic gain. This trend has only been accelerated by the disenchantment with the new brand of American cultural imperialism and diplomatic policies motivated by the power of petrodollars. Unfortunately for women, democracy and equal rights are branded as two contaminating Western influences, and so a return to female seclusion, veiling, and totalitarian sharia law is seen as the most effective way to distinguish the East from the West.

Fatima Mernissi's memoir of a harem girlhood not only is a beautifully written book, replete with humor, integrity, and hope, but also provides us with very good insight into a life that has been the subject of countless speculations. Indeed, it is a valuable corrective to the images of the harem that have been prevalent in the West for three centuries. The book reinforces the stylistic and thematic concerns of Mernissi's other works by offering a different balance between the personal and the scholarly voices and by exploring issues central to women's lives in a postcolonial Muslim context. In the process of telling her personal story, she simultaneously creates a rhetorical construction of her nation that both exposes its faults and extols its virtues. Throughout her works, she adamantly asserts that a critique of aspects of Muslim culture does not necessarily mean she advocates a wholesale adoption of Western ways. It is an aspect of her work already gaining critical appreciation: Winifred Woodhull notes in the works of Mernissi and Assia Djebar a dual resistance to "the homogenizing repressive forces of fundamentalisms while also countering Orientalist imperialisms" (1993, 32). Although Mernissi critiques the national, patriarchal customs that limit women's access to education, divorce, and travel, she yet defines a culture that has an integrity and value of its own and is fully capable of reform and progress.

8

To Undo What the North Has Done

Fragments of a Nation and Arab Collectivism in the Fiction of Ahdaf Soueif

MRINALINI CHAKRAVORTY

> Participation. Life. Students from Egypt, Libya, Sudan, Algeria, Morocco, Iraq, Jordan, Palestine, Syria and Yemen all sit around the same table. News of unrest comes from the universities of Europe and the United States of America. Poetry and Politics. Never mind the defeat. Never mind the "Setback" and Sinai and what remained of Palestine gone. The young have a voice and the voice shall be heard. Bassam, the Palestinian, and Hani, one of the Harley-Davidson boys, both play the guitar and the campus rings to songs of exile and yearning.
>
> —Ahdaf Soueif, *In the Eye of the Sun*

There is optimism yet. As well as political purpose. It is December 1967 in Cairo, and Arabs have just lost a massive military conflict with Israel over sovereignty and shipping rights in the Strait of Tiran and the Gulf of Aqaba. Still, in her novel *In the Eye of the Sun* (1992), Ahdaf Soueif describes the students gathering at Cairo University in the wake of this "defeat" in unequivocally enthusiastic terms. There is "Life," she writes, and "Participation." Soueif's protagonist, Asya al-Ulama, a young upper-class student of English literature in Cairo in the 1960s, is in the thick of this social tableau, full of life, and eager to participate. The critical element here that seems to make such optimism possible, and to infuse this otherwise dreary historical moment with much political purpose for Asya and her fellow students, is the representation in this scene of almost all of the Arab world. Students they are all, but most notably students whose national identities converge in this moment to produce a sense of ethnographic Arab solidarity that overrides all the depression of "defeat" and "loss." In this moment, the coming together of Egypt, Libya, Sudan, Algeria, Morocco, Iraq, Jordan, Palestine, Syria, and Yemen over questions of "Poetry" and "Politics" acts as a salve over the wounds of war and the excesses of Western imperialism.

What Ahdaf Soueif, like other Arab women writers such as Fadia Faqir, Nawal el-Saadawi, and Hanan al-Shaykh, is also able to imagine here is the possibility of a Pan-Arab, secularist identity that disrupts Western, and even Islamist, stereotypes of Arabs as united only by religion. This is not to say that Soueif is unaware of the cultural importance of Islam in the Arab world.[1] Rather, what Soueif represents in her work is a postcolonial worlding of Arab culture based on language, shared history, and sociality that forms a discursive alternative to the often prevalent, and false, notion that Islamic fundamentalism is all that motivates Arab political struggles. Writers such as Soueif persistently open up another world of Arab existence and political motivation: an Arab world that is marked especially by an awareness of colonial and neoimperial oppression, and one where the domain of the realpolitik is constituted on the basis of a heterogeneous ethnic and gender solidarity that exceeds, and at times even interrogates, the constraints of national, religious identification. For these postcolonial Arab writers, sociocultural Arab unity is the main catalyst of the Middle Eastern struggle against Western imperialism.[2]

1. Indeed, I am not claiming that Ahdaf Soueif and other Anglophone Arab writers represent an Arab culture that is artificially separated from Islamic practices and that the characters in these books are wholly devoid of religious affiliations. On the contrary, most characters in Soueif's novels, such as Asya, Saif, Chrissie, Bassam, Noora, Lateefa, and others in *In the Eye of the Sun* and Amal, Sharif, Layla, and Omar in *The Map of Love*, are, in fact, Muslim. However, this aspect of their cultural identity, I would argue, remains just that, one aspect of Arab culture among others for these characters. Further, I would argue that these novels are deliberate in portraying faith as largely disconnected from the political aspirations and actions of these characters. A "jihad" versus "McWorld" (see Barber 1993; and Huntington 1996) attitude toward Arab literature is already politically proscriptive insofar as it aligns Islam with tradition and the West with modernity. I would mark my own reading here as refusing to participate in this construction of binaries.

2. For example, Leila Ahmed in *A Border Passage* writes, "My schoolmates at the English School in Cairo included Syrians, Lebanese, and Palestinians. . . . One of my two best friends

Soueif's novel traces the life of a young Cairene, Asya al-Ulama, through her formative years in Nasser's Egypt, her life as a student of literature and linguistics in England, and her subsequent return to Cairo. The novel is formally realistic, focusing as it does on an almost month-by-month detailing of Asya's life from 1967 (Nasser's Egypt) to 1979 (Egypt under Sadat). It is almost eight hundred pages in length, and, in this regard, in form, it can be said to be modeling the great Nahda (Arab Renaissance) styles of late-nineteenth- and early-twentieth-century Arab *bildung* novels by the likes of Jurji Zaydan, Muhammad Muwaihili, Muhammad Haykal, Yahya Haqqi, and even the early Naguib Mahfouz and Tayeb Saleh, which were written in the genres of romantic historical novels. It is important to my project to acknowledge Soueif's formal likeness with these Arab writers as a way of mapping an Arab literary influence on her oeuvre, even as I make the argument that Soueif's work, despite its allegiance to realism, is also marked by a sense of "crisis," a lens on modernity, a voice for feminism, and an unrelenting emphasis on the present, all of which are unique to contemporary Arab fiction. Comparisons of Soueif with Dickens and George Eliot simply miss the episodic, journalistic, multiple diary forms (the many voices) that fashion her narrative and echo works of Arab "crisis" literature such as later works by Mahfouz and Saleh, as well as Khoury, Kanafani, Munif, el-Saadawi, al-Shaykh, Faqir, and more.[3] Soueif, along with these others, and especially by writing in English, creates an intertext within Arab fiction between a long tradition of past Arab

---

through my school years was Jean Said, who would later write *Beirut Fragments;* she was the younger sister of Edward Said, the well-known theorist and literary critic. They were Christians of Palestine and we were Muslims of Egypt, but their attitudes were not discernibly different from ours" (1999a, 6). Although Ahmed's point here is about the European-style education system of the Egypt of her childhood, the scene she presents in her memoir is essentially one of Pan-Arab unity that transcends issues of nationality, ethnicity, and religion.

3. As Hind Wassef remarks, Soueif has been "hailed as Egypt's George Eliot," and her novel "has been called Egypt's *Middlemarch*" (1998, n.p.). But as Edward Said has pointed out, "In many ways Asya is her own Casaubon" (1992, 19). Said's comment works to undo the common practice of reading non-Western writers only insofar as they measure up to a Western canon. The important point that needs to be made is that Soueif is not George Eliot—her gender politics are not from the nineteenth century, and she, as Said notes, is capable of turning *Middlemarch* on its head.

literature and a more immediate one whose focus has been to represent the turmoil in the Arab world as itself productive. What is produced is a Pan-Arabism that is contracted by the historical fractures experienced by Arab people, and whose platform must be ever shifting, ever newly articulated, so as not to prefigure Arab experience as in any way static or homogenous.

Edward Said famously concludes *Culture and Imperialism* with the caveat, "No one today is purely one thing" (1994a, 336). Said's is not a simple and happy claim to hybrid identities. Rather, what Said's scholarship is at pains to show is that the disruptions produced by colonialism and imperialism "consolidated the mixture of cultures and identities on a global scale" (336). In representing the politics of an Arab collective, writers such as Ahdaf Soueif perform the delicate task of showing how such collectives are paradoxically born of the very "mixture of cultures and identities" produced by colonialism. Moreover, a sense of Arab collectivism becomes possible only with the recognition that it is a collective of the present, continually in the making, and without any essential foundations. If anything, it is the incoherence of universalizing colonial ideologies of the nation, patriarchy, and religion that makes it possible for Soueif and others to imagine a collective in terms of difference. Pan-Arabism is worlded in Soueif's novel as always and incessantly mapping the limits and tensions of its own constituency as a collective, and as in dialogue with the failures of nationalism, religion, and patriarchy in making sense of what it means to be Arab.

It is my argument that postcolonial Arab writers such as Soueif see the quotidian negotiations of cultural identity that happen within the Arab world as an impetus toward Arab unity and as the main catalyst of the Middle Eastern struggle against Western imperialism. The Pan-Arabism of contemporary postcolonial Arab fictions comes in the aftermath of the period of high nationalism after the Second World War when national identity and nationalist ideologies were the primary tools for countering colonialism. The paradigm of the nation, especially for Arab women authors today, seems to offer a very limited scope for coping with the exigencies and fossilized remnants of the colonial power structures and their continuity with neoimperial forms of oppression. The historical moment in which postcolonial Arab women are writing now is very different from the moment in which Frantz Fanon first imagined the forceful expulsion of the colonizer from the world of the colonized. Moreover, although the term suggests an affinity, Pan-Arabism as represented in these texts constitutes a more dynamic engagement with the cultural and historical realities of the present-day Arab world than the late-nineteenth- and early-twentieth-century versions of the "Arabism" that Fanon dismisses. For one, the Pan-Arab politics evoked by these novels is not atavistic or blindly universalizing in that it does not seek to idealize a distant and sterile epoch of some common past that is unavailable to the realities or "events of today."[4] In addition, Arab identity is also carefully represented as a predicate of various and often divergent national and ethnic belongings. And finally, Pan-Arabism is also shown as a literal expression of the ethnocultural and religious heterogeneity that is the lived experience of the Arab world and the source of a political force that informs the Arab struggle against Western hegemony.

I believe that it is important at this juncture, and to the political goals of this project, to explicitly recall those voices within the Arab world that are crucial in developing the notion of Arab "connectedness" along heterogeneous, and non-European, lines. Although I see Rifaa al-Tahtawi as an important figure in developing the concept of Arab unity as also secular, this position is given coherence and new direction by scholars such as Sati al-Husri (1880–1964), Abd al-Rahman al-Bazzaz (1913–?), Michel Aflaq (1910–), and Hichem Djait (1935–), to name just a few among a host of others. Indeed, writers such as al-Husri, al-Bazzaz, and Aflaq gradually distill ideas of Pan-Arabism already imbricated in the works of traditionalists (Sayyid Jamal al-Din al-Afghani, Muhammad Abduh, and others)[5] and modernists (Rifaa al-Tahtawi and Taha

4. For a succinct and indeed excellent discussion of traditionalist versus progressive (read: European-style) scholars, Albert Hourani (1988, 1991) and George Antonius (1939) offer more detailed but essentially similar analyses of the polarities of Arab thought in the twentieth century.

5. Al-Afghani is widely regarded as the father of modern Muslim nationalism and an advocate of Pan-Islamism who privileged Muslim laws *(shari'a)* and established traditions *(hadiths)* above any "tribal solidarity" or forms of ethnic nationalism. Although he significantly influenced those recent Arab scholars termed "traditionalists" or "fundamentalists," his position is complex; he also seems to echo proponents of the Nahda, "hoping that Mumammadan society will succeed in breaking its bonds and marching resolutely in the path of civilization after the manner of Western society" (1968, 87). Along with al-Tahtawi, al-Afghani was among the first to suggest a linguistic basis for Arab unity, asserting "that the unity of language is more durable for survival and permanence in this world than unity of religion" (56). Although in his other writings (see,

Husayn)[6] alike in order to mark a path for Arab autonomy that is indebted neither to religion nor to the West for guidance.

This chapter deals mainly with issues of Pan-Arabism and gender, especially as they are inscribed within frames of individual and collective

---

for example, *The Emergence of the Modern Middle East: Selected Reading* [1970]), al-Afghani refutes these claims for science and language, he furthers them in the context of his writing against imperialism. Such context-oriented positions are what allies al-Afghani with a certain thread of Pan-Arabism that becomes increasingly prominent among later scholars such as al-Husri (1982), al-Bazzaz (1982), Aflaq (1982), and Djait (Donohue and Esposito 1982): a Pan-Arabism that distances itself from notions of Muslim fraternity and nationality in favor of a unity based on language and culture.

Abduh was al-Afghani's most famous disciple who in turn drew a large following among younger Arab thinkers of the twentieth century. As a mufti of Egypt, Abduh advocated a return to the purity of an Islamic past as the only way in which to make Islamic cultures commensurate with modern times. He used examples from classical Islam to argue for human rights and women's rights and against class prejudice. It was this mode of regressive, progressive argument that drew his many followers, including Ali Abd al-Raziq (1888–1966), Rashid Rida (1865–1935), Amir Shakir Arslan (1869–1946), and Ahmad Lufti al-Sayyid (1872–1963), all of whom used Islam as universal justification for why any other type of unity among Arabs is too limiting and exclusionary. For specific excerpts from Abduh, and his followers, see Donohue and Esposito 1982.

6. Those individuals in favor of a Nahda such as Taha Husayn (1889–1973) and Sadiq al-Azm (1936–) go so far as to argue that Arab culture is essentially European in its practices and sensibilities. "The dominant and undeniable fact of our times," Husayn insists, "is that day by day we are drawing closer to Europe and becoming an integral part of her, literally and figuratively. This process would be much more difficult than it is if the Egyptian mind were basically different from Europe" (1954, 119). For Husayn, and other supporters of the Nahda, Europe was the central measure for judging Egyptian/Arab accomplishments, and European modernity thus became the goal to which Arabs needed to aspire. Hence, Saree Makdisi, Albert Hourani, and others are again not incorrect in assuming that the Nahda school of scholars saw Arab culture as civilizationally underdeveloped in comparison to the more industrial Europe. I am not disputing this criticism of the Nahda movement. What I am claiming, rather, is that there have always been among some Arab thinkers a more complex understanding of the relationship between Europe and its Arab colonies that makes it necessary to situate Arab responses to colonialism and Arab calls of resistance outside of a dichotomous framework. Makdisi characterizes al-Tahtawi as one "who regarded tradition as something to move beyond rather than return to" (1995, 89n7), thereby clearly placing him in the company of those individuals who perceived a future modernity for Arabs that proceeds out of a teleological line of progress from barbarism to civilization.

responses to imperialism in contemporary Arab contexts. The issue of representing collective women's subjectivities in terms of individual "life development" is crucial to Soueif's representation of feminist contexts within the Arab world. My effort has been to resite sexual and gender subjectivities within other forms of life development (political, academic, and so on) that the novel presents as a means for representing Arab collectives, especially in the decade leading up to the millennium. Soueif's *In the Eye of the Sun* refracts narratives of displacement and war through the prism of gender and self-articulation offered in her novel to arrive at alternate possibilities for reading the public sphere within Arab contexts in terms of secular and collective responses to the imperatives of imperialism.

Reading Soueif's work as implicitly engaged in the task of self-articulation, as well as in the collective representation of contemporary Arab identity politics, requires a singular reconception of how this work handles the terms of self-presentation or autobiography. The narrator's life story runs together with the author's to a point where one seems to largely frame the other: Asya, like Soueif, comes of age in Nasserian Egypt, is the child of affluent university professors, is raised on a political and intellectual diet of Arab socialism, and leaves Egypt for England in order to earn an advanced degree. Both also begin to reflect on their expanded situations as Arab women within a global political locus during the time of their relocation. Out of place, writer and narrator seem to slip in and out of the common experience of being Arab, women, and dislocated in the West. Yet the collapse between author and narrator also remains of necessity incomplete: Ahdaf Soueif escapes the frames of her fiction, whereas Asya remains bound in them. Soueif's life text doubles the life text of her narrator and in so doing impresses the work with a signature that is specifically autobiographical in these two senses: coding the book as the author's fiction and presenting the author as also fictional. This double gesture of the author's presence-absence inscribes *In the Eye of the Sun* as an effective measure of binding together the authority of the autonomous, self-presenting subject and the encumbered, collective subjects of history that a book about being Arab in the world today demands.

What the self-aware writer/narrator of *In the Eye of the Sun* confirms are the radically unexpected terms for conceiving autobiography within the Arab context. The author's shadowing of the narrator's life with her own well-publicized but marginally different one foils any attempt to test the gestures of self-articulation made by Asya on the exhausted turf of authenticity. The problem of presenting the Arab situation in this novel sidesteps the issue of authenticity for an alternative approach that considers the voice of the narrator as the voice of a self-possessed individual but declaims the liberal terms of autobiography and authenticity that confer this voice with agentive subjectivity. Rather, what this novel demands is a placing together of fiction and its narrative claims to self-articulation as tandems to the consideration of collective historical claims as such. Asya cannot speak herself as every Arab woman, but her story echoes the traces of a collective struggle that does not need the "true fit" of autobiographical claims to truth and witness. The fiction of Asya's life narrative begins with the premise that "you cannot have a true fit of identity in the political" (Spivak 1992, 788).

Without the easy sanction of the authentic subject, or the authentic self-voicing witness, Asya's story unfolds as in proxy to the numerous others within the novel. Asya's story of affluence, dislocation, and growing political sensibility both speaks for others and, because of its claim to fiction over truth, is able to claim itself as an approximation of others' experience. Certainly, as Gayatri Chakravorty Spivak notes, such claims to approximation are indispensable to the writing of collective struggle: "To achieve autobiography in the double bind of the practice of the conqueror's writing is to learn to be taken seriously by the gendered subaltern who has not mastered that practice" (1992, 771). Asya re-presents herself in English but also, beyond this presentation, presents herself as different from both the English (who are alien to her) and the subalterns such as Bassam, Toota, and Dada Zeina (who are alienated from her). Her narrative practice is to illuminate precisely the ways in which these others remain outside of the means of self-articulation that is her privilege. The mode of self-articulation as inauthentic, unoriginal self-inscription that Ahdaf Soueif presents in *In the Eye of the Sun* substantiates the grounds for the larger historical platform of Pan-Arabism as a means for negotiating individual and collective struggles against imperialism in the Arab world. In place of truth claims for the self, and indisputable witness testimony, this novel re-presents "autobiography" most fully as "a wound where the blood of history does not dry" (Spivak 1992, 795).

DISPLACEMENT

In Soueif's novel, Asya's coming of age is a coming to recognition of the scars of dislocation and migration. Bassam's songs of "exile and yearning" punctuate the narrative of *In the Eye of the Sun,* offering a narrative counterfocus to Egyptian experiences of nationalism. Bassam is Palestinian and lives in Cairo as an emblem of Arab unity over the disfranchised status of Palestine. At the same time, Bassam's liminal position within Egyptian society emerges as the condition for negotiation that makes Pan-Arabism in this novel the basis of an identity that is constantly being reshaped. Asya's Egypt may seem inflected by the nationalisms of Nasser and Sadat, but Asya's lived experience of Egypt, a place with many who are out of place, bears witness to the fragility of nationally "imagined communities" in the Arab political context.

Bassam's presence within Soueif's novel stirs Asya to sustained contemplation on the plight of the "Abdel," the dispossessed. It is a contemplation that is all the more important for its gyrelike logic, seeing Bassam as wholly other, seeing him as herself, and then expanding outward into a kaleidoscopic awareness of the multitudes around her who are without a sense of permanent belonging. Soueif writes of Asya's preoccupation with Bassam at a study session: "Asya closes the book gently and glances at Bassam. She had wondered since she had met him—what was it really like to be him? To be so displaced?" (1992, 233). For this question, Asya has no immediate answer, and Soueif's tactic here is to place Bassam elsewhere in Asya's thoughts, at least for the moment: "He was born in 1949; one year after the partition and the war. He'd grown up in Nablus and since 1967 his family—and he in the summer holidays—had been living under occupation" (233). This thought then is a movement in representation toward origins; for Asya to understand Bassam, he needed first to be identified as Palestinian, someone born into a state of dispossession that Asya, as an Egyptian, has never experienced. Yet his proximity to her, moving as he does in her circle, makes Asya go further: "Actual physical occupation. What would that be like?" she asks, and ventures, "To have . . . the Israelis themselves, stop you, . . . and say, 'Sorry. You can't come in here any more. You are banned" (233). This point, it seems, is the political moment, opposing disempowered Arabs to Israeli aggression, in Asya's still youthful ruminations. Asya here others herself, for a time imagines herself in Bassam's place, without place, and is able next to enunciate a politics of Arab unity, a way of seeing herself, Bassam, and countless others in a place of political vulnerability. Bassam, Asya realizes, "appeared almost—maimed. One of the bruised people. All those bruised people: Palestinians, Armenians, Kurds, and of course the Jews themselves . . . What can be done?" (234). There is a shift in Asya's new expression of Pan-Arab solidarity. The inclusion in this list—"Palestinians, Armenians, Kurds"—of "Jews" is important because Asya here recuperates Pan-Arabism from becoming religiously divisive and foregrounds instead a certain pathos of displacement, an empathy toward the "maimed" and "bruised" as sufficient grounds for unity and action. Across time, Soueif and al-Tahtawi echo each other, situating the refugee as an integral aspect of *watan* (country, home). And regardless of religious affiliation, Soueif and al-Tahtawi make refugees the source of political impetus, without at the same time completely dissociating, or ignoring, historical specificity. Palestinians, Armenians, Kurds, and Jews all have very distinct experiences of unrootedness, and, for Asya, their historical differences must be acknowledged in any attempt to consider them together, to ponder the active question, "What can be done?" Asya will have none of what Michel Aflaq has called the "abstract humanity" of European colonialism that "consider[s] peoples as blocs of static, homogenous humanity with no roots in the earth, unaffected by time" (1982, 111).

"What can be done?" Asya asks. What Soueif shows Asya doing is in fact negotiating, confronting, and arguing with the people in her circle who would deny Palestinians a space of legitimacy and inclusion within Egyptian society, even as they denounce the occupation of Palestine. In a typical scene from the novel, Asya argues with her friend Chrissie's mother, Tante Muneera, about Bassam's love for Noora, one of Asya's college friends who is also the daughter of a prominent Egyptian minister. To Muneera's outburst, "'Palestinian?' . . . 'Palestinian? And he's going and falling in love with Noora al-Manesterli? I swear her father will have him jailed,'" Asya replies, "'Yes, well, he realizes all that. That's why he's so hesitant about speaking to her. But in fact he's from a good family. He's a Huseini. His uncle is the governor of Gaza and they have houses and lands in Nablus'" (1992, 115). In an attempt at conversion, Asya tries to translate Bassam's status as an exile into the common parlance of class privilege, and lineage, in which Muneera speaks. In this instant, it seems that Asya's strategy is to pit attitudes of class, and origins, against Muneera's bias toward Palestinian refugees. This tactic, at least momentarily, allows Soueif to represent Bassam as a product of his own history, belonging as he does to a land and family. Still, Muneera remains unconvinced: "'Governor of Gaza? Houses and lands in Nablus? Houses and lands in the palm of the Devil. Are you all mad? Don't you live in this world?'" What is urgently felt in Muneera's refusal to yield, to accept Bassam, is the emergency of his condition as an exile. Palestine is under siege, and many Arabs like Muneera (and later even Asya's husband, Saif)[7] are unable to recognize Palestinians in their midst as anything but forsaken people. Soueif's portrayal of Asya's response, "'So what does that mean, Tante?' Asya knows this is not the moment for arguing but she cannot help it. 'That Palestinians shouldn't fall in love?'" (115), emphasizes the need for persistence in making a case, even if now "is not the moment," for the dispossessed. Although Asya's strategy seems to fail with Muneera, on a metanarrative level, *In the Eye of the Sun* makes the unstable circumstances of this refugee an ever present lens through which its protagonist is compelled to view the world.

The novel's intermittent gaze on Bassam and Noora's life together—Noora disowned from her family, Bassam working precariously for the *Voice of Palestine*—shapes the political ethos of Pan-Arabism within it (233). Bassam's forceful deportation from Egypt becomes a way for Soueif to implicate representations of displacement in representational critiques of U.S. influence over the Arab region. On her return to Egypt from England, Asya tells of Bassam's last night in Egypt: "Bassam is gone. Picked up the night of Camp David and given twenty minutes to pack a bag and then driven off into the night leaving a distraught Noora helplessly to cry her heart out. . . . As far as anyone could tell he would not be able to come back for a long time—perhaps not ever" (775).

7. Significantly, even on her wedding night, Asya confronts Saif's attitude toward Bassam's alliance with Noora (252). Saif's inability to embrace Bassam becomes one of the first signs of difference between Asya and Saif and shadows their eventual separation. Here Soueif, it seems, makes a sense of accommodation toward those individuals such as Bassam indicative of both a gendered perspective on Arab unity and an internal opposition that all visions of Pan-Arabism such as the one Asya espouses will have to deal with, if only to distance themselves from these others.

The year is 1980, and Asya returns to a very different Egypt, one that is no longer nonaligned; Sadat is very much in the U.S. camp, and, politically, it seems Egypt has steered clear of Nasserian visions of "Socialism, Arab Unity, The Palestinian Cause" with which the novel opens (17). Still, Asya's attachments are with Bassam and Noora, and the novel keeps open the need to interrogate the kind of national politics that seeks to write them out of Egypt's history. As Amin Malak notes, "What is particularly engaging about the heroine, Asya, is that her sharp political sensitivity extends beyond Egyptian nationalist concerns to embrace other dispossessed peoples of the Middle East such as Kurds, Palestinians, and Armenians" (2000, 146). This "sharp political sensitivity" characterizes Soueif's call to consider Arab unity beyond national borders.

DISPLACEMENTS: THE WORK OF WOMEN

Already we have, with Asya, a gendered focalization of the social instabilities attendant on living out of borders. Asya herself is faced repeatedly in *In the Eye of the Sun* with being outside, in places of nonbelonging, first in Beirut and subsequently in England (1992, 143, 511). In her novel, Soueif codes the shifts of migration and movement, both as experiences of refuge seekers such as Bassam and as an economy of gender within the Arab world.[8] Women, such as Asya's mother, Lateefa, and Asya's nanny, Dada Zeina, are figured in terms of transnational labor and are agents of Egypt's encounter with modernity within this narrative. Women as migrant workers, leaving one Arab country to work in another, pre-scribe women's desires, needs, and autonomy within the contours of Pan-Arabism in this novel. For Soueif, it seems that in order to have a viable politics of Arab unity with which to address the extreme pressures of Islamization and Westernization at work in the Middle East, a Pan-Arab coalition must first account for those realities, of the displaced, of displaced women, often marginalized by the first two hegemonic paradigms.

Asya's own return to Cairo, her place of belonging, for example, is poignantly marked in Soueif's text by her mother's departure from it. On the eve

8. Even in Bassam's case, as Soueif shows, it is Noora who suffers a parallel loss of family and home, as she is denounced by her family for marrying Bassam and suffers economic hardships in bringing up their child on her own, after Bassam's deportation.

of her return, she receives this letter from Lateefa: "I have signed a contract to go to the University of Kuwait next year. The way the economy is going here now, somebody in this family had better make some money. . . . As for your father . . . [h]e does not, of course, approve of my going to Kuwait. He believes I am 'selling out' . . . and proposing to prostitute my brains and my training to a few ignorant nouveau-riche Arabs" (731, 732).

Lateefa's decision to move to Kuwait is transcribed here as economic need and gender autonomy within an otherwise patriarchal familial-national structure. Lateefa's labor, in this case intellectual labor, it seems, not only is marketable elsewhere, in other Arab places, but also reifies her position as woman and wage earner within her family. It is not surprising that her decision to leave Egypt is explicitly economical and that it engenders an accusation of "prostitution" by her husband, Mukhtar "al-Ulama," or Mukhtar "the scholar." Soueif makes clear that Mukhtar's scholarship is intractably nationalistic, unyieldingly focused on a limited, developmental Nasserism for Egypt, and Egypt only, in contradistinction to even Nasser's own larger visions of Arab unity. Lateefa's insistence on leaving inaugurates a sort of transit space for women as family members, workers, and migrants within *In the Eye of the Sun:* a transit space of the present whose very ephemerality enables modern Arab women to challenge the permanence of the old templates of nationalism, and patriarchy, while keeping open directions to the future.

So even as Asya returns, Lateefa leaves. And this circumstance is the new situation for Arab women—between coming and going—that Soueif's novel presents for us as the dynamic domain to which any attempt to write a politics of empowerment for Arabs must bear witness. The space of transition that Lateefa chooses to inhabit is not an easy one, contested as it is by her desires for self-assertion and her own cultural conditioning that as yet—despite her willingness to leave, question her husband's judgment, and Egypt's national project—is still weighted by a divisive view of the Arab world. This divisiveness, as Soueif shows, at once stems from feelings of cultural superiority and the very real problem of economic disparities between Arab states that any vision of Pan-Arabism, in order to be effective, needs to acknowledge. Thus, in the same letter in which Lateefa reaffirms her decision to leave nation and family, she also writes, "I do not feel that bad about it—after all, you could see it as continuing a tradition: it was always us Egyptians who educated all those Arabs and civilized them; us and the Levantines" (731). Lateefa's prejudices here may be based on her own internalization of colonial and Egyptian nationalist discourses on "civilized" and "uncivilized" or "developed" and "underdeveloped" Arabs, but it is also shaped by her awareness of the economic rift between Arab countries. "So now," Lateefa writes to Asya, "[the Kuwaitis] have money and we don't—and they can pay us and we need paying" (731).

This situation is a difference within the Arab scene, of economic disparity in Arab-Arab relations, that Soueif's representation of Pan-Arabism foregrounds and critiques. The division of the Arab world between the haves and the have-nots takes on, in Lateefa's words, a rhetoric of tradition and modernity, of progress and backwardness, that echoes Islamist and colonial attitudes toward Arabs. However, this disparity in wealth is a real one that exists and frequently impedes the coherence of a Pan-Arab claim to identity.[9] In Soueif's

9. Middle Eastern newspapers frequently note the wide disparity in wealth in the region. In "Riding for a Fall," Wael Gamal of *Al-Ahram* writes of the poverty line in the Middle East based on two reports, the ILO's *Working Out Poverty* (2003) and *The World Wealth Report* (2003), issued by Merrill Lynch and Cap Gemini Ernst and Young, which measures "key trends and developments in the global HNWI [high-net worth individuals] market." "The Middle East," writes Gamal, bringing these two status reports together, "is a stark example on both sides. 'The number of people in the Middle East living at or below the $2 a day line rose from 50 million to nearly 70 million in the 1990s,' the ILO report said. At the same time, according to the HNWI report, 'the number of HNWIs increased by 4.7 per cent—nearly double the international rate—to 300,000 . . . to reach $1.1 trillion" (2003, n.p.). Comparative economic analysis of this type—drawing on both social and corporate "wealth management" findings to view the bigger picture—is rare. Most economic reports ignore labor-based reports that allow for conclusions such as Gamal's: "There is no safety net and little state support. After all the poor do not cause poverty. Poverty is the result of structural failures and ineffective economic and social systems. It is a product of inadequate political responses, bankrupt policy imagination and insufficient international support. . . . The work of the poor is largely invisible. Far too much of women's work is still uncounted and undervalued" (n.p.). Instead, they confirm policies of trade liberalization and tariff reduction that, though supposedly intending to reduce economic disparity, continue to focus on a corporate system too centered on individuality and profit generation—that is, the maintenance and regeneration of HNWI. Social change is hence made dependent on an ethos of individuality that merely uses the rhetoric of change and communitarianism to stabilize the status quo: the domination of world markets by the West according to Western conservative market principles. See, for example, the implementation of the Egypt-EU Association Agreement of 2003 and the *2003 Trade Investment and Development* report for the Middle East and North Africa region

novel, this problem of economic difference is represented as the differential matrix of Pan-Arab experience that allows for a simultaneous critique of excess, excesses of wealth in particular, while signaling the possibility of seeing this division as also palliative, also in effect regenerative of mutuality among Arabs. Hence, Asya and her sister, Deena, are able to engage in a fierce critique of "the Kuwaitis spending millions creating a stock exchange that they don't need" (473), as Lateefa modifies her earlier appraisal of the Kuwaitis somewhat: "They can pay us and we need paying—it's no reason to stop helping them" (731). For Soueif, it seems as important to launch an internal Arab response against superficial capital accumulation and modernization as it is to recognize the ways in which the possession and flow of capital, of oil money, magnify interdependencies and create alliances among Arabs.[10]

Dada Zeina's departure from Egypt for Saudi Arabia is cast in a similar aspect, conjoining elements of critique, need, and reciprocity. Her emigration is met with skepticism and accusations of "greed" within the Ulama family, where she has been in service for years (269). The incentive for Dada Zeina, according to Tante Soraya, seems to be so overwhelmingly monetary that considerations of loyalty, love, and an age-old alliance with the Ulama family with whom she has been so long seem to slip. Yet, as Soueif is at pains to show, Asya's encounter with Dada Zeina's sister, Sett So 'ad, yields a very different explanation of

---

(both of which facilitate a lowering of tariffs within Arab countries and the opening of Arab markets to foreign import and export) and Egypt's 2003 entry into the Patent Cooperation Treaty, which checks all Egyptian innovation against a standard of intellectuality and intellectual rights established by the U.S. market system.

10. I would note Soueif's strategic compromise here as against more critical works such as Ghassan Kanafani's *Men in the Sun* (originally published in 1962), which takes a much more stringent view against the oil-rich states. Kanafani's novel represents the experiences of Palestinian workers who attempt to cross into Kuwait without papers for work, in hopes of a better life. The novel has a dark end: the workers die of heat and suffocation when their truck, driven by an Iraqi human trafficker, is unexpectedly held up at a customs checkpoint. Kanafani's conclusion here is about the impossibility of a collective Arab experience, given the manner in which colonial borders between Arab states are still rigidly enforced by Gulf states who, in Kanafani's account, make it impossible for rich Arabs to identify or aid those other, dispossessed, poor Arabs outside their borders. Soueif's novel avoids such neat divisions, and with them a singularly apocalyptic commentary on the Arab experience.

the circumstances that shape Dada Zeina's going away, being away: "She went away with her Saudi family, my darling. They had to go and they couldn't do without her, the children loved her so. So she left her kids in safe keeping with me—they're big kids now, may God protect them—and went. She sends me a hundred pounds a month for their expenses. The Saudis value her so" (371). There is a lot invested in the operative term *value* here. Soueif's emphasis seems to be as much on the "value" of the Saudis for Dada Zeina as her "value" to them. To this aspect is added the dimension of "love"; after all, Sett Um Sobhi or Dada Zeina is only "Dada," or nanny, to Asya, and in so far as Asya "loves" her, the Saudis too "couldn't do without her." Soueif's is an incisive commentary on class privilege within the Arab world, Saudi and Egyptian, and at the same time an affirmation of the bonds that are born of such social contradictions, bonds that are not necessarily made or broken by nationality.

There is a not unintended parallel here that Soueif makes between Lateefa's position and Dada Zeina's. But still, it is not a parallel where the experience of an upper-class intellectual as she moves between universities and cities comfortably telescopes the experience of a menial worker moving between homes and countries. Both are motivated, to a large extent, by need, and both gain some economic autonomy within the narrative for the work they do as women. Certainly, a reductive criticism of Soueif's novel would be to dismiss her overt move to crisscross the paths these two women take as simply a token gesture that still ignores the enormity of the vastly different social conditions that are the lot of each of them. Soueif's delineation of the work that Lateefa and Dada Zeina do, as workers away from home, but also as women making active, involved choices at home, builds the gender-scape of contemporary Arab fiction. Not only Bassam, the Palestinian living out of land, but equally the likes of Lateefa and Dada Zeina, together with him, seem to give voice to the multiplicity of positions that intersect in Soueif's making of an Arab polity.[11]

11. Even in *The Map of Love* (1999) we encounter Amal who, having lived in England, has returned to Cairo at the turn of the millennium and is coping with the land problems of the *fallaheen* that were inherited from the days of British colonialism and are now exacerbated by the trade relations among Egypt, Israel, and the United States. Alongside this narrative, we see her interactions with Isabelle, an American journalist come to Cairo to write about the Egyptian experience of the millennium, and both their engagements with a nineteenth-century story of

REINSCRIBING DESIRE

Ahdaf Soueif's *In the Eye of the Sun* is also a slow and deliberate exploration of female desire. The novel's rhythm fluctuates between Asya's very personal and detailed articulations of desire, both material and sexual, and a choppy reportage of Egypt at war. Soueif places women's desire at the heart of questions of displacement, class mobility, Islamization, and Western hegemony. For its open contemplation of Asya's virginity, her premarital experimentation with sex, her worries over her sexual performance, her rejection of her ensuing pregnancy, her masturbation, her adultery, and more, the novel has engendered predictable responses from both Islamic conservatives and Western commentators. As Hind Wassef notes in her review of *In the Eye of the Sun* for the *Cairo Times*, "On this side of the divide, [Soueif] is accused of being immoral, defaming the image of Egyptian women. . . . The sexual detail proves a little shocking for some readers. . . . Because English was her medium, the easiest thing has been to denounce her as not part of Arab literature at all." Further, Wassef elaborates on Soueif's reaction to this criticism: "The novel was declared immoral, and an insult to Arab women, by what [Soueif] calls . . . the 'loony fringe,' whom she insists have not read it at all" (1998, n.p.). As Soueif herself indicates, she considers this type of censure a "fringe" reaction to her work. Nevertheless, it is a real "fringe," "loony" or not, whose presence shapes perceptions, conditions, and limits of Arab femininity, and thus is confronted within the space of Soueif's novel itself.

For instance, when Asya returns to Cairo, having completed her doctorate in northern England, she finds in her class on seventeenth-century English poetry a woman "who sat shrouded in the front row," *tarha* clad, and who in response to a question about the value of English writes, "I want to learn the language of my enemy" (1992, 754). Beyond this statement Asya cannot get the girl to say more, because as one of her classmates explains,

---

interracial love and politics. The "map" here between Egypt, the United States, Britain, Israel, and also Palestine seems to be acutely drawn and fractured by strains of nationalism, colonialism, and present-day transnational capitalism. It is from within these fissures that Ahdaf Soueif nevertheless also attempts to represent a political alliance between Arabs that is not the stereotypical one of Islam.

"She cannot speak . . . because the voice of a woman is 'awra'" (754).[12] This moment is significant in the novel for the way in which such conservatism seems to freeze the frames of existence for Arab women as spectacular representations of either a pure, veiled East or a degenerate West. Not only is the woman in *tarha,* who cannot speak, frozen when confronted by Asya's question, "Why is English the language of your enemy?" but Asya too finds herself fixed by this confrontation: "So as far as this girl—and the others who thought like her—were concerned she was doing a sort of porno-spread up here for the world to see. . . . So now it was . . . a class holding people who were sitting and scrutinising her and thinking she was doing something shameful . . . something for which the fires of hell were being stoked in readiness" (754). Both the woman whose voice is *awra* and Asya, who dares to lecture publicly, seem to be locked as counterspectacles of one another in this scene, performing a femininity that is seen, from the other side, as entirely "spooky" and restrictive or "shameful" and base (755, 754).[13]

A similar type of gender locking and freezing seems apparent in Western discourses about Arab women, as evidenced by the stereotypical Western responses to the sexual content of *In the Eye of the Sun.* Western reviewers of the novel seem most "surprised" by Soueif's "candid" discussion of sexuality vis-à-vis an Arab woman protagonist, and it becomes the operative basis

12. *Awra* means "parts of the body which should never be shown in public" (787).

13. Even Asya's later admission, "I do have a kind of sneaking admiration for [veiled women]," recognizes the East versus West attitude that seems to typify conservative Islamic responses to the role of women in the public space. Asya's observation that in spite of being "spooky" "they've sorted out some kind of answer to what's happening all around us—all the manifestations of the West that they see here are no good for them, for the way of life they want to hold onto. . . . And their answer is genuine" is immediately challenged by her sister, Deena: "How genuine is it, though? . . . I mean, it's essentially an urban phenomenon" (755). What *In the Eye of the Sun* clarifies, at this point, is that such politics of "veiling" seem predicated on binary divisions of the world that itself seem to spring from imported movements of capital and urbanization. See Leila Ahmed's *Women and Gender in Islam* (1992) for a discussion of Western colonialist and Islamist patriarchal discourses on veiling and Homa Hoodfar's essay "The Veil in Their Minds and on Our Heads" (1997) for an astute analysis of the contrary cultural practices of veiling—as orientalist/colonialist tradition, as sign of protest, and as pragmatic practice enabling women's entry into the workforce—that Muslim women negotiate.

for their praise of Soueif's work as quintessentially more liberated than other Arab writing, which for them, it seems, is still very much under the influence of the veil. "Probably the most candid and erotic discussion of sexual politics in Middle Eastern fiction," declares a reviewer in the *San Francisco Chronicle* (Soueif 1992, book jacket). A critic for the *Boston Globe* writes, "Unlike other Arab Muslim writers, Soueif deals with Asya's sexuality, and the complex sexual and emotional dynamics with the men in her life, in candid, even blunt terms" (ibid., front matter). There is a complex erasure at work in these comments that is just as debilitating to the Arabic literary canon as is the excision of Soueif's work from Arabic literature at the hands of Islamic "fringe" critics. These reviewers either have not read or choose to ignore that whole body of Arab texts by authors such as Nawal el-Saadawi, Tayeb el-Salih, Hanan al-Shaykh, and the later works of Naguib Mahfouz that unhesitatingly deal with issues of Arab women's sexuality.[14] Soueif's discussion of Asya's sexuality in these terms is seen only as a momentary glimpse past a veil that can never really be lifted, a cultural exception that is most "unlike other Arab Muslim writers," and therefore serves only to establish the rule: that Arab fiction is silent on questions of gender and that the repression of women is a cultural norm for the Arab world.[15]

14. Even *A Thousand and One Arabian Nights* here is forgotten in attempts by the Western press to keep Arab fiction sterile and, for the most part, disengaged from any commentary on gender.

15. Evidence of such attitudes in Western readers of Soueif is commonplace. This reader's question on women and Islam is typical of what Soueif faces at book readings: "I appreciate that you're trying to promote awareness, among presumably mainly western women, about how poor people who are uprooted could be driven to sympathize with Islamic fundamentalists, partly because of their economic problems now, and possibly partly because of the atrocities committed in the not so distant past by the British government, for example. But I partly expected for you to comment much more on how Islam oppresses women, and on the fact that they're segregated. Do you tackle that much in the book?" (Burnett 2001, 107). The reader, along with reviewers of Soueif's work, seems, on the one hand, able to register some of the complex grids of minority fundamentalism and economic and colonial oppression that condition the representation of women and sexuality in these texts. What is impossible for some readers and reviewers to overcome, on the other hand, seems to be their "expectations" of a discussion of women's oppression and Islamic fundamentalism that they see as endemic to Arab cultures. This conditioning of an attitude toward Arab women as always veiled prevents an engagement with the terms of

"Sexual imperialism" is Asya's scathing characterization of this tendency in the West to deny any agency, or historical contingency, to Arab women. Asya's confrontation and break with Gerald, the crude, needy, and overly possessive Englishman with whom she commits adultery, are telling of Soueif's attempt to address the symptomatic effacement of Arab women that happens in the West. Asya's final and only tirade against Gerald seems deliberately to echo a much larger problem of control and gain that underlies Western attitudes toward women from other parts of the world. Asya's first question to Gerald invokes the absurdity in his presumption of better knowledge: "You are going to stand here and tell me about Egypt? Tell me what was wrong with how I grew up?" (1992, 723). But she is quick to the inquisition, to discern the profiteering orientalism that produces the East for the West and infects even individual perceptions:

> "Gerald," Asya says quietly, "why have all your girl-friends been from 'developing' countries? . . . [T]he reason you've gone for Trinidad—Vietnam—Egypt—is so you can feel superior. You can be the big white boss—you are a sexual imperialist— . . . You pretend—to yourself as well—that it's because you don't notice race—or these cultures retain some spiritual quality lost to the West— . . . but that's all phony. . . . The hypocrisy of it. 'I know you better than you know yourself'—shit—what you mean is that the way you think I should be is better for you than the way I am." (723)

The struggle here is between imagism and reality, between a program of production practiced in the West that induces dependency, and gain, and rejects the assertion, time and again, of the gender autonomy and self-representation possible in the East. Asya as she "is," a sexually aware, mobile, active, and outspoken Egyptian woman, is incommensurable with the production and consumption in the West of images of passive and hidden Arab women, that which Asya "should" be.[16] And as Soueif shows, this repeated investment

---

Soueif's work that resites women's sexuality beside the veil and in contestation with discourses of displacement, capitalism, and colonialism.

16. It is not insignificant that Edward Said, one of the foremost critics of Western presumptions about Arabs, had the following to say about Soueif's work: "Soueif is one of the most extraordinary chroniclers of sexual politics now writing" (1992, 19).

in keeping the veil on Arab women is in the West just that—a profitable investment.[17]

In the Eye of the Sun, like other novels of what Saree Makdisi has called "Arab modernism," works in the interstices of these two prominent, and equally restrictive, paradigms of Arab femininity, namely, Islamism and neo-orientalism, in order to sanction a politicized space of desire from which Arab women respond to historical conditions of patriarchy, displacement, economic hardship, and war.[18] Soueif's fiction endorses, expands, and even feminizes Makdisi's label of contemporary Arab fiction as a "literature of crisis." Makdisi writes of the historical "rupture" and "discontinuity" of the numerous wars in the Arab world that shape and are shaped by novels that focus on the lived realities of war. "This literary trend," Makdisi says of modern Arab fiction, "helps to produce not merely the expression or the articulation of crisis but rather the reality of crisis itself; it does not replicate reality but rather contributes to the production of the real in the Arab world" (1995, 98). Soueif's fiction too realizes this "crisis" within Arab representation, and for the representation of Arab women in particular, as continually bound by the ideologies of religion and imperialism. Further, *In the Eye of the Sun* is also engaged in the "production

17. I am reminded here of the Coca-Cola advertisements that were aired in the aftermath of 9/11 showing two burka-clad Arab women walking on Venice Beach, thirstily looking for a drink. This ad supposedly was to raise awareness and increase sensitivity in the United States toward Arab culture. The ads were revoked after conservative Muslim groups protested what they saw as an unseemly exposure of Islamic women to American-style consumerism. What is lost in this media clash between American corporatization and Islamic traditionalization of Arab women is that the vast majority of Arab women would want to sell neither Coke nor religion. Veiled as the Arab women were, the images being sold here were designed to be ambiguous and homogenous so as to be interpellated into multiple consumer discourses, of racists (who saw them as wholly "other"), of orientalists (who would find their passivity empathetic), and of Islamists (who saw them as symbols of purity). The resulting and public conflict between the last group and Coca-Cola served only to ossify the opposition of the U.S. and the Arab worlds for the first two types of consumers, in the bargain, I speculate, increasing sales of the cold drink.

18. Makdisi's canon of Arab modernists includes Naguib Mahfouz, Al-Tayeb Saleh, Ghassan Kanafani, Elias Khoury, Nawal el-Saadawi, Hanan al-Shaykh, Abdel Rahman Munif, Emile Habiby, Sahar Khalifa, and Sherif Hetata, among others. Although Makdisi's list is mainly confined to Arab writers writing in Arabic, I would include here Arab writing in English by the likes of Fadia Faqir, Leila Aboulela (1999), Leila Ahmed, and, of course, Ahdaf Soueif.

of [a] real in the Arab world" that worlds the Arab situation as radically heterogeneous, marked in its quotidian minutiae by displaced peoples, economic strife, and colonial and imperial wars but still all within the realm of women's activity. Pan-Arabism too is figured within this new grid of reality as a political gear for Arab unity that must continue to engage with circuits of disunity and difference within it, imploding models of "tradition" and "modernity" in order to keep in play an alternative that, despite being distinctly present for Arabs, is also not less than the Arab present.[19]

MARGINAL SOLIDARITIES: PAN-ARABISM, BEYOND THE NATION

Soueif's narrative is textured by the crisis moments in Egypt's history such as the Suez Crisis of 1956, the Arab-Israeli colonial conflict of 1967, and the Pax Americana of the Sadat years. But these crisis moments of Egyptian history, between Nasser and Sadat, are perceived only through the filters of their representation—in the media, in this novel, and in the reaction of the people who inhabit the space of *In the Eye of the Sun*. The effect is the absence of a meganational narrative. In its place, the coming together of divergent collectives (exiles, migrants, women, the fellahin, the effendiya, students), always at odds with any attempt to write Arab history in terms of singular national development, suggests a radical rethinking of the place of the nation for Arabs. What Soueif's account suggests is that even a schizophrenic history of Egypt, from one crisis to the next, as one nation's reactions to colonialism or imperialism, is an inadequate way to historicize Arab representation. What is opened up instead are new histories, new diplomacies, modern spaces of cohabitation among Arabs, within and without particular national bounds, that make urgent a politics of regional coalition.

19. Here I am borrowing from Makdisi's temporal formulation of the "alternatives" that Arab modernism makes possible: "The texts," writes Makdisi, "I am calling 'modernist' point only to an uncompromising and inescapable present, a historical present that can only be modified and changed when Eurocentric constructions and understandings of 'modernity' and 'tradition' are dropped forever, and when alternative constructions and formulations of history, a history in which Arabs are not mere 'added' or 'included' as subordinate or 'underdeveloped' elements, have come to replace them" (1995, 99–100).

What is written ultimately in the novel's snapshots of war is dissonance: dissonance between the nation and its people, between an event and its construction, between history and its representation, and finally between an earnest ethos of collectivism and its fraudulent practice.[20] The narrative splinters on various levels—Soueif's representation of the chaos in the war rooms is rendered incongruent with narratives of nation spun by the media for consumption by people on the street, Arab commoners—'Am Salih, Asya, Bassam, and others.[21] The outcome of the weeklong 1967 Arab-Israeli conflict was monumental military losses of territory, people, and property for Egypt and its Arab allies, losses that within the novel are translated into a recognition of both what Nasserism could have aspired to (or rather purported to aspire to in its calling for Arab unity and so on) and its very real shortcomings.[22] Nasserian goals for Pan-Arab solidarity, socialism, and nonalignment fail because

20. Even Nasser's initial military ousting of the British from Egypt in 1954, after seventy-two years of occupation, had, as Rashid Khalidi observes, "powerful resonance in an Arab world still dotted with French bases in Morocco, Algeria, Tunisia, British bases in Libya, Jordan, Iraq, Aden, and the Gulf, and American bases in Morocco, Libya, and Saudi Arabia" (1989, 379). Hence, Nasser's influence on anticolonial programs throughout the Arab world and the ready reception of his ideas for Arab unity in most of the Middle East cannot be underestimated.

21. Examples of such inside-outside depictions of war abound in Soueif's work. Egypt's retaking of parts of the Sinai in October 1973 is also presented in Pan-Arab fashion from the perspective of occurrences in and reports from the Sinai, Jerusalem, Damascus, Beirut, and Cairo, as well as media reports from *The Times* (London) and *Al-Ahram* (Cairo) and Asya's living of the events as they filter to her in university in the North of England (337–43). Here narrative strategy itself becomes representative of a certain Arab identity that operates across national borders—a certain cultural basis on the part of those individuals in the previously mentioned locations, and even for Asya far away, for following closely developments in the Arab world and attaching themselves to an affirmative political outcome for Arabs. Yet this identification is not consumed in any sense by some theoretical sameness of existence. Rather, it operates on the basis of difference, of location, religion, gender, that is strategically evoked to show the diverse positions that serve to produce coherent Arab-Arab relations.

22. It is relevant to note that, in 1956, the United States supported Egypt against the tripartite attack over the Suez Canal. Even so, Nasser, in an effort to remain nonaligned, stressed Soviet support for his agenda and deliberately undermined Washington's privileged status. Thus, this period between colonialism and later American imperialism witnessed a determined move by Arab leaders to avoid a sense of indebtedness to any one external power. See Khalidi 1989.

of an absolute, inward turn toward the nation as the only source and support for these collectives. *In the Eye of the Sun* makes clear that Pan-Arabism under Nasser is ultimately ineffectual because Pan-Arabism is heralded mostly as a rhetorical form of Arab political activism, whereas an exclusive, and punitive, style of nationalism, complete with "purges," "concentration camps," "the torture of both the leftists and the Muslim Brotherhood," and the use of "Mukhabarat, the huge intelligence organization that has been turned against the people," warrants the nation as the only mode of belonging in Egypt (1992, 63). Individuals such as 'Am Salih and Asya, and all those students at Cairo University, such as Bassam and Hakim, who continue to hope for more despite the Arab defeat in this war represent another reality within the novel, a reality that makes Arab-Arab relations (across borders and religions) a lived experience, a condition of Arab modernity that is always already present and to which any effort to launch a campaign on behalf of Arabs must speak.

The distance *In the Eye of the Sun* travels over time, from Asya's adolescence to adulthood, from Nasser to Sadat, is also the distance in history from colonialism to a nouveau imperialism, dominated by the rise of U.S. corporatization. If Soueif is critical of Nasser's authoritarian leftism and its unaccounted-for margins, she presents Sadat's "getting cosy with the Americans" as a deliberate giving in to an imperialism that views the Arab world itself as wholly marginal (218). Religious factionalism and oppositional politics, in both instances, become manipulated by the state in order to build legitimacy for its own policies. Where Nasser sees leftist opposition and Islam as a counterforce against nationalism, Sadat, as Soueif suggests, encourages Islamists to undo precisely the coherence of the Left that would oppose his open-door policy with regard to the United States (472). It is the critical shift between Nasser's uniform persecution of the Left and religious factions in order to promote a unilateral, nation-centered vision of anticolonialism and Sadat's manipulation of these two movements against each other in order to advance U.S. interests in the Arab world.

Both Nasser's socialism and Sadat's conservatism fail to assimilate their politics to the unevenness and difference present within the Arab world. What is institutionalized in both instances is an effacement of differences of religion, gender, and class in favor of an opaque rhetoric of nationalism and sameness that ignores the presence of multiplicity within the civic sphere. Nasser, despite his vision of Arab unity in difference, unable actually to incorporate difference within totalitarian rule, becomes a purveyor of "torture," persecutes opposition (even by students), imprisons religious factions, and is assessed in the novel as "the Chief" "who didn't concentrate too well on liberty" (235, 105, 220). Sadat too is implicated in a planned betrayal of students and workers who resist his policies (103–4) and blind compliance with the United States, whose main goals in the region are the supply and control of oil. From Asya's perspective, then, Sadat's negotiations for peace with Begin and Carter appear to be mere puppetry, as it becomes clear to her that "the United States does not want to see," and she quotes Jimmy Carter, "'a fairly radical new independent nation in the heart of the Middle East'" (714). Soueif's critique of Sadat's liberalization, or, rather, Americanization, of Egypt comes as an echo from the past in the war in Iraq today. Oil was then, as it is today, a major motive of U.S. actions in the Middle East. Asya, in 1979, reflects on the recent coup in Iraq: "London and Washington have got Kuwait and Saudi and Gulf Oil. Plus their own. Do they have to have Iraq's as well?" (17). The distance from colonialism to U.S.-style imperialism, from Suez to Knesset, it seems, is not so far: London and Washington still stand as centers of power and control over the Arab region, and the motive is, as always, profit. Arab life, it seems, is lived in the shadow of these Western imperatives, and the worlding that Soueif attempts in her work is an acute response to these external power plays: a response that makes it possible to see often derided Arab practices, such as the practice of giving *baqsheesh* (tips) to the poor, as subversive of Western corporatization. At the annual pilgrimage to the "City of the Dead," Tante Soraya hands out food and money to the poor children who live there, and Asya reflects on what Gerald Stone would have made of this scene: "What would he have said? That it was seigneurial? Patronising? Perpetuating the evil system of privilege?" (746). Asya's reflections, however, lead away from this critique often made by the West to suggest the worse possibilities of ignoring this ritual: "Of course it would be best if there were no children living among the tombs, if they all lived in clean little houses . . . like in some Bavarian village—and who would look after the graves? . . . a company—an 'open-door' company to run the City of the Dead—well, they've given Transport to the French, Sewage to the British, Telecommunications to the Germans and Defence to the Americans; they could give the Cemeteries to the Swedes or the Japanese" (746). Soueif's words here are a stinging portrayal of the want and absurdity that an overreliance on a free-market economy benefiting the West would create for Arabs. Certainly, the "Bavarian villages," it is implied, are only an ideal that would never materialize for these children by the tombs, and corporatizing the dead is an absurd solution to the morbidity that already exists for these Arab poor. No, *baqsheesh* must be kept in circulation, Soueif suggests, if only to prevent the sort of contract poverty that would replace it.

Finally, *In the Eye of the Sun* is a studied work in representing Arabs as unified, despite their many differences, in the interest of self-representation. Pan-Arabism in this regard is much more than a nostalgic yearning for resurrecting Nasserism. It is a politics of thinking about Arab identity in terms of change, as heterogeneous, critical of imposed constructions, and invested in the very act of disseminating its own self-images in the world. Consider, for example, the connotations of this scene: Asya, a student of literature, plays a bootlegged tape of Sheikh Imam, "an elderly blind man who is a protest singer, more or less banned by the government," in a cottage in the North of England (495). Deena; Gerald, Asya's English lover; Marzouk, a Yemeni student; Hisham, suspected of being in sympathy with the Mahabith, or the Egyptian secret police; and his casual lover, Lisa, are in the audience. Asya pauses the tape every few seconds and translates Sheikh Imam for the rest. Her efforts run for pages. Every pun and parallel, all ironies, are explained, flushed out, and made discursive. Soueif's is a painstaking insistence on representation and critique and rerepresentation through translation and critique. Sheikh Imam, it turns out, sings a jibe: at Nixon, at Watergate, at sultans, at oil money, at Hitler, at Makka, and at the wealth, poverty, and political prowess within the Arab world.[23]

23. I thank Ahdaf Soueif for her gracious reading of my work and her perceptive responses. This chapter has been shaped by her generosity. I also thank my mentors, Gabriele Schwab, David Lloyd, and J. Hillis Miller, for their careful evaluations of this project. Lindon Barrett's friendship and scholarly guidance continue to be vital, as is Leila Neti's sustained personal and intellectual support.

9

Weaving Poetic Autobiographies

Individual and Communal Identities in the Poetry of Mohja Kahf and Suheir Hammad

CAROL FADDA-CONREY

> The dark side of who we [Muslims] are will not stay covered up, nor does it help us to cover it up, and asking the disturbing, subversive questions is a noble jihad. Fear is not a basis for any art and never can be.
>
> —Mohja Kahf, "Poetry Is My Home Address"

The U.S. Census Bureau's racial categorization of Arab Americans as non-European whites becomes a pertinent and even ironic issue when compared to the current perception and reception of Arab Americans in the United States as a marginalized ethnic group. The negative stereotypes that have become common in the experience of Arab Americans not only relegate this group to the margins of American society but also render it invisible, denying it access to unbiased representation. The Arab American experience, then, becomes a site to be probed and questioned (by way here of some of its poetic articulations), with the ultimate purpose of producing a knowledge about what historian Joan Scott calls "the complex and changing discursive processes by which identities [here specifically Arab American ones] are ascribed, resisted, or embraced" (1993, 408). Through a close analysis of the autobiographical elements in the works of two contemporary Arab American poets, Mohja Kahf and Suheir Hammad, this chapter pursues such a mode of questioning, focusing on the discursive and autobiographical construction of an antiessentialist Arab American subjectivity rooted in the Arab American experience. In their respective poetry collections *E-mails from Scheherazad* (2003) and *Born*

Palestinian, Born Black (1996), Kahf and Hammad, the first of Syrian and the second of Palestinian heritage, foreground the paradoxical and contradictory place that Arab American women, and by extension Arab Americans in general, are allotted within the United States, thus upholding Audre Lorde's belief that "poetry . . . [is] a revelatory distillation of experience" (1984b, 37). By drawing on their experience of living in the United States as women of color, both poets discursively contest and undercut the majority's preconceived notions of what constitutes Arab American subjectivity, thus creating their own poetic versions of individual and collective Arab American identity.

My analysis of the poetic constructions of various Arab American identity formations in this chapter proceeds from the assumption that Kahf and Hammad, although living in the United States and identified as racially white, still occupy and speak out from a third world woman's minority stance, a positionality that I delineate in conjunction with the cartographic explanation of the term *third world* outlined by Chandra Talpade Mohanty as being "defined through geographical location as well as particular sociohistorical conjunctures . . . thus incorporat[ing] so-called minority peoples or people of color in the U.S.A." (1991, 2). Kahf and Hammad, then, by speaking out from the ranks of the minority, foment a coalition with other people of color in the United States, forming what Mohanty conceives of as "an 'imagined community' of third world oppositional struggles." "The idea of imagined community," Mohanty continues, "is useful because it leads us away from essentialist notions of third world feminist struggles, suggesting political rather than biological or cultural bases for alliance" (4).

In analyzing what can be described as the autobiographical elements in Kahf's and Hammad's works, I am not implying that these two poets *consciously* incorporate elements of their personal lives into their poetry or that the poems are *purposefully* shaped to act as direct reflections of their lives. Instead, I suggest that the poems are, to a large extent, informed by the poets' experiences as women of color living in the United States, pointing to the manner in which ethnic and religious adherences as well as the varieties and convergences of physical location influence and shape the poems included in this study.

Susan Stanford Friedman points out in "Women's Autobiographical Selves: Theory and Practice" that "individualistic paradigms of the self ignore the role of collective and relational identities in the individuation process of women and minorities" (1988, 35). This chapter follows Friedman's analysis by arguing that "in taking the power of words, of representation, into their own hands, women [writers like Kahf and Hammad] project onto history an identity that is not purely individualistic. Nor is it purely collective. Instead, this new identity merges the shared and the unique" (40). Such a reformulation of autobiographical writings, in content and form, ultimately subverts the limited tools of self-representation available to female minority writers and "creat[es] an alternate self in the autobiographical act" (41).

In this way, extending the boundaries of autobiography to include the poetic genre is of particular importance to minority women's writing, which often transcends the self to trace connections between the writer's individuality and her ties to specific communities, whether they are outlined by ethnicity, race, or sexuality. The poetry of Kahf and Hammad, as argued in this chapter, deeply evinces the creation of such "an alternate self," one that is both "unique" and "shared" and transcends the negative representation of Arab Americans in the United States. The rest of the chapter closely analyzes specific poems from Kahf's and Hammad's first poetry collections to highlight the varieties and convergences of Arab American individual and collective experience. Examining these poetic articulations as forms of autobiography helps question and eradicate the negative and erroneous images plaguing Arab Americans in the United States.

WRITING SELVES, WRITING COMMUNITIES

The Arab American self portrayed by Kahf and Hammad is reflected in the array of nuanced themes and motifs carefully woven into the poems' fabric, presenting the reader with lingering images of love, difference, exile, and religion. Both Kahf and Hammad possess a strong poetic voice that resonates with the experience of what it means to be Arab American in the United States, including what it means to be a veiled Syrian American Muslim feminist (Kahf) or a Palestinian American political activist (Hammad)—what it means to be daughters of exiles and immigrants living in racially diverse places like New Jersey (Kahf) and Brooklyn (Hammad).

Having emigrated as a child to the United States with her parents, Kahf grew up in Indiana and later moved to New Jersey, where she earned her Ph.D.

in comparative literature from Rutgers University. Her academic publications include *Western Representations of the Muslim Woman: From Termagant to Odalisque* (1999), as well as several articles on Arabic literature and Muslim identity. She is currently an associate professor of English at the University of Arkansas, where she teaches courses in comparative literature, Arabic literature, postcolonialism, love and eros, and the Quran. Her upcoming publications include her first novel, about growing up in the Midwest, and a second collection of poetry, *The Hagar and Aisha Poems.*

Hammad also emigrated to the United States with her parents, when she was five years old, growing up in Brooklyn until the age of sixteen, after which her parents moved to Staten Island. Her work has been published in various anthologies, including *In Defense of Mumia* (1996), *Listen Up!* (1999), and *The Space Between Our Footsteps* (1998); zines; and poetry journals such as *Essence, STRESS Hip-Hop Magazine,* and the *Middle East Report.* She currently performs on Russell Simmons's *Def Poetry Jam* and has been claimed as the first Palestinian woman to star in a Broadway show. In addition to *Born Palestinian, Born Black,* Hammad has also written a memoir titled *Drops of This Story,* both of which were published by Harlem River Press in 1996, and she recently published her new collection of poetry, titled *ZaatarDiva* (2005). Her work as an activist has also led her to speak at several university campuses, prisons, and antiwar sit-ins, and she is featured in movie projects such as *Lest We Forget* (2003) and *The Fourth World War* (2004).

By drawing on their individual repertoires of experience, showing in the process how "subjects . . . are constituted through experience" (Scott 1993, 401), these two poets bring about an important development in the shaping of Arab American subjectivity. In doing so, they effect a reconfiguration in the identity(ies) and portrayals of Arab and Arab American women in particular and Arab Americans in general by mixing their poetry with an autobiographical element that strongly encompasses communal relations. It would be simplistic and shortsighted, however, to claim that these authors' works merely replicate or represent their experiences and thereby uphold an "authentic" Arab or Arab American subjectivity, which in itself is too complex and multilayered for such essentialist categorizations. Instead, what Kahf and Hammad accomplish through their incorporation of autobiographical references in their poetry is not an isolated reconstruction of the self, "singled out as a separate entity, standing independently on its own and defined in terms of its own merits," but an attempt to establish a solid relational component to their Arab American identity (and by extension to other minority groups), a mapping of the "I" within the "we," situating solid interrelational ties within a community while staking an individual space within it (Golley 2003, 57). The autobiographical representation of this individual space, then, is not limited to the parameters of these two poets' experience but encompasses a range of voices belonging to racially and ethnically marginalized individuals, including an assortment of Arab Americans and other peoples of color. By incorporating distinct and varied articulations from within the Arab American communities, the poetry of Kahf and Hammad achieves both an individual and a communal voice that resists stereotypes and discriminatory appellations.

In her edited collection titled *Scheherazade's Legacy: Arab and Arab American Women on Writing,* Susan Muaddi Darraj discusses the diversity of the emerging Arab American literary voice, stating, "The multitude of styles testify to the variety of ideas, opinions, and experiences within the community of women writers of Arab descent, a fact that tears down the stereotype of Arab women as uniformly similar: silent, acquiescent, unthinking" (2004, 3–4). The poetry of Kahf and Hammad, for instance, although poignantly political in theme and content, diverges in its application of varying textual strategies and poetic styles. With a playfulness thinly overlaying an unabashed and challenging stance, Kahf infuses her poetry with a worldview informed by a delicious mix of themes and images, intricately mining and intermingling English and Arabic words, as well as experimenting with and revising traditional conceptions of creativity and sexuality, upending them in the process.

Donna Seaman describes *E-mails from Scheherazad,* Kahf's first book of poetry, as "brilliantly wry and utterly irresistible," portraying Kahf as "an earthy, playful, and purposeful poet who writes with as much sass as sensitivity about what it is like to be a woman, a person of color, an immigrant, and a headscarf-wearing Muslim in a non-Muslim country" (2003, 1141). Born in Damascus, Syria, and having immigrated to the United States with her parents at the age of four, Kahf writes poems that directly oppose the predominantly negative portrayal and perception of "headscarf-wearing Muslim[s] in a non-Muslim country," and thereby creates a space that reconfigures Muslim

American women's identity,[1] reshaping its predominantly simplistic and one-dimensional representation by investing it with nuanced and multilayered characteristics.[2] In lieu of a fate dictated by subjugation and repression, the nuances among Arab and Arab American women generally, and Muslim American women specifically, are complexly drawn by Kahf in a manner that teases out the fine ethnic, cultural, and religious distinctions within this multifaceted group as well as between it and other minority groups in the United States

E-mails from Scheherazad skillfully handles a multiplicity of themes that elucidate and balance these individual and collective voices. As Kahf's first poetry collection, this volume spans more than a decade of her poetry, encompassing, for instance, some of her earlier poems dating back to 1990 ("Lateefa," "Move Over," and "From the Patios of Alhambra"), whereas other featured poems tackle more recent events such as 9/11 ("We Will Continue Like Twin Towers" and "The Fires Have Begun"). The poems included in this volume weave a telling tapestry of stories, portraying the newly arrived immigrants still carrying the journey's dust "on their shoulders" ("Voyager Dust," l. 2) and the seasoned ones for whom the homeland has become only a memory ("Word from the Younger Skaff").

1. I realize that the parameters of Muslim American identity are much wider than the Arab American context, but for the purposes of this chapter, I read Kahf's poetry as reflective of primarily an Arab Muslim-American experience, focusing on Muslim Arab-Americans as a subgroup of the Arab American community.

2. As a regular contributor to "Sex and the Umma," a column on sexuality and Islam featured on the *Muslim Wakeup!* Web site, Kahf uses the short-story genre to address a wide array of topics addressing sexuality and Islam in an extremely frank and unabashed style, covering issues of premarital sex, homosexuality, and sex education. In one short story, for instance, "The Rites of Diane," a group of Muslim American girls, congregating for a bridal shower, have a heated discussion about masturbation, virginity, and the hymen, whereas in "Lustrous Companions," a Muslim American woman asks the sheikh at her local mosque in New Jersey, "Do women get to have sex in paradise too?" (2004a, n.p.). In this way, Kahf, as a progressive feminist Muslim who wears the *hijab* (head scarf) "out of pride in my heritage, but . . . [not] in the required Islamic way anymore" (2003, "Ask Mohja"), challenges and revises the deprecating characterization of Muslim women by a U.S. majority (subsequently revising the self-same characterization applied to all Arab women, since Arabs and Muslims are more often than not conflated in the American mind).

Kahf also mixes metaphors and languages to bridge the differences between places as disparate as Damascus and Arkansas in "Fayetteville as in Fate," or outlining, on a smaller scale, "a clash of civilizations" in the poems "My Grandmother Washes Her Feet in the Sink of the Bathroom at Sears" (l. 22) and "My Babysitter Wears a Face-Veil." Outlining this "clash of civilizations," embedded in ethnic, religious, and racial differences in the United States, becomes a way to counter the negative stereotypes faced by Muslim Americans, who can then claim their share in the possessive "My" in the titles of the two latter poems to signify a collective experience. Such a confrontational poetic stance, however, is not meant to solidify religious difference. Instead, poems such as the ones in the numbered "*Hijab* Scene" series, with a great amount of wit, show how religious difference (here embodied by the *hijab*) is constructed by way of a majority's tendency to demonize the unfamiliar, thus highlighting the irony and futility of divisive stereotypes. Pointing out the contradictions inherent in being part of a Muslim minority in the United States, Kahf writes in her poem "Move Over" (2003):

> We are the spreaders of prayer rugs
> in highway gas stations at dawn
> We are the fasters at company banquets
> before sunset in Ramadan
> We wear veils and denim,
> prayer caps and Cubs caps
> . . . .
> We will intermarry and commingle
> and multiply, oh, how we'll multiply
> Muhammad-lovers in the motley
> miscellany of the land (ll. 1–6, 16–19)

The repetition of the word *we* here becomes an incantation denoting a Muslim American voice that challenges the exclusionary limits of homogenous white Christian culture in the United States. The intermarriage and "commingling" of Muslim and white Christian America infuse religious difference with racial overtones in such a way that the intermingling of religion comes to parallel the mixing of races that complicates American identity.

By focusing on a collective mosaic of Muslim American experience rather than its individualized equivalent, Kahf performs what Bernice Johnson Reagon terms "cultural autobiography" (1982). Susan Stanford Friedman, paralleling works by critics such as Regina Blackburn, Stephen Butterfield, and Mary G. Mason with works by theorists such as Sheila Rowbotham and Nancy Chodorow, deems the "individualistic concept of the autobiographical self" too limiting for women and minorities, stressing "collective identity . . . [as] a source of strength and transformation" (1988, 34, 39). Kahf's articulation of a suppressed minority's voice not only contributes to such positive transformation but also leads to the constant (re)formation of a dynamic and shifting Muslim American identity, one that defies the kind of static characterization generated by stereotypes and the fear of the Other. More important, the type of hybridity portrayed in the intermingling of "veils and denim" and "prayer caps and Cubs caps" in Kahf's "Move Over," rather than pointing to a juxtaposition of disparate religious and cultural markers, indicates instead an irreversible change enacted upon the constructed notion of a "pure" and essential American mainstream identity. In other words, the hybrid intermarrying of Muslim and white cultures in the United States, a parallel to racial commingling, revises American identity so that ensuing feelings of national belonging and inclusion encompass the otherness of the Muslim American. Such a change, by affirming that cultural, social, and religious assimilation is not the only option available to U.S. ethnic communities to achieve recognition, literally alters the face of the American hegemonic center, injecting it with an ethnic, racial, and religious fusion, with hybrid heterogeneity being the ultimate outcome of the "intermarry[ing] and commingl[ing] and multiply[ing]" referenced in the poem.

The title itself, "Move Over," which might initially be taken to mean a Muslim American's call to "take over" a center dominated by white Christian Americans, lends itself to a more intricate and complex reading, denoting a much needed shift in cultural, racial, and religious mappings that would not only ease up a space for ethnic and racial minorities but allow new mappings to emerge as well. Creating a "cultural autobiography" of Muslim Americans, however, in no way contributes to the fixing of this group's identity, but allows room for fluidity and transformation, even for indeterminacy. Kahf reflects on the in-betweenness plaguing Muslim Americans living across and between two cultures when she writes in the same poem (2003),

We don't know what to do at weddings:
wear white and cut the cake?
wear red and receive garlands?
rap songs or tambourines?(ll. 8–11)

The answer to these questions, though, a mere "It doesn't matter" (l. 13), reaffirms the validity of both options, confirming the right to choose either or neither. Thus, the overwhelming importance placed on tradition and cultural continuity shifts and "moves over" to accommodate change and multiplicity.

The notion of a unifying "we" signifying a communal "cultural autobiography" also looms large in Hammad's poetry, which, in comparison to Kahf's, takes on a more combative stance in delineating and reflecting on Hammad's ethnic and racial outlook from both a personal and a collective point of view: born in Jordan to Palestinian refugee parents, moving to a Palestinian camp in Beirut, and growing up in racially diverse Sunset Park in Brooklyn, while in a broader sense identifying with globally disfranchised people of color. Hammad's poetic stance in *Born Palestinian, Born Black* (1996), though equally confrontational, departs from Kahf's in its stark harshness, intermixed with pain and anger propagated by a raw and unmitigated poetic honesty.[3] Published in 1996, when Hammad was twenty-three years old, this volume of poetry mirrors the intermixture of influences in Hammad's life, including Palestinian displacement,[4] connections to African American and Puerto Rican cultures that Hammad was exposed to while growing up in Brooklyn, and the various forms of violence she has experienced and been a witness to, manifested, for example, through the Arab-Israeli conflict, as well as through the harsh circumstances surrounding urban youth culture in New York and the disfranchisement of peoples of color all around the world. In this way, Hammad's first

3. The title refers to African American poet June Jordan's "Moving Towards Home." In this poem, reacting to the Sabra and Shatila massacre that killed hundreds of Palestinians in Beirut, Jordan writes, "I was born a Black woman / and now / I am become a Palestinian" (Hammad 1996, ix).

4. Palestinian exile in fact denotes a double displacement because the Palestinian American not only encounters dislocation in the diaspora but also feels cut off and "out of place" even when back at "home" in Palestine, owing to the transformation of much of the once-familiar landscape into Israeli territory.

volume of poetry features poems that are laced with the palpable anguish of uprootedness and displacement affecting not only Arab Americans but other communities of color in the United States and across the globe as well. Noting the difference in tone between Hammad and other Arab American poets, Susan Muaddi Darraj writes, "The steady, reflective voice of Naomi Shihab Nye . . . stands in contrast to the hip, edgy voice of Suheir Hammad" (2004, 3). Barbara Nimri Aziz extends this comparison to Hammad's thematic deviation from preceding Arab American writing, emphasizing how "Hammad's work represents an important step away from nostalgia and toward a face-to-face maturity of what it is to be Arab and American" (2004, xv). Thus, instead of Darraj's aforementioned reference to a "silent, acquiescent, and unthinking" Arab and Arab American woman, there emerges in the poetry of Kahf and Hammad a provocatively vocal, challenging, and intelligent female counterpart that shrewdly transcends the "individualistic autobiographical self" to become more autobiographically communal.

What fellow poet Nathalie Handal describes as Hammad's "different lives and her union with people of many cultures" informs the core of Hammad's work, leading her, like Kahf, to locate her individuality within communal concerns and struggles, thus explicitly situating the poetic "I" within a "we" (Hammad 1997, n.p.).[5] The connotations of this "we" may shift from one poem to another, thus widening the boundaries of collective identity. The collectivity that we encounter in Hammad's poem titled "open poem to those who rather we not read . . . or breathe" (1996) goes beyond the Muslim American community depicted in Kahf's "Move Over," so much so that the "we" in this poem represents a united but multiple-colored voice denouncing American white hegemony. In an intriguing shuffling and coupling of words and their multilevel meanings, true to her "slam" style,[6] Hammad creates a double entendre on the word *fashion:*

5. I am indebted for this distinction between the "I" and the "we" to Nawar Al-Hassan Golley's *Reading Arab Women's Autobiographies: Shahrazad Tells Her Story,* in which she states, "Writing for women is a process and a quest for dialogue, social change, and the possibility of saying 'we' as well as 'I'" (2003, 61).

6. Hammad performs on *Def Poetry Jam,* produced for HBO by Russell Simmons, "perhaps the most powerful rap producer and promoter in the industry." Hammad says about the show,

fascism is in imperial fashion
but we be style
our tongues   long slashed to keep silence
wear blood jewels
our heads sport civilizations
hips velvet wrapped in music
and you can see the earth running
right under our skin (ll. 21–28)

By coupling fashion with the fascism inherent in white racism, and wresting an irrefutable communal style for colored minorities, including Arab Americans, Hammad overthrows the enslaving demands of fashion, which stifle individual expression. Instead, people of color express their individual and communal resistance to "fascist" racism by literally wearing their heritage as raiment and weaving their own visual and vocal style, all the while infusing it with meaning and molding it into historically significant, rather than short-lived and empty, fashion statements:

we   children of children exiled from homelands
descendants of immigrants denied jobs and toilets
carry continents in our eyes
survivors of the middle passage
we   stand
and demand recognition of our humanity (ll. 4–9)

Such a powerful testament to a collective past fraught with subjugation and discrimination (extending to the present) shows that, for Hammad, her own Palestinian history of exile cannot be disengaged from the larger history of imperialism and colonialism that scatter peoples across the world and sever them from their homelands, whether they are exiles, immigrants, or descendants of slave-trade victims. The particular reference to "survivors of the

---

"Hip-hop is absolutely a part of who I am, its aesthetics and its content. Hip-hop has a tradition of speaking within your own vernacular and cadence, of imparting your parents' historical legacy when that history has been marginalized in schools and in the mainstream. I understand the Palestinian diasporic situation better through hip-hop" (Farah 2004, 34).

middle passage" links the Palestinian diasporic experience to the hardships faced by Africans uprooted from their homes and made to suffer through the Middle Passage and the brutal slavery awaiting them in the New World. Such a jolting comparison is meant to underscore the changing face of human subjugation, which nevertheless maintains the same kernel of inhuman treatment meted out to powerless peoples, whether they are Africans or Arabs.

The bond generated from such racial, gender, and ethnic groupings constructs a "cultural autobiography" that extends beyond one minority group to encompass multitudes, offering the tools for resisting racism and oppression:

> We   braid resistance through our hair
> pierce justice through our ears
> tattoo freedom onto our breasts
> The bluesy souls of brown eyed girls
> clash with blood on the pale hands of
> governments of war (ll. 135–40)

Again, here, as in Kahf's "Move Over," physical markers of difference, whether they are racial, cultural, or religious, manifested in skin color, African braids and head wraps, or veils and prayer caps, prove to be powerful tools for confronting the center's homogeneity, effecting ripples of change by reaffirming the strength inherent in the unification of marginalized voices. Hammad reflects on the personal gratification she attains from such a unity, thus reinstating the deep and elemental connections between self and community, when she says, "[I remember] the first time I wrapped my hair in a gele, an African head wrap. Using material from Senegal, I wanted to wrap myself in the beauty of sisterhood. The ancestors remembered my name and whispered it to me under the material" (1997, n.p.). This theme of sisterhood manifests itself in another of Hammad's poems, titled "we spent the fourth of july in bed" (1996), in which the boundaries of the marginalized collective are extended to encompass third world, predominantly female, victims of racial and imperial oppression. Here again, the connecting "we" supersedes the collective Arab American identity, linking the plights of Iraqi, Malaysian, Filipina, Puerto Rican, Yemeni, and Palestinian girls, women, and youth, as well as women from Nagasaki and Hiroshima, thus creating a solid unity out of their suffering. Nathalie Handal, in the introductory comment to her interview of Hammad, insightfully comments on this poet's ability to establish unity among peoples even in the absence of homogeneity: "Her profound desire to transcend cultural and religious barriers have [*sic*] given birth to a poet who unifies diversity" (1997, n.p.).

Kahf's poem "Disbeliever" (2003) also enacts a unifying identification with victims of conflict and wars across the world, including men, women, and children. The speaker laments the mass atrocities committed against bodies of helpless and unarmed peoples in the third world, reverting to a powerful reassertion of humanity that is reinstated and reflected in simple and everyday expressions of love:

> By the limping of the people of Iraq
> By the wound of frantic running in Qana, in Kosovo
> By the men and boys of Hama massacred
> By the swollen bodies in a river in Rwanda
> And Afghani women and the writers of Algiers,
> I am a disbeliever
> In everything that refuses to kiss
> Full on the lips the ones still living
> And receive them in the bosom of the self,
> No matter the religion or the nation or the race (ll. 1–10)

Such a denouncement of world suffering resulting from neoimperial as well as domestic aggression and abuse of power portrays the speaker's empathy and human understanding of such horrifying experiences. This kind of empathy can be linked to Susan Stanford Friedman's analysis of "the relational model of female selfhood in Chodorow's work," a study that sets the stage for "a consciousness of self in which 'the individual does not oppose herself to all others,' nor 'feel herself to exist outside of others,' 'but very much withothers in an interdependent existence'" (1988, 41). In "Disbeliever," this very form of "interdependent existence" is manifested in the speaker's adamant transgression of a self-sufficient individuality, branching out to foment collective selfhoods shaped by race, ethnicity, history, marginalization, and gender. In this way, Kahf reaffirms the inclusiveness inherent in the concept of "others" as delineated in Friedman's female autobiographical cadre, adding to it a transnational aspect that cuts across spatial and temporal borders to enact global forms of collective identifications.

The "interdependent inclusiveness" embedded within the self's relation to others as depicted in Kahf's "Disbeliever" is disrupted in her poem "Hijab Scene no. 7" (2003) by an alienating and discriminating U.S. mainstream, which, instead of existing "withothers," "oppos[es itself] to all others," including Muslim American minorities. The speaker confronts the mainstream's erroneous assumptions that render her mute and invisible by virtue of her color, appearance, and religious affiliation, stating,

> No, I'm not bald under the scarf
> No, I'm not from that country
> where women can't drive cars
> No, I would not like to defect
> I'm already American
> . . . .
> Yes, I speak English
> Yes, I carry explosives
> They're called words
> And if you don't get up
> Off your assumption,
> They're going to blow you away (ll. 1–5, 11–16)

The repetition of "no" and "yes" suggests that these answers are tiredly offered in response to a set of hackneyed questions reminiscent of cross-examinations rather than constructive dialogue, with the end result being to instill difference instead of overcoming it. But more often than not, as these responses show, the mainstream's knowledge of a minority group such as Muslim Americans is extremely restricted, reflecting the widespread prejudices and generalizations about this group that the U.S. majority accepts at face value. Instead of being subsumed by such negative stereotypes, the speaker vocalizes a counternarrative that stresses a Muslim American collectivity that incorporates seemingly opposite entities, such as the intermingling of Islamic and American identities, on the one hand ("No, I would not like to defect / I'm already American"), and feminism and the *hijab,* on the other hand. Such honest answers uncover the intricate fantasies embedded in the U.S. mainstream's perception of the Other (represented here by the veiled female), fantasies that repeatedly evoke the Muslim woman as endlessly mysterious and exotic, in need of being rescued from a tyrannical patriarchy.

The collective autobiography that Kahf relates in this poem affirms that Muslim Americans are entitled to belong in the United States, with their various identifications (as Muslims, Americans, feminists) complementing rather than contradicting each other. Such connections disrupt the simplistic stereotypes that mainstream America has bought into, showing the limitations of binary representation. The poem's confrontational tone culminates in what seems to be the speaker's confession to being guilty of terrorism charges: "Yes, I carry explosives." However, in another swift rhetorical move, Kahf strips "explosives" of their literal meaning, reascribing their power in words instead of bombs. But wielding words instead of bombs is not a benign act, for it uncovers a deep anger that escalates as the poem progresses, representing the frustrations of a minority group whose identity is largely determined by negative stereotypes. The speaker exploits the self-same power embedded in negative labels ("terrorist," "fanatic," "oppressors," "backward culture") to dislodge such stereotypes, answering the mainstream's probing questions with her own interrogations to highlight the small-mindedness of prejudice:

> What else do you need to know
> relevant to my buying insurance,
> opening a bank account,
> reserving a seat on a flight? (ll. 7–10)

AUTOBIOGRAPHY OF/IN PLACE

In quoting and applying Sheila Rowbotham's "theor[y] of women's selfhood to women's autobiographical texts," Friedman describes this theorist's analysis of how "women can move beyond alienation through a collective solidarity with other women—that is, a recognition that women as a group can develop an alternative way of seeing themselves by constructing a group identity based on their historical experience" (1988, 35, 40). In borrowing this concept of "collective solidarity" and "group identity" and applying it to the Arab American community as a whole, my analysis of Kahf's and Hammad's communal autobiographies becomes closely intertwined with a sense of place that hinges on "historical experience," at the same time including the concepts of collectivity and individuality discussed earlier. Arab Americans' attitude toward both their host land and their homeland, however, remains a complex matter, simply owing to the multiplicity of origins included under the Arab American umbrella, as well as the various conditions driving Arabs to emigrate to or seek exile in the United States. In "Lateefa" and "Argela Remembrance," Kahf and Hammad, respectively, offer a glimpse of what it is to live between worlds. For both speakers in these poems, the pull of Palestine as a homeland occupies a central place in their consciousness, opening up a tension between here (the present) and there (the past), even when "there" is a place that is purely constructed from stories handed down from one exilic generation to another. Hence, any move to assimilate into the "here" of the United States, and its acceptance as a permanent home, becomes a betrayal of the lost homeland.

In "Argela Remembrance" (1996) Hammad grounds the autobiography of a Palestinian American community within a very tactile and tangible exilic setting, which in its every aspect becomes the antithesis of a lost Palestine that permeates the poem but is never named or described. The speaker, referred to as "my father," articulates himself through the character "suheir," offering a communal testimonial that emphasizes, through the repetition of "we" and "we are a people," the collective experience of Palestinian Americans. The positive cohesiveness of this "we," however, is outweighed by the shock of dispossession, so that the definitions following the recurring line "we are a people" demonstrate the painful experience of maintaining a collective Palestinian identity while being a "people" without a land:

we are a people
name our sons after prophets
daughters after midwives
eat with upturned hands
plant plastic potted plants
in suffocating apartments
tiny brooklyn style
in memory of the soil once

laid under our nails
. . . .
inhaling strawberries in argelas
we've become a people of living room politics and tobacco
stained teeth . . . painfully
reminding each other
reciting quranic verse and
um kolthom scripture
of how jasmine can
fill your head on a clear night and
mint tea dawned you to morning (ll. 21–29, 34–43)

The overwhelming sadness punctuating this poem's stark and brutal imagery revolves around a gaping absence that pervades every aspect of Palestinian relocation. The absence of a home place is reflected in fragments symbolizing the larger whole that was left behind. "Plant[ing] plastic potted plants," an act that embodies the truncation and rootlessness of exile, mirrors the artificiality of the speaker's new surroundings. Potted plants, disheartening replacements of Palestine's olive trees and fruit orchards, and metaphors of displaced Palestinian identity, possess no roots and bear no fruit. They are plastic and sterile, an extension of an alienating location to which the speaker feels no connection. Moreover, the alliterative repetition of the letter *p* at the beginning of every word in this line does not make for easy reading, encompassing the exile's cumbersome navigation of a foreign language.[7]

Hammad's effective use of synecdoche also conveys the fragmentation of Palestinians' collective memory. Offering bits and pieces of the whole (that is, Palestine, which in itself remains unmentionable), Hammad's poem beautifully makes traumatic experience immediate and tangible. "Plant[ing] plastic potted plants," the speaker testifies, is "in memory of the soil once / laid under our nails," giving memory a vivid and earthy texture. This soil, a synecdoche

7. The fact that the letter *p* does not exist in the Arabic alphabet makes even more pertinent the line quoted here, which depicts some of the difficult linguistic and cultural navigations of Palestinian and, by extension, Arab exile.

of Palestinian tilled farmland, conveys the severance of a deep attachment to the earth, a bond passed down from one generation to another. The absence and loss of this land are augmented and rendered intolerable when juxtaposed against the "suffocating apartments / tiny brooklyn style." This poem's Palestinian American autobiographical collective, then, is one that registers communal mourning, which instead of resulting in acceptance and acquiescence insists on re-creating images of the homeland through memory:

> . . . painfully
> reminding each other
> . . . .
> of how jasmine can
> fill your head on a clear night and
> mint tea dawned you to morning (ll. 37–43)

Carol Bardenstein highlights the recurrence of such fragmentation in Palestinian narratives, describing it as "the selective appropriation of what is perceived as part of a repertoire of past collective memory, or tradition, which is incorporated and activated within a discourse in the present" (1998, 1). Such "Proustian recollections," according to Bardenstein, "conjured up repeatedly, revive and re-articulate the memory of Palestinian rootedness in a Palestine before displacement and dispersion" (19).

In its delineation of an Arab American communal autobiography, Hammad's "Argela Remembrance" anticipates "Move Over," the poem by Kahf discussed earlier, with its enumeration of various juxtapositions that contribute to the formation of a collective Muslim American identity. However, whereas "Move Over" concentrates mostly on the constant negotiations that Muslim Americans undertake owing to religious difference, "Argela Remembrance," as a collective autobiography of multigenerational Palestinian Americans, locates the survival of exilic identity in the continuation of cultural as well as religious tradition: "reciting quranic verse and / um kolthom scripture" to incite memories of the homeland. The weighty coupling of religious verse and traditional Arabic song acts as a painful but nevertheless powerful deterrent against collective amnesia, so much so that cultural heritage (signified by Um Kolthom's "scripture") is on par with the "quranic verse."

Born in a humble village in Egypt, Um Kolthom (1904?–1975) is known as "the star of the East" and "the diva of Arabic song." Trained to sing traditional Islamic songs with her father, Um Kolthom rose to stardom during the 1930s and 1940s to become "unquestionably the most famous singer in the twentieth-century Arab world" (Danielson 1998, 1). The choice of Um Kolthom as a cultural signifier goes beyond the love-torn and melancholic incantations of her well-known songs, and extends to this singer's role as a symbol of Arab nationalism. (After the Arab defeat in 1967 in the Arab-Israeli war, for example, she organized a series of concerts and donated the proceeds to the Egyptian government. Supporting Gamal Abdel Nasser and Arab nationalism, she became "the voice and face of Egypt" as well as the Arab world [1]). In addition to the important implications of these religious and cultural reminders, however, coupling "quranic verse" and "um kolthom scripture" interestingly enough portrays the way in which both are heard by the second-generation Arab American speaker, whose limited exposure to the recitation of "quranic verse" and the long, prayerlike musicality of Um Kolthom's songs renders the two almost indistinguishable (and also alludes to Um Kolthom's training in traditional Islamic songs), so much so that they come to carry equal weight in representing a displaced Arab cultural and religious heritage in the diaspora.

In contrast to Hammad's "Argela Remembrance" (1996) in which the memory of the lost homeland permeates and even threatens to engulf the present of a Palestinian American community, Kahf's poem "Lateefa" (2003) offers the perspective of a first-person narrator who is torn between the allegiance that she was taught to uphold toward a lost Palestine and the connectedness that she feels toward her adopted country, more specifically New Jersey, the state she was born and raised in:

> I was born here—BORN!
> INNA YOU-ESS-AY—oh Bruce,
> oh Connie, I
> got nowhere to go back to
> *(Daddy, you can talk to me*
> *all you want about Palestine*
> *and I'll be faithful to the end*
> *but I don't know it, never*

smelled its rainwet streets, don't know
its stoops and backyards and chicken coops.)
. . . .

I know New Jersey. I've run
my fingers up and down its spine,
scaled the vertebrae of official buildings
on Broad Street, in Newark,
taken Uncle Ali to Immigration. (ll. 36–45, 52–56)

By demonstrating an immediate and palpable familiarity with Bruce Springsteen's grounded and down-to-earth "INNA YOU-ESS-AY," the speaker lays claim to this land, in all its physicality, thus rooting her identity in a solid place, not the imaginary one that her father creates for her from memory. This rootedness, demonstrated through anthropomorphic imagery used in describing New Jersey, asserts a tactile rapport between the speaker and the state. Running her "fingers up and down its spine, / scal[ing] the vertebrae of official buildings," the speaker savors an intimate and sensual relationship with her surroundings, one that is based on deep firsthand knowledge, as opposed to her father's memories of an intangible Palestine, which, although she is fiercely dedicated to many of its causes, remains for her an idea and not an actuality.

In "Argela Remembrance," the repetition of "we are a people" and the descriptive imagery following this phrase end up underscoring the lack (of place and roots) that plagues Palestinian Americans in exile. A similar type of reiteration occurs in Kahf's "Lateefa," but instead of accentuating disconnection, it emphasizes the speaker's belonging-through-knowledge:

I know New Jersey
. . . .
I know where the Sister Clara Muhammad Schools
. . . hold their fairs,
and where the Ansar Allah
peddle Islam in little vials
of odiferous oils
. . . .

I know like uncles the bearded immigrant sheikhs
. . . .
I know the storefront mosques in the neighborhoods (ll. 52, 57–61, 63, 74)

The repetition of "I know" and the descriptions following it embody an openness and freedom of movement that come in direct contrast with the overwhelming sense of confinement inherent in the "suffocating apartments / tiny brooklyn style" of "Argela Remembrance." Moreover, such repetitions outline a clearly demarcated sense of place, represented by concrete physical landmarks that connect the individual and the community to an immediate present.

Both "Argela Remembrance" and "Lateefa" involve an exchange between a daughter and her father. However, whereas in "Argela Remembrance" the father ruminates about the memory of Palestinian displacement, including his own—

he tells her
baba
we once stood on the edge of our sea
but they made us leave (ll. 49–52)

—in "Lateefa" it is the daughter addressing her father, portraying the point of view of the second and third generations of Palestinian exiles whose image of the lost homeland is constructed from secondhand memories that they do not identify with. The necessity to keep alive the pain of displacement and dispossession described in "Argela Remembrance" is transformed in "Lateefa" into the second-generation exiles' guilt resulting from their relinquishing of their parents' past. This past is replaced by a present that new memories could be built on. After all, for the poem's speaker, there is no going back to her father's homeland (since Palestine has become for her and her generation more of an imaginary place), and she feels rooted in New Jersey, where she was "BORN."

In an interesting discussion of Palestinian memory, Carol Bardenstein points out the possible existence of "multiple memories inhabiting the 'same' sites . . . [with] one set of memories gain[ing] ascendancy and legitimacy in the constructed present, and other layers of memory [being] submerged to varying degrees, giving rise to the phenomenon or sense of a memory-site or memory-object being 'haunted' by those submerged memories" (1998, 2). The confluence in "Lateefa" of multiple realities and memories occupying the same site of exile points to the variance within communal Palestinian American voices, with the difference between one generation and another being reflected in their experience of the location of exile. Thus, the intricacies of communal and individual autobiography in a poem such as "Lateefa" become more pronounced, pointing to the different levels of experience that inform such autobiographies.

Kahf's and Hammad's creation of communal and individual poetic autobiographies emphasizes what Chandra Talpade Mohanty describes as the role of "writing in the production of self- and collective-consciousness" (1991, 33). Kahf herself states, "Writing is the way I know how to be in the world, although there are other equally worthy ways to communicate and to create beauty and truth. . . . Words are my thing" (2004b, 8). Nawar Al-Hassan Golley stresses the revisionary aspect of writing autobiography, stating, "When a woman writes about herself, she is immediately engaged in a double process of writing and rewriting the stories already written about her as a woman, as passive or hidden. . . . Writing for women becomes a double act of self-discovering and self-making" (2003, 61). In the case of Kahf and Hammad, such self-discovery and "self-making" extend beyond the self to emphasize through poetry a collectivity of Arab American experience, an act that develops into a complex act of creation and discovery since it involves the peeling back of historical and cultural layers through the writing process.

By doing so, these poets unveil a strong political commitment, giving a strong poetic voice to a minority that currently experiences invisibility. After all, as Scheherazad states in Kahf's "E-mail from Scheherazad," "Where I come from, / Words are to die for" (ll. 5–6). Barbara Nimri Aziz states in her foreword to *Scheherazade's Legacy* that the Arab American community has reached the conclusion that other minorities, including African Americans and Italian Americans, had reached before it: "Write or be written," for to be written is to be stereotyped and rendered powerless. She cites Toni Morrison's description of writing "as a process by which a person goes to a place and moves the dirt in order to understand why he or she is there at all." And this is where Arab American writers find themselves today, "moving the dirt" and "sifting through the little things overlooked or abandoned or discolored by others"

(2004, xiii). Mohanty also emphasizes the important link between political commitment and writing, delineating the solid "relation of writing, memory, consciousness, and political resistance . . . [affirming] the creation of a communal (feminist) political consciousness through the practice of storytelling . . . and . . . the redefinition of the very possibilities of political consciousness and action through the act of writing" (1991, 35). The interconnectedness of storytelling-through-writing and a burgeoning political consciousness, then, become evident and necessary tools of expression and resistance in the works of Kahf and Hammad, important members of the widening group of Arab American poets, contributing to what the Arab American poet Naomi Shihab Nye describes as "parts of a giant collective poem" (2002, xiv).

PART FOUR

The Personal and the Political in Autobiographical Writings

There are many different kinds of Palestinian experience, which cannot all be assembled into one. One would therefore have to write parallel histories of the communities in Lebanon, the occupied territories, and so on. That is the central problem. It is almost impossible to imagine a single narrative: it would have to be the kind of crazy history that comes out in *Midnight's Children*, with all those strands coming in and out.

—Edward Said, "On Palestinian Identity"

10

Arab Women Write the Trauma of Imprisonment and Exile

DAPHNE M. GRACE

This chapter will examine the effect of the traumatic experience of imprisonment and exile on Arab women writers, taking as examples the Egyptian writer and doctor Nawal el-Saadawi and the Iraqi writer and artist Haifa Zangana. Both women write their autobiographical experiences from a perspective of political prisoner and exile, where exile is an experience of having "endlessly to choose between submission and submission" (Zangana 1991, 10). My study of the two writers will address notions of how autobiography can, as Sidonie Smith (1998, 433) points out, be a "culturally disruptive" writing process, in addition to one that can replicate and induce trauma in its focus on and exposure of painful memory. Memory, however, is itself problematic, as Zygmunt Bauman argues in the context of war victims: "Memory is a mixed blessing. . . . Memory *selects,* and *interprets*—and what is to be selected and how it needs to be interpreted is a moot matter and an object of continuous contention" (2003, 86; emphasis in original).

Autobiography as a genre is perhaps best suited to negating or collapsing the existence of the binary opposition that distinguishes history from fiction. Whereas postcolonial theorists have grappled with the idea of "truth/untruth," the writer of autobiography is justifiably at liberty to manipulate his or her construction of a past out of the fragments of memory. This reconstruction, or "re-membering" as Toni Morrison terms it, emphasizes the provisionality of history and has both problems and advantages. Concepts of what constitutes history have, of course, been challenged and rewritten by and following

Hayden White and Robert Carr, and further deconstructed by writers such as J. M. Coetzee, Isabel Allende, and Salman Rushdie. Although history and fiction are "language games deployed in different contexts," in the case of autobiography this differentiation may not be so clear-cut (Ashcroft 2001, 136). The situation in autobiography is as paradoxical and contradictory as in some postmodern fiction, where "lying is never simply opposed to truth, but is a sort of hybrid overlapping of different registers of narrative, a 'rhetoric'" (136).

This discussion will also draw on some of the debates inherent within writing autobiography, including problematic cultural choices as well as difficulties involving the reliability or stability of the narrator. It also reveals the importance of women from the Arab world rising above the fear of censorship and punishment frequently incurred within the act of writing and publishing.

Sidonie Smith proposes autobiography as a type of manifesto, a public performance or announcement of an individual's interpretation of experience on behalf of and as part of the larger group, accessing and mapping borders of public-private and personal-political. Such writing is aimed as a critique "motivated by the autobiographical subject's desire to contest dominant discourses" within the framework of creating counterpublics (Smith 1987, 436–37). Although this approach may be a contestable interpretive strategy (which rules out solipsism), autobiography for Arab women cannot be written merely as an exploration of individual life experience, since the individual always implicates the group: it is written as political and social comment, to create empathy in the reader, and to protest. "We write to avenge ourselves against the world," declared Hoda Barakat in a conference presentation in 2005. Arab women write, she suggested, because they have no other weapon, no other power. They write to remember and to forget. Writing can protect from madness or suicide; it can be a way of "writing away the prison" (Hamida Na'na in Faqir 1998, 91)—which can be interpreted as both metaphorical and literal. This chapter will also explore to what extent writing is successful for cathartic purposes, as a way of exploring the experiences and implications of violent experience in formulating strategies of women's resistance.

Postcolonial theory as a way of conceiving and analyzing literature has largely been inspired by the work of Frantz Fanon, the main instigator of psychic and social rebellion in North Africa and beyond who urged the native academic and intellectual to take an active role in revolution. Violence as a legitimate tool of the oppressed has thus been condoned in both academic and revolutionary discourses. Moreover, most critics would not disagree that Fanon's work is as relevant today as it was when written, since the urgent requirement is in reworking the present as well as rewriting the past. Although writing autobiography is a way of reappropriating the past and a methodology of redressing the enforced silencing of the colonized "subaltern," it has also been seen as an active strategy for political empowerment (Smith 1987, 433). The post-Fanon world for a half century had been largely characterized by decolonization from the imperial powers in Africa, India, the Middle East, and so on, decolonization bringing with it, as Fanon writes in *The Wretched of the Earth,* "a natural rhythm into existence, introduced by new men, and with it a new language and a new humanity" (1961b, 178). Recent invasions and the colonization of countries such as Afghanistan and Iraq could be seen as a reversal of this hope.

The texts of the two Arab women writers I discuss here deal with experiences in the 1970s and 1980s, yet the issues they address are of continuing relevance, resonating with not only events replicated today but also events and experiences that are becoming more, rather than less, commonplace for women, and especially for both male and female writers and academics. Whereas Fanon urged the academics and intellectuals of a colonized country to become involved in the struggle for independence, it is these writers and intellectuals who are often seen as the main threat and among the first to be assassinated by the occupying powers. Zangana highlights how many journalists, newspaper editors, and academics (many of them women) have been killed since 2003, since "for the occupation to last, or for its aims to be fulfilled, independent minds have to be eradicated. We feel that we are witnessing a deliberate attempt to destroy intellectual life in Iraq" (2006, 46).

Writing as a weapon is still valid in the post-Iraq-occupation world. My main focus on the work of Haifa Zangana has particular relevance to this contemporary positioning both of women and of writers. Zangana originally left Iraq in 1976 under the regime of Saddam Hussein; "I can't go back to Iraq," she wrote in 2002, "because, like many Iraqis, I was imprisoned and tortured. When I was released I was haunted by howls of pain and memories of the dead" (9). In 2006, since she is a writer who dares to voice her criticism of the occupation of her homeland as a journalist in the "free world," she found herself on a list of "terrorists" recently published on the Internet. Her exile, therefore, continues.

PROBLEMS OF AUTOBIOGRAPHY

In *Women Claim Islam: Creating Islamic Feminism Through Literature,* miriam cooke (2001) argues that Arab women write autobiography as a search for a sense of empowerment either social or political, writing as a means of locating themselves within a master/male-oriented narrative and language. In her book *In the House of Silence,* a title suggestive of the "traditional" placing of women within a prisonlike sociohistorical positioning, if not the literal incarceration of women,[1] Fadia Faqir enumerates some of the problems and reasons cited in the writing of autobiography of Arab women. Questioning the validity of the genre in terms of its literary or historical value, she argues that self-representation is a means to explore issues of gender, history, and psychological "reality," a means of performing a "multiple translation of the darkness" (1998, 6, 22).

Yet whatever the reason for putting pen to paper, the choice of writing autobiography entails a problematic positioning. Within the Islamic world, the concept of autobiography is itself problematic, or even impossible, one that violates the concept of *'umma* (nation) and validates the idea of the individual as outside, or even above, the community. Not only is the genre of autobiography fraught with notions of an adherence to "truth," but it could be argued that only those Arabs who have adopted a "Western" lifestyle—and the concept of individuality—would be likely to use this form of writing. By choosing to write their lives, these authors (whether male or female) have set themselves against the Islamic sense of society.[2] Autobiography thereby becomes both an act of assertion

1. Other titles of autobiography, such as Raimonda Tawil's *My Home, My Prison,* also endorse this position—one that often is overemphasized in the sensationalization of Arab women as "victims" in European best-sellers. In England, for example, bookshop shelves frequently display the now overfamiliar image of a veiled face revealing only a pair of anguished eyes above the title of yet another terrified "escape" narrative from an Islamic culture. How indicative they are of "Arab women's" life stories could be called into question.

2. Thanks to Ghada Karmi for her comments to me on Arab women's autobiography at the Edward Said Memorial Conference, University of Sussex, England, May 14, 2004.

of one's individual identity as opposed to and distinct from the social identity within the group—an "act of defiance"—both personal and political (9).

For the Muslim woman, the writing of fiction or fact is equally fraught with problems. Writing remains for Arab women a key means of subverting dominant hegemonies and reasserting agency, a means of voicing their "silenced" narratives. Women write to negotiate a "textual, sexual, and linguistic space" for themselves, though writing itself remains for many secret and subversive (22). Risking censorship, slander, or possible imprisonment, the Arab woman writer is a dissident, crossing into the traditionally male space of language. Such violations of sacred sexual/textual space impinge on a woman's honor *(sharaf),* which is contingent on her silence and invisibility, and challenge both cultural concepts of women and the "master narratives" that always assume the speaker is male.[3] Thus, women's task in writing is subversive of patriarchal structures of language and society. "Within theocratic, military, totalitarian and neopatriarchal societies writing . . . becomes an act of defiance and assertion of individual identity" (9). Autobiography in particular is considered both bold and indecent in Arab society, especially when written by a woman. As a genre, autobiography is not considered "literature."

Autobiography, therefore, is often an informed choice, one used as a political tool with the object of exposing Arab society and its problems through personal narrative. The personal as part of the community is still endorsed, but functioning as a synecdoche, as a tool to expose society through individual experience. It is therefore all the more powerful as a tool of indictment of a social system when the autobiography entails the narration of the trauma of imprisonment and torture. Many Arab women writers have, to greater or lesser degrees, attempted to write about their prison experiences. Jennifer

3. Interestingly, this tendency to silence personal narratives involving traumatic individual and social memory is also discussed by Ronit Lentin in the context of Israel and survivors of the Shoah (Holocaust). The writing of women's memories was in fact instrumental in bridging the "memory gap" in social discourses and perceptions of traumatic experience, which had previously remained unnamed and silenced (Lentin 2000, 3). Women's testimony as survivors had been excluded from historical accounts, and writers had to "break the conspiracy of silence" that surrounded the masculinization of Israeli discourses and the "feminization" of the Shoah victims.

Langer cites the group of women exiles she meets in London in the poetry workshop Exiled Writers' Ink: "How is the experience of being a victim of violence in conflict articulated in their writing? Is exile a safe space in which to describe horrific experiences and accompanying emotions? Generally, the silence of the women in this area is significant" (2005, n.p.).

The problem of silence is not only one of fear of reprisal, or of stepping outside the culturally accepted prelates of the *'umma.* Here, as Langer again explains, "the omissions may be too painful or unacceptable to articulate, such as rape. Denial may be a way of dealing with atrocities too terrible to confront. The function of the work is both cathartic and declamatory serving to bring an understanding of the brutality of systems to the outside world in a way that a newspaper article cannot because it describes the innermost feelings and experiences of the individual woman" (n.p.).

Haifa Zangana describes the cathartic aspect of writing in the following terms: "Is it my charm for curing the leprosy that permeated my body on the day it was touched by whatever I hate; my charm for warding off forgiveness that comes with the passing of time, for repelling widespread failing memory, repelling the return to a country where they still practice insulting rituals, repelling the conscious emptying of memory of its rage, repelling oblivion, oblivion, oblivion?" (1991, 53).

Within the framework of autobiography written by women in the third world, as Barbara Harlow delineates, their personal struggle, interrogation, imprisonment, and often torture are placed in a historically situated narrative, a part of a "collective enterprise" (1987, 455). Women's prison literature in general combines fictional forms with the documentary record and expresses experiences not based on categories of gender, race, or ethnicity (453). As these repressive conditions proliferate out of the "third world," these narrative documents gain relevance out of their specific politicogeographical locales. In general, the prison experience gives writers "both their own main message and the motive to communicate it" and is described with the intention of showing that "the author's individual experience is not unique or even extraordinary" (Franklin 1978, 249–50).

Prison literature can express national-liberation struggles or resistance movements and has wider ethical and social implications. Works of historiography such as Assia Djebar's *Fantasia: An Algerian Cavalcade* (1993) also demonstrate how narratives of women's political prison experience and torture expose the ethics of colonial forces. Both men and women writers of prison experience utilize their personal experience as motivation to write and as their main message, to show the reader that "the author's individual experience is not unique or even extraordinary" (Harlow 1987, 455). Like slavery with its symbol of the "ship" discussed by Paul Gilroy (1993), the traumatic space of prison can be viewed as a symbolic "shared experience of terror" that lies at the heart of communities in Africa, the Middle East, and the diaspora. Indeed, "the cell"—though it is the apparent ultimate refutation of liberatory space—could be compared to "the ship" as a transcultural space of trauma and reassessment of selfhood.

Although such experience is not gendered, in our masculinist world of terror and war, women are frequently the victims of international, national, or community violence. In the Middle Eastern world in particular, they are targeted by both the international community—since it has largely been women who bear the greatest impact of sanctions that limit the availability of health care and education or even safe drinking water. Women and children form the greatest percentage of the one hundred thousand Iraqi civilian war casualties. Women are also often the targets of local patriarchal forces that locate women as the upholders of family honor;[4] they have now become the target for arrest by U.S. troops who use them in order to access male relatives.

In her article "Staying Alive," Ahdaf Soueif meets with some of the women in Baghdad to find out what they are doing in these "critical times." She explains: "They are doing what they've always done: toughing it out, spreading themselves thin, doing their work, making ends meet, trying to protect their children and support their men, turning to their sisters and their mothers for solidarity and laughs. There was a time, I guess, when women's political action was born of choice, of a desire to change the world. Now, simply to hold on to our world action is thrust upon us" (2004, 119; the article was originally written in 2003).

In the Middle East, Soueif concludes, the women are also history keepers: the ones who record, document, and remember the "demolitions, expropriations,

4. I have discussed the concepts of honor and shame and the implications of violence against women in the Middle East and India under the guise of religious or nationalistic hegemonies elsewhere (Grace 2004).

arrests and killings." She continues, "Keeping the children alive. Keeping culture alive. Preserving history and telling the story—these seem to be at the heart of [our] women's concerns right now" (119). Meanwhile, women are victims as well as witnesses. "Lack of security and fear of kidnapping make Iraqi women prisoners in their own homes," writes Zangana (2004b, 13). Similarly, in a country where women never wore the veil, now women are covering up for invisibility, security, and protection. Noga Efrati examines the implications of the abolition of the Personal Status Law in Iraq, which would eradicate the present law of equal rights between men and women, replacing it with sharia law: "In the 'new Iraq,'" she writes, "women have found themselves running just to stay in place" (2006, 595).

The propagation of fear is a tactic of war; for some, it is a daily phenomenon in society as a means of controlling the collective consciousness. Writing of the context of life in Iraq under the Saddam regime, Zangana explains, "Fear is our friend and our comrade, we grow up with it, it is closer to us than anything else. We have lived so long with fear, we cannot live without it" (1991, 9), and similarly, "Torture has left a deep scar on our collective memory, and death is no stranger. We wanted to put an end to both" (2004, 9). Nawal el-Saadawi, commenting on the situation of African writers, argues that those individuals who escape prison are very often haunted by a lifetime of fear and by "the spectre of prison walls looming over the horizon, even if they have never engaged in political activity and never wielded anything but a pen. People in our countries are nurtured on fear" (1999, 205). Both these examples from writers are endorsed in the 2004 Reith Lectures given by Wole Soyinka on the topic of the escalating "climate of fear" throughout the world.

Yet how is the experience of an upbringing in fear or being the victim of violence articulated in Arab women's writing? How is it possible to describe horrific experiences and their accompanying emotions? Jennifer Langer explains, "Denial may be a way of dealing with atrocities too terrible to confront. The function of the work is both cathartic and declamatory serving to bring an understanding of the brutality of systems to the outside world in a way that a newspaper article cannot because it describes the innermost feelings and experiences of the individual woman" (2005, n.p.).[5]

5. See http//www.swan.ac.uk/conferences/transcom/htm.

Two women writers who have breached the barrier of fear in writing about traumatic experience are Haifa Zangana and Nawal el-Saadawi, writers who draw on and expose their experiences in Iraq and Egypt, respectively, to elucidate a woman's witness of and resistance to violence. Born in Iraq, Haifa Zangana became politically active, working with a young communist faction working to overthrow the Ba'athist regime and was arrested. As a result, she was imprisoned and tortured under Saddam's Ba'ath regime. Because of the constant threat of further violence, she left Iraq, first going in 1975 to Syria where she joined the Palestinian Red Crescent. Since 1976 she has lived in London. Nawal el-Saadawi, an Egyptian doctor and author, remains a forceful advocate of women's rights around the world and a tireless campaigner for human rights. Her books, articles, and lectures have been crucial in shaping ideas about women's oppression in Egypt, creating a feminist discourse that seeks to redefine patriarchal structures of history, culture, and identity.

As Arab women writers of fiction and autobiography, both Nawal el-Saadawi and Haifa Zangana were jailed in their countries, under the regimes of Anwar Sadat and Saddam Hussein, respectively. Having both lived for many years in exile, they write about their traumatic experiences of exile and utilize them in both fictional and autobiographic texts. El-Saadawi was jailed for being a writer, a fact that Barbara Harlow (1987) interprets as influencing the significance of her writing, while also linking el-Saadawi to other political prisoners as well as her own characters.

El-Saadawi's two autobiographical works, *Daughter of Isis* (1999) and *Walking Through Fire* (2002), address the social, cultural, and political problems of her country, Egypt, while problematizing both her own and Arab women's identity. Her book detailing her prison experience, *Memoirs from the Woman's Prison* was published in 1983 (and translated into English in 1986). Many of her fictional works also draw on her own life experience. As el-Saadawi points out, "Prison literature is one of the distinctive areas of creative writing in all African countries, and reflects the oppression exercised against thought. Prison, in fact, for hundreds of years has remained a part of our daily lives. But now this is more so than ever. It has become one of the heroes of contemporary novels" (1997, 205).

Although other women writers have written about the prison experience, the purpose of such documentation is all-important for my discussion here.

A prison memoir such as Zaynab al-Ghazali's *Days of My Life,* for example, was written from the perspective of a "spiritual awakening" and religious conversion (cooke 1998, 129). As the "number-one" enemy of President Nasser, al-Ghazali was imprisoned as a representative of the active jihad of the Muslim Ladies Association, an organization she founded to be an equivalent to the Muslim Brothers. Al-Ghazali's testimony is intended to elucidate how her survival of torture and imprisonment is owing to her implacable faith, her ritual of prayer, and her steadfast belief system. As miriam cooke comments, al-Ghazali's agenda is to present her experience as a religious testimony of her "descent into hell, the purification through torture and the re-ascent to earth to minister to the world" (127). In contrast, el-Saadawi and Zangana write about their incarcerations explicitly with the purpose of exposing the regime, the horror and the trauma of their experience, in an attempt both to come to terms with it personally and to share it with a greater public.

HAIFA ZANGANA

A frequent commentator for *The Guardian* newspaper in Great Britain and a high-profile activist for international human rights, Haifa Zangana has written editorial articles and letters on the sanctions against Iraq and the current U.S. occupation of Iraq, where "torture as an instrument of submission is a vital part of continuing occupation" (2004a, 13).[6] Implicating how writing life can influence fiction, Haifa Zangana's first book, *Through the Vast Halls of Memory,* is based on her experience of imprisonment and torture in Iraq (published first in English in 1991 and in Arabic in 1995). Zangana writes to expose the core of her ordeal and extends her narrative to encompass a more universal experience of compassion for others who may still be suffering similarly today. The time line of her narrative is the present, her trial and imprisonment an ongoing existence from which she cannot be freed, even in the relative safely of her present exile. Coming to terms with the past is problematic, as is the ability to explain the experience to others. Memory is denied

6. See also, for example, the articles "Bombs Will Deepen Iraq's Nightmare" (Zangana 2002); "Iraqis Have Lived This Lie Before" (*The Guardian,* June 29, 2004), and the letter "Iraq Elections Are Not Free" signed by Zangana and nineteen others (January 20, 2005).

or remains unarticulated. As she explains in her article, "I, Too, Was Tortured in Abu Ghraib," "How can you talk about your humiliation, your weakness, letting yourself and others down, your reduction to an animal sleeping with urine and faeces? Can you explain how your mind loses its grip on nerves and muscles, how fear grows inside you like a weed? Silence becomes your refuge while carrying your shame and guilt for still being alive. Thirty years on I still wake at 2am every morning. That is the time they used to lead me out of my cell for interrogation" (2004a, 13).

The power inherent within Haifa Zangana's writing is that she is able to work through the trauma of recollection to expose and challenge her past experience. Trauma theory acknowledges the inadequacies of language to articulate such events; the experience of trauma is beyond language (Gilmore 2005, 102). In the context of Zangana's experience, it is the very denial of torture and the degradation of abuse that paradoxically confirms their occurrence. Yet as Leigh Gilmore suggests, "speech of all sorts spills from the site of trauma" (2005, 102), and for Zangana the averted empty gaze of the abused man or the banality of her conversation with her parents when they visit her in jail speaks volumes. What happened is not as important as what the person feels she has become. Degradation, powerlessness, and pain can render the documentation of an event meaningless. Yet individual trauma transforms into a "deep scar" on the collective memory (Zangana 2004a).

It is for this reason that Zangana's account of events at the now infamous Abu Ghraib, where she was interrogated and abused, is nonlinear, taking into account childhood memory as well as dreams and nightmares. One dream experience comments on how the body registers fear "before fear reaches the brain, recognizing images of torture, stored not in the memory but in the body's very cells" (1991, 10). Her recollected memories are rehearsed and repeated in an attempt to access all the possible multifaceted views of what happened, to review what really happened in light of the fact of forgetting. What interests her is the problematic selectivity of memory: how truthful are the images? Zangana emphasizes the importance of memory retaining its integrity to the truth, and it is for this reason that *Through the Vast Halls of Memory* cannot be called "autobiography," since that term implies notions of "truth." She emphasizes that the ethics of writing is a responsibility to ideals but above all to retain the truth of her dead comrades. "What one is trying to do is to realize what was the truth and to maintain and be true to that truth of the group and their work" (Grace 2006, n.p.). (The Arabic edition of the book includes two additional chapters, one extended version of her childhood memories and a further concluding chapter that discusses the role and elusive nature of memory.)

In her text, shifting through memory, Zangana writes openly about her prison ordeal: the horrific sight of her tortured friends and comrades, her own physical squalor in the filth of her cell. Her memories create an enduring state of fear that overwhelms normal physical and mental function. "What do you do if you have inside you a wound as big as yourself? What do you do if the wound inside you is your very existence?" (1991, 11), she asks, conjuring up the definition of autobiography as "a wound where the blood of history does not dry" (Spivak quoted in Gilmore 2005, 99).

Emphasizing that during her time incarcerated she was the only political prisoner among the women, since the government officially denied the existence of any "politicals," she also implies that the violations of her body and psychological persecution against her were gender-specific violence. Although she shares with the reader her experience of life in a hot and dirty cell with the other women "lifers," she has little in common with the other women, save an intrinsic understanding of the social situations that had made most of these women turn to murder of their husbands. This text is not specifically "feminist," in the way that a campaigner of women's rights such as el-Saadawi is often read, but an account of a vicious and sadistic regime that allowed no adversaries to survive, either male or female.

This type of document, however, in many ways must defy traditional narrative forms and is often a combination of fact and fantasy, autobiography and dreams. The interfusion of fact, fiction, and dream is both a deliberate narrative device and an artifact of the nature of memory. Zangana sees this fusion as necessary because of the unreliability of memory and the need of the adherence to truth where exact details of events may be blurred or forgotten. The nature of memory is both fascinating and problematic, in particular the selectivity of memory (Grace 2006, n.p.) and how remembering can be triggered: a list of missing persons in an old newspaper evokes a sudden flood of memories of people and events apparently long forgotten.

In her memoir, the time line switches between memory and comment from the perspective of her present exile in London. Yet the present and her memory of the past blur, as do waking and dreaming. Every night immediately on returning home, in order to reduce the number of waking hours in the day, she takes sleeping pills, but "on awakening the dream is always the same, the past" (1991, 28). Her book provides testimony to the ongoing psychological damage done by imprisonment, the terror of dreams and nightmares that persist years after her confinement. The lack of a linear narrative, switching both time and place references, is part of her strategy for writing that involves various defense mechanisms whereby the full impact of the brutal details can only be alluded to; full exposure is further than she is prepared to go. Even so, she comments on how the writing of her book took several years, as the process of recollection remained perpetually fresh and traumatic. Similarly, she describes how much later when she attempts to tell a friend about her time in jail, her friend comments, "But you talk about it as though it happened to somebody else!" Again, although she attempts to portray the terror of her arrest and interrogations, the fear of torture and execution, she tells us that the terror has never been forgotten, even after twenty years. Recollecting the past is far from a healing mechanism, as suggested by Frantz Fanon; memory is pain. "I look at the past as it approaches, falling on me, enfolding me, as though in layer upon layer of concrete. I look in silence. . . . I want to scream. The scream becomes a whisper: memory, draw closer" (Grace 2006, n.p.).

Suggesting that the catharsis of writing is ultimately ineffectual, since "the past is the present is the future" (ibid.), her attempts to ward off oblivion are reminiscent of the themes explored by Assia Djebar. For Djebar, writing can forge an intellectual and emotional space that helps to "lift the taboo, to lift the veil. To lift the veil and at the same time keep secret that which must remain secret" (1993, 62). Yet sharing the burden of her experience with the reader is also a method of sharing guilt regarding our own responsibility for the world situation. Since "history has striven to repeat itself around a single axis: man," Zangana queries, "is there any guarantee that we too will not wear the faces of the torturers of the future?" (Grace 2006, n.p.).[7]

7. Compare the current situation in Iraq, where "torture has been practiced since day one of

Although the past remains ridden with pain, the present situation of exile is also burdened with feelings of alienation and displacement with its associated sociocultural and psychological trauma, even when she recounts meeting with other "comrades who survived" and sharing memories. Dreams merge with reality in the isolation of the exilic experience within an alien culture. Even a bus ride through London becomes a terrifying experience, one that summons up the demons of loneliness, insomnia, and claustrophobia. Sleep contains the terror of dreaming. The narrative ends with details of three vividly remembered dreams: the memory of torture, the sadness at lost and unreachable family, and loss and fear as she vainly tries to find her way home—reiterating the futile attempt to escape such memories. Zangana recently commented that the third dream—a vision of Baghdad as a stinking city of ruins covered in dust—has now become a reality (ibid.).

As the use of trauma and terror (and terrorism) has become central to the future of human life on this planet, the discussions within the field of trauma studies are concerned with solidifying the difference between perpetrators and victims, terrorists and the terrorized, inhuman atrocities and what may constitute legitimate retribution. They have highlighted a need to focus on various historical moments as well as projecting future outcomes.

Dominick LaCapra (2001) emphasizes the dichotomy between event and experience, how the original experience is translated into emotional trauma through the role of memory. The original traumatizing event cannot be confused with the traumatized effect; one cannot necessarily invoke the effect of the event in terms of affect. He analyzes formulating ways and means of "working through" trauma—emphasizing the distinction between "working through" and "acting out." Performativity, or acting out the trauma, may not be a working through of the events in terms of healing or closure. Many historians disavow the role of mimesis or repetition, and theories of trauma are thus problematic. Historiography in a limited way may be a way of working through of the past. LaCapra also discusses the differences between historical and transhistorical trauma. Historical trauma can possibly be lived through and healed; transhistorical trauma cannot be healed—one just has to learn to

---

the occupation. . . . But the occupying forces have chosen not to see Iraqis as humans. . . . Iraqis did not struggle for decades to replace one torturer with another" (Zangana 2004a).

live with it. Historical trauma relates to being a victim, transhistorical to being vulnerable.

In the theoretical context of the healing of trauma, it is significant that Haifa Zangana denies any cathartic or healing process taking place through writing or working through trauma. For Zangana, writing does not provide a paradigm for any healing process. The memories are not healed; they remain fresh and painful. Neither do they fade with reliving or retelling them. "Things are not healed or worked out through revisiting memory," she explains. "They remain fresh and vivid." Writing *Through the Vast Halls of Memory* took more than eight years because of the difficulty of thinking about that time in her life and the painful process of revisiting the memories of that experience. She describes how, like opening the drawer of a desk in which something has been hidden, the memories are always there, and do not change. She is also concerned with how consciously we use our memory. Memories themselves do not change; what the writer attempts to do is realize what the truth is and maintain this truth (Grace 2006, n.p.).

The problematic nature of Zangana's journey through the halls of memory is revealed ultimately through the framing device of the text. Just as she discloses the need for talking about personal traumatic memories as if they had happened to another person (1991, 32), the book opens with the framing device of an introduction to letters and papers written by exiles and now in Zangana's possession. The reader must decide if she is merely the editor of these documents or the author. This pose of the narrator being merely a "friend" of another woman writer is a distancing technique, a technique for surviving memory, of being able to come to the end of an exhausting journey and for the mind to "sleep in peace" (2).

This avoidance technique is indicative of the types of approaches to how personal testimony may be recorded and validated in the face of loss or fragmentation of memory (a typical response to a traumatic event), denial, and the passage of time.

NAWAL EL-SAADAWI

Whereas Haifa Zangana uses dream material to access and simultaneously deny traumatic memory, Nawal el-Saadawi further problematizes the borders of fact and fiction in her autobiography. El-Saadawi was arrested and imprisoned in 1981 along with other Egyptian intellectuals under Anwar Sadat's regime. She was eventually released after Sadat's death and shortly after founded the Arab Women's Solidarity Association, an international organization dedicated to "lifting the veil from the mind" of Arab women. Following a career as a doctor and writer, she and her husband have been consistently persecuted and frequently forced to live in exile in the United States. Her books, articles, and lectures have been crucial in shaping ideas about women's oppression in Egypt, creating a feminist discourse that seeks to redefine patriarchal structures of history, culture, and identity. Her feminism is uncompromising in the forcefulness of expression, and her writing and her "voice," as Nadje Sadig al-Ali puts it, "constitute a discourse of rebellion. It is directed against patriarchy and all other forms of oppression." (1994, 33). El-Saadawi's imprisonment in September 1981 by the direct order of President Sadat was, as she describes in her book *Memoirs from a Women's Prison,* an illegal act and a violation of human rights. Incarcerated without being charged or tried, she describes her life in the jail and the relationships that were forged with the other female political prisoners—also there without charge or indictment for any "crimes." The Kafkaesque quality of her experience is highlighted along with the development of her relationship with the other women, who, despite their ideological differences, formed a close community behind bars.

El-Saadawi's text of her memoirs from jail emphasizes the community spirit and the interpersonal exchanges between the women. Her description of her encounter with "the authorities" in the form of the chief prosecutor is narrated in only one out of the six sections of the book ("Out to the Investigation"), and it is written in an almost humorous tone in order to emphasize the ridiculous nature of the "charges" levied against her, the inconsistencies of the "law," and the sham structure of the judicial system under the Sadat regime. Although emphasizing her outrage and sense of injustice, the purpose of the text is remote from the horror and sense of fear inherent in Zangana's memoir, together with the sense of the difficulty of putting the personal experience into the concrete form of words, or sharing the horror and shame in order to gain cathartic release. El-Saadawi's jail experience reveals her egotism, yet the experience forces her to be introspective, to evaluate her stance of always being "right" in the face of "wrong." She writes that the worst of prison is not the walls and the inconvenience of being deprived liberty, but the "prison that is doubt. And doubt is the most certain of torture. It is doubt that kills the intellect and body—not doubt in others, but doubt in oneself. . . . The baffling, crushing question for the mind: was I right or wrong?" (1986, 136).

The experience she cites as being the worst torture is that of being without pen and paper—neither had she imagined that "pen and paper could be more dangerous than pistols in the world of reality and fact." When another woman inmate asks to write to her mother, the prison head responds, "[That is] utterly forbidden. Anything but pen and paper. Easier to give you a pistol than pen and paper" (49). So rigorously was this rule enforced that the women were forced to undergo body searches if suspected of hiding any paper. El-Saadawi herself wrote her prison journal on toilet paper, which she carefully hid under a tile in the bathroom. Her journal was her "escape" from the reality of the incessant noise and squalor of the jail (129), and in it she explored her *de profundus* thoughts and experiences. El-Saadawi argues that "pen and paper are a thousand times more threatening to the system than a bullet fired from a gun. When a tyrant dies he can be replaced. When an idea survives it can move a nation" (1997, 204).

Such philosophizing is not available in the face of real terror and the dehumanization of physical pain. Zangana's text reveals as much in its omissions and aporias as it does by what is written in the slim volume. Unlike Nawal's intense sense of injustice against herself, Zangana's main concern is for the suffering of her fellow inmates, as one by one her friends and former colleagues are dragged in after being tortured to identify her and for her to be tormented by their unimaginable suffering. The image of one man turned by torture into a "disfigured mass of flesh" continues to haunt her, and her text reads as the struggle of a human mind to come to terms with such witnessing (1991, 32). Similarly, her account of the months spent in a tiny cell with the other women is self-effacing, revealing without emotion details of her physical state while imprisoned.

The honesty of the book induces in the reader a profound sense of empathy, and it is empathy that Dominick LaCapra suggests as both an opposite to objectification and a "counterforce to victimization," one whose role "is important both in historical understanding and in the ethics of everyday life" (2001,

219). Working through the past involves and challenges dimensions of both history and self-understanding.

Self-understanding is a prerequisite for the elaboration of the self in autobiography. Without self-knowledge, autobiography is at best superficial and at worst egotistical. To write one's life is a form of primeval offering of the self, a sacrifice on the paradigm of the self/other altar. It is an act of symbolic mutilation (where the one is divided into many so that the parts may be once more gathered into a meaningful whole); the self is lost in order that it may merge with the greater identity of society and its understanding of itself. It is a procedure that requires some basic ritual tools such as honesty and an openness to change and growth within the process of analysis and working through. The writer is both Isis (the seeker of wholeness) and Orisis (that which must be restored to wholeness).

El-Saadawi's narrative *Memoirs from the Women's Prison* is not without its critics, and the text itself is not unproblematic when viewed as "factual," since much seems to be omitted, interpreted idiosyncratically, and avoided or even trivialized. She fails, for example, to point out that she was arrested along with fifteen hundred others in a purge of intellectuals who refused to support the Camp David agreement. Her arrest seems to be an isolated experience in which she alone has been victimized. In her 1986 review "In the Beggar's Cell," Ahdaf Soueif shows that el-Saadawi also fails to credit the other women in the prison for their own achievements as famous writers and protestors. Her cell mates, "all of them distinguished, fighting, articulate women . . . are here reduced to the role of a chorus providing backing for Sa'adawi's courageous outspokenness" (2004, 205). Soueif also takes el-Saadawi to task for making her memoir "a vehicle for self-promotion" and hopes that what she lacks in taste she makes up for in accuracy of information (206).

Significantly, el-Saadawi's other autobiographical works give scant reference to her prison experience but emphasize how such experience is extended in exile. Her autobiography, *Walking Through Fire,* alternates between personal details of her quotidian life and explicating episodes of her search for love relationships, her marriages, children, and divorces. Here again, episodes based on dream sequences and her imagination, her projections of near reality and what might have happened, are juxtaposed with graphic details of events and experiences that did, apparently, occur. These juxtapositions elaborate the narrow threshold between fact and fantasy, between memory and invention. This problematic point of view is one seen elsewhere in Arab women's approach to autobiography: the status of the identity of author/narrator and character is problematized and is often, ultimately, lacking an identity, exemplifying how woman's life script aims to overcome being "a non-story, a silent space, a gap in patriarchal culture" (Smith 1987, 50).

Nawal el-Saadawi uses fiction and autobiography to challenge and undermine both history and history-as-myth and to expose everything she determines to be present-day violations of human rights. Despite emotive exclamation, her prison diary reveals the heavy responsibility she feels in her writing: "Nothing in my life is more precious to me than writing but I think it requires even more courage than killing" (1986, 164–65). Though emphasizing her outrage and sense of injustice, Nawal el-Saadawi's extensive body of writing acts as a border crossing to access and challenge topics and experiences that have previously been held as taboo or as "culturally" acceptable. Generalizing her experience beyond the bounds of gender, class, ethnicity, or nationality and her technique of blurring fiction and reality are el-Saadawi's means of universalizing the prison—an attempt at crossing the boundaries of racial and cultural experience.

CONCLUSION

It is possible to place Arab women's autobiography within the framework of the global (and feminist) ethics of nonviolence, tolerance, truthfulness, and respect for life (see, for example Dower 2003). Yet the inconsistencies of Arab women's writing of trauma are indicative of both the nature of the "postmodern" world, fraught with self-doubt and the negation of transcendental certainties, and the manipulation of social and national identities by coexisting religious and neoimperialist forces. The politics of writing and publishing is responsible for criticism of any woman attempting to articulate personal and social "meaning," and especially women hoping to bridge academic boundaries of color and culture. At worst, Arab women face trial and imprisonment because they have dared to put their thoughts and experiences into writing; at best, they face criticism and misunderstanding, whether from political authorities or Euro-American academics and feminists who are often supporting a political agenda, as Haifa Zangana documents in her article "Colonial Feminists from Washington to Baghdad: Women for a Free Iraq as a Case Study" (2005).

In the account of atrocity and in the discourses of human rights, the novel, autobiography, and journalism merge as narrative forms. Writers take on the role of witness bearers and documenters of their own traumatic experiences as well as the wider sociopolitical implications of that historical moment to the community. The identity that is forged through such texts transcends gender and race; the women writers form a transnational group (within a framework of potential resistance) regardless of national identity or ethnicity. As Sidonie Smith comments (in the context of the testimonies by women sex prisoners in the Second World War), such women writers "testify to the embodied connection they feel to one another, a connection that carries the ethical force of collective witness" (2005, 128–29). Although Zygmunt Bauman (2003, 86) voices the very real danger of the tendency of victims to become victimizers, of the failure of victimization to humanize its victims, writers such as Haifa Zangana are not alone in their ethical concerns for our global society. Testimony, the power of remembering and retelling personal events, transforms apparent "victimhood" into a powerful act of human connectivity. The whole past (with its quotidian repetition as present) is never totally recaptured by memory; if it were, as Bauman argues, "memory would be a straightforward liability rather than an asset to the living" (87). The purpose of testimonial autobiography is, after all, "lest we forget."

11

A Journey of Belonging

A Global(ized) Self Finds Peace

NAWAR AL-HASSAN GOLLEY
AND AHMAD AL-ISSA

I do not think anyone in the West . . . knew what to make of me. I was an anomaly and therefore defied easy categorization. I had been born and raised in America, to be sure, but at the same time I was now a Jordanian citizen, I was addressed as "Your Majesty," and my perspective had broadened to include Arab and Muslim sensibilities. At the same time, I looked like an American, spoke like one, and understood American cultural references. I was married to a head of state who had inherited his position and his commitment to represent Jordan for a lifetime, not merely for four years. And so, as his wife, had I.

—Queen Noor, *Leap of Faith: Memoirs of an Unexpected Life*

Our age is characterized by two related phenomena: globalization and postcolonialism. Taken as broadly cultural phenomena, both have had a great impact on most academic disciplines, including, most important, literary studies, as both have great implications for the negotiation of identity, the processing of subjectivity, and the representation of the other—all essential paradigms of personal narratives.[1] This chapter looks at the personal and political memoir of Queen Noor of Jordan, *Leap of Faith: Memoirs of an Unexpected Life* (2003), in which the global and the postcolonial self meet in one persona at peace with itself and the world around it. Queen Noor's persona is a good site for

1. On how globalization and postcolonialism meet and differ, see Jay 2000.

examining global and postcolonial issues, mainly multiculturalism or cultural hybridity, transnationalism, and multilingualism.

Like some of the Arab women's works studied in this book, Queen Noor's story encompasses both her personal and her political selves as she charts her journey from the cultures in which she was brought up into her husband's, the conflicts in her multicultural childhood having forged a self-reliant and determined person who was able to make this transition. However, in contrast to many other autobiographical works studied in this book, because Queen Noor identifies so completely with her husband, we are given a portrait of a relationship in which the wife supports her husband both in his private life, in striving to make the family relationship work, and also politically in helping him in his work.

It is true that memoirs are not supposed to be comprehensive life stories. William Zinsser argues: "Unlike autobiography, which moves in a dutiful line from birth to fame, memoir narrows the lens, focusing on a time in the writer's life that was unusually vivid, such as childhood or adolescence, or that was framed by war or travel or public service or some other special circumstance" (1998, 15). Queen Noor probably would have written her life story, she acknowledges, later, toward the end of her active life when there would have been almost a complete story to tell (2003, ix). However, on the death of her husband, King Hussein of Jordan, on February 7, 1999, many people encouraged her to share her memories and her perspective on Hussein's legacy at a time when they might be of particular relevance. The writer does not dwell much on her childhood or discuss many other issues a full autobiography might have included. However, *Leap of Faith* is a five-hundred-page text that describes the personal and political life of not only the queen but also her husband, the king, in one book.[2]

Queen Noor's story is undoubtedly unique; however, she resists portraying a unique sense of self, as her full identification with her husband, manifested in the way she combines his life with hers in her book, confirms all critical debates on how the autobiographical self presented by women "renders inadequate not only generic definitions of autobiography, notions of the

2. Inasmuch as, and even more, Winnie Mandela's *Part of My Soul Went with Him* (1985) was about Nelson and Winnie Mandela, *Leap of Faith* is about King and Queen Hussein.

'completed' self, but also the notion of the unique individual self" (Golley 2003, 66). Throughout the book, we live with the king and queen in a rich narrative marked by the fusion of the personal and the political, the interjection of "he" and "I," the interlacing of anecdotes, the interlude of events, and the intermission of interrelated ideas. Indeed, the first chapter in the book, "First Impressions," is neither about the writer nor about her birthplace; it is about her future husband and his birthplace, the country she is soon to adopt. Her fascination and identification with Jordan, its history, traditions, and beauty, are expressed as early as page 2: "I had found myself spellbound by the serene expanse of desert landscape washed golden by the retreating sun at dusk. I was overwhelmed by an extraordinary sensation of belonging, an almost mystical sense of peace." This sense of belonging remains with her until the last page of the book.

Unlike the myriad political memoirs currently available, especially in the United States where everyone has a story to tell, and everyone seems to be telling it, Queen Noor's story is very special. It may not be written in the best literary style, but it is a story of an "unexpected life"; after all, she did not inherit her royal title. Rarely does one become a queen overnight. Hence, her memoir is also an account of a transition: from being an ordinary person to becoming a celebrity. Moreover, with the exception of Hanan Mikhail Ashrawi's *This Side of Peace* (1995), Queen Noor's memoirs are probably the first modern political memoirs of a female Arab politician. *Leap of Faith* is a rich and complex personal narrative in which most postcolonial issues can be examined, from multiculturalism and hybridity to border crossing, the notion of the self in relation to the other and otherness, the issue of the personal and the public, alterity, and English versus local languages. This reading of her memoirs shows how Queen Noor emerges in her memoirs as an icon but a no less real, global person. Written with the specific political purpose of bridging cultural divides and although not a complete autobiography, Queen Noor's *Leap of Faith* nonetheless offers a notion of the self and identity processing by a woman in the age of globalization and postcolonialism. Her transnational self defies all assumptions about the impossibility of belonging in a global postcolonial world.[3]

3. On how the concepts of globalization and belonging interrelate, see Croucher 2004.

QUEEN NOOR: A MULTICULTURAL AND TRANSNATIONAL IDENTITY

The persona revealed in *Leap of Faith* is an excellent model of the multicultural self with a transnational identity. The writer first learned about her multicultural roots, Swedish on her mother's side and Syrian on her father's, at the age of six. This multiple heritage gave the young Lisa, the queen-to-be, a new sense of identity, and for the first time she felt connected to a larger family and a wider world.[4] However, much to her mother's long-standing frustration, Lisa was drawn to her Arab roots rather than her mother's Scandinavian heritage. Queen Noor does not write much about her Swedish background and ancestors, but she writes at length about her Arab ancestors. However, her short reference to her grandmother's racist remarks is very symbolic of her rejection of her maternal roots (24). Being taunted about her Arab background by university colleagues might have caused the young Lisa to withdraw from society (36), but it also made her keener to identify with her Arab roots. She symbolically refers to how her Mediterranean Arab instincts surfaced in the (Greek) marketplaces, where she learned to bargain over every price and how it "was not easy to suppress the Halaby brothers' entrepreneurial genes" (31).

After marrying King Hussein, Queen Noor manifested her sense of belonging to Arab culture by intensifying her efforts to learn Arabic and by adopting Islam as her religion. Having been brought up to choose her own spiritual path, she was determined that the decision to adopt Islam would be hers and hers alone. Her paternal grandfather made a similar spiritual conversion from Greek Orthodoxy to Christian Science when he emigrated from Syria to settle in the United States. Unlike her father's family, though, who, as immigrants, had felt the need to assimilate and de-emphasize their Arab roots, Queen Noor would willingly and on her own terms grow to identify with and adopt Arab culture.

4. We have to apologize to Queen Noor for referring to her as Lisa, the name she has not used since her marriage to the king. We are using the name to refer to the queen before her marriage.

Indeed, her memoir is a personal expedition: a crossing from a state of liberalism into a life of spiritualism.[5] As a converted Muslim, Queen Noor feels, for the first time, a sense of belonging to a larger community, for which she was humbly grateful. She did not adopt Islam for convenience's sake. In fact, this sense of belonging to the Muslim community was to stay with her throughout her life with King Hussein, and a year after his death, she performed *umrah,* a shorter version of the hajj. The pilgrimage to Mecca, she says, was "an opportunity for me to distance myself from the material and temporal world and to reconnect with the purity of faith that had sustained and guided me throughout Hussein's illness and beyond. I also experienced another deeply comforting and uplifting dimension of my faith—solidarity with the larger Muslim community, or *Umma,* a community profoundly unified and at peace in Mecca, the birthplace and heart of Islam" (501).

The genuineness of the queen's true and wholehearted embrace of Arab and Islamic culture is demonstrated by the lengths to which she went to learn Arabic: a true Muslim should preferably know Arabic, the language of the Holy Quran. She demanded books on Islam and Jordanian history so she could study and learn as much as possible. Although she had been studying Arabic since she had first arrived in Jordan, after her marriage she redoubled her efforts to read and become fluent in Arabic, a difficult and demanding language. Eventually, she felt secure enough in the language to converse in Arabic and even to deliver formal speeches, but it was a long, difficult process, and even today she still has a raw feeling of inadequacy, constantly frustrated by her inability to master the language at a truly sophisticated level of fluency.

She was also insistent that her four children, Hamza, Hashim, Iman, and Raiyah, should be fluent in Arabic, defying the royal tradition of bringing in British and European nannies and hiring instead Jordanian nannies to help raise the children, causing consternation among family members. Queen Noor's insistence on learning Arabic and teaching it to her children is part of

5. Indeed, the journey that liberal Lisa makes into Muslim Queen Noor is the opposite of Saint Augustine's journey of conversion to Christianity in *Confessions,* which remains the model for all memoirists.

her awareness that culture and language are inseparable, an issue at the heart of most postcolonial literature.[6] It reflects her genuine desire to assimilate and adopt Arabic culture.

The queen-to-be not only willingly embraced Islam as her religion and took Arabic as her second language but even welcomed a change of name, from Lisa al-Halaby to Noor al-Hussein. It is not customary in Arab cultures to change a woman's family name after marriage, as in some Western traditions. Arab women keep their full names after marriage. The queen does not explain why even her first name was to be changed at all. She simply welcomes it and considers it the most precious gift the king ever gave her. "Noor" means "light" in Arabic, so her full name would be Noor al-Hussein, the "Light of Hussein." She confesses that her family, particularly her mother who gave her her birth name, had much more trouble accepting her new name. Although she understands this difficulty, eventually she became adamant that her mother use her new name. Because of her mother's continued resistance to the change, Queen Noor felt her mother was refusing to acknowledge her new life and the commitment she had made: "What she did not understand, until I explained it quite forcefully, was that I had made a lifelong commitment when I embarked on marrying King Hussein, and if she loved me and supported me, she had to recognize and accept that commitment as well. She never called me Lisa again" (110–11).

Acceptance of a totally new name is evidence of Queen Noor's willingness to adopt her new identity. She found it harder to adjust to her new title, though. This challenge came as a surprise, one not necessarily as pleasant as her new name: "I heard the announcement that he was giving me the title of Queen. . . . I was the only person, it seems, in Jordan and the Western world who was not fixated on what title I would have. The newspapers had been filled with conjecture ever since our engagement had been announced" (119–20).

The quest for identity formation necessitates a look into one's past. In her absolute embrace of Arab culture, Lisa was not anti-American. In fact, she loved her country, but her trust in its institutions had been badly shaken, especially after the Ohio National Guard shot four Kent State University students who were protesting America's secret intervention in Cambodia in 1970.

6. On the centrality of the question of language, see especially Ashcroft, Griffiths, and Tiffin 1989; and Thiong'o 1981.

America's military involvement in Vietnam, which she opposed vocally, and American racism against blacks, symbolized especially in her maternal grandmother, infuriated the young Lisa. She was to look elsewhere for a home. Her work experience in Iran made her aware of a fundamental lack of understanding in the West, especially the United States, of Middle Eastern cultures and the Muslim faith. Disenchanted with American politics, Queen Noor was more than happy with her new Arab and Muslim identity.

A COLLECTIVE SENSE OF IDENTITY

Leap of Faith, like many women's autobiographical writings, fits into women's self-writings that have been described as "a way to provide spaces within which women can talk about the complexities and pluralities of their selves" (Golley 2003, 69).[7] It has been accepted by many scholars that, unlike men's self-narratives where "characters and events are little more than aspects of the author's evolving consciousness," "the self discovery of female identity seems to acknowledge the real presence and recognition of another consciousness" (Mason 1980, 210). *Leap of Faith* presents a living model of a collective identity. The queen depicts her total and lifelong identification with her husband, country, culture, faith, and dreams.

The king and queen were to become political partners for life. In return for her devotion to the king's mission for peace in the Middle East, the king would trust the queen wholeheartedly: "I have complete faith in you," he would tell her. "You have never made a mistake" (148). For Queen Noor, this statement was an unequivocal vote of confidence. From the very beginning of their marriage, she acted as a sounding board for his international speeches. After the king's illness at the end of 1997, he asked his queen to speak on behalf of both of them at formal occasions, such as the Global Ottawa Land Mine Ban Treaty (469). Toward the end of their life together, the queen writes of her husband as her best friend, her dearest love and inspiration: "For twenty years we had been husband and wife, father and mother, life partners through international crises and domestic turmoil in Jordan. I had joined him with all my heart in

7. In her book, Nawar Al-Hassan Golley (2003) reviews critical debates on women's collective identity.

his quest for peace in the region and experienced with him every achievement and setback" (463).

The persona in *Leap of Faith* asserts the fluid identity that women represent in their self-writing as they define themselves in relation to others. Queen Noor's identification with her husband is the principal force in her life and in her memoir. However, this identification is not unprecedented. As discussed earlier, before meeting the king, Queen Noor, then Lisa, identified with her father and his culture. This connection was at the expense of her relationship and seeming lack of strong association with her mother and her culture.

Queen Noor does not go into many details about her family and childhood but is candid enough to refer to her parents' troubled marriage. The dysfunctional family atmosphere was so tense that the young Lisa begged her parents to divorce and, surprisingly, pleaded to attend a boarding school (34). However, these family tensions were also a positive driving force in Lisa's life. Her emotional distance from her parents would turn her into the independent person with an appreciation for communal relationships that she needed to be in her unique marriage. Queen Noor emerges in her memoirs as an ideal wife, mother, and stepmother. An independent young woman commits herself, out of sheer love and conviction, to a man with a history of three marriages and eight children and a whole country to rule under very difficult political circumstances.

Her self-reliance, wisdom, and determination to create a strong family, unlike the one within which she was raised, are evident throughout her memoir. Her sense of and respect for the king's privacy deny her the luxury of consulting family members and friends about accepting his marriage proposal:

> I felt a growing need to respond to the King's proposal. It would have been helpful to have someone to talk with, to help me sort things out, but there are no secrets in Amman. It was not that I doubted the discretion of my few close friends; however, I instinctively felt that it would be an infringement of his privacy for me to speak about him to anyone. Apart from his inner circle and his sister, Princess Basma, and her husband, Major Timoor Daghastani, whom we visited occasionally in the evenings, no one knew I was seeing him. Nor did I feel this decision was something I could thrash out with friends and family in the United States over the telephone. It would have to be my decision alone. (99–100)

Almost selflessly, Lisa was more concerned about making the right decision inasmuch as how her decision would affect the life of the king rather than herself:

> I agonized over my decision for the next two weeks, trying to work out in my mind whether I should question [King Hussein's] judgment in considering me to be the right choice for him and for the country. Although none of his previous wives had been born in Jordan either, what might be the negative implications for him in the Arab world if he married me? Would it matter that I was born in the United States? Was I suitable? I had lived an independent life, traveled in many different cou ne [*sic*] necessary to make a good wife for a king. (93)

She also thought of the political implications of this marriage:

> There were other considerations. America had long since replaced Britain as the major influence in the region, and its unflinching political support for Israel was highly unpopular in the Arab world, including Jordan. Might his own people feel antagonistic toward their King, even betrayed, by his choice of an American woman, albeit one with Arab roots? This was not a frivolous concern. The King's image had already been deeply affected in the region when an article in *The Washington Post* the year before alleged that he was on the United States Central Intelligence Agency payroll—a critical charge in a region where anti-American sentiment ran so high. The last thing I wanted to do was add fuel to this kind of damaging slander. (94)

She then worried about her social role, still in a dutiful manner: "I had always worked, not only out of necessity, but also because it was important to me to contribute to society" (93). And last, "on a more personal level, I wondered where I would find the strength for the difficult times that were bound to come. Would I be able to cope?" (93). But her main concern, which has never entirely dissipated, was whether she would be able to fulfill the role of the king's wife and consort and be worthy of his faith in her (109).

Upon hearing of the king's proposal, her father expressed some political fear about her safety, and her mother was concerned about the difference in cultural backgrounds. In the end, her love for the king with the beautiful eyes would win. King Hussein and Queen Noor would start a partnership in marriage that would last for more than twenty years, ending only in his death: "I had an incomplete picture of what the future might be, but I knew that no matter what happened, I would always have my work and the contributions I could make to the country to see me through. The King had let me know in so many words that he was offering me a partnership. That realization, too, helped me make up my mind. I had a job to do for a country I already loved, and an extraordinary man as a partner. Together we could make a difference" (104). Having made this decision, Noor would work very hard to prove that she had made the correct decision. She would willingly and fully devote herself to the well-being of his extended family but, at the same time, find a public role through which she could also fulfill her sense of achievement. Twenty years later, the queen is still as adamant in her loyalty as ever. During the king's sickness, she devoted herself wholeheartedly to making her husband well, protecting him from the outside world so that he could use all his energy to battle his illness. During this partnership, the queen was a devoted mother to her eight stepchildren and mother to four of her own. She made sure to offer love and understanding to all from the very first days. In fact, before taking off to Scotland on her honeymoon, she organized a gathering for all the king's children and their mothers, hoping to create a loving, secure, nurturing family spirit (119).

The queen's identification with her husband did not overshadow her attempt to identify with other members of the family. She tried hard to keep a complex family together, becoming a godmother figure in the royal household. Queen Noor might have overshadowed her own mother in the book, but as a mother herself she followed in her mother's footsteps, for, among the few references to her mother, she credits her with pursuing a "courageous if painful struggle for family peace" (34). In this sense, Queen Noor's memoirs assert the cultural empowerment of the maternal stance.

PUBLIC VERSUS PRIVATE: A PUBLIC MARRIAGE

Leap of Faith is a story of a transition from ordinary to royal life where the negotiation of the private and the public is at its best. Adjusting to a royal lifestyle was not particularly easy for a private and independent person like Lisa. A simple person by nature, Queen Noor had never really liked the lavish lifestyle of royalty. Indeed, her criticism of royal ways and her rejection blinded her judgment in some circumstances. For example, she mistook the royal lifestyle for cultural differences: "It was jarring to walk out of even my bedroom to immediately face a valet or a waiter or my husband's aide-de-camp. . . . Though some people might yearningly fantasize about such personal attention, I found it quite unsettling and intrusive. Over the years to come I would realize that some of this dissonance was cultural—the difference between a Western sense of privacy and personal space and an eastern emphasis on communal identity and space" (147). She did not reflect on the issue of lack of privacy connected with the lives of celebrities in any culture, not even when, many years later, she met Bill and Hillary Clinton and learned about their own "intense lack of privacy and the running commentary by the media and political opponents about every aspect of their life" (415). Queen Noor made another error in referring to a further aspect of royal life as a cultural difference when she criticized the palace staff for not conserving energy and for leaving lights on throughout the night. Forgetting that the palace staff were all British, headed by a British comptroller of the royal household (149), Queen Noor mistakenly considered this issue cultural rather than a difference between ordinary and royal lifestyles: "Perhaps our disparate views on the subject were partly cultural; the energy crisis in the United States had made Americans, including my family, quite conscious of the cost of consumption" (149–50). A strong believer in privacy, Queen Noor became resigned to the fact that the king and his family were public property (157) and that the most private of issues, including her first miscarriage, for example, was fodder for public consumption (185). Although she made many accommodations as she strove to find an effective balance between her natural inclination to privacy and the practical value of sharing enough of their private lives with others so those others could understand what the king and queen were trying to accomplish, she still continued to find the intrusion of the world into her private life very challenging. In fact, it caused her a lot of grief and sometimes depression (314–15).

The expectation that a queen might be expected to present a glittering image also caused her some problems, as it was neither in her nature nor what she considered useful as a representative of Jordan. Using Queen Sofia of Spain as a role model, she sought a style that balanced understatement and the need to look regal. As she became active in public life, she also learned to provide the type of public image she wanted the media to have. She started to "pick and choose what to emphasize, planning [her] schedule to achieve a balance between [her] more traditional ceremonial roles and [her] desire to focus on significant development initiatives—cultural, social, and environmental" (159). As a result, she became a queen who set her own priorities, establishing her own projects and speaking publicly on her own initiative. It would not have been possible for Lisa, the private person, to have published her memoirs, which is in itself "a gesture toward publicity, displaying before an impersonal public an individual's interpretation of experience" (Smith 1998, 436), had she not learned, as Queen Noor, the art of being a public person. Unlike many modern autobiographical writings by women who struggle to prove the personal is political, Queen Noor does not have to be personal because her life was a struggle at becoming public.

In examining the cosmopolitan identity of Queen Noor's persona, her memoirs, as a text, can be seen to be multiple in that they combine the genre of biography with personal and political memoir.

KING AND QUEEN AS ONE

It is the king whom we first meet, with Queen Alia before her tragic death, through the camera lens of the future queen in the winter of 1976 on page 1 of *Leap of Faith*. From page 3 on, we learn as much about the king as we do about the writer or probably even more. Before visiting Jordan, Lisa knew that the king had a "unique position in the region. He was a pan-Arabist with a deep understanding of Western culture, a consistent political moderate, and a dedicated member of the Nonaligned Movement" (3). In Jordan, she learned about the special respect the king had achieved among Muslims owing to his Hashemite descent from the Prophet Muhammad, peace be upon him. Having known him as a wife for more than twenty years, the queen writes about the king's family history: his special relationship with his grandfather King Abdullah; his early succession to the throne of Jordan; his political dreams, achievements, and frustrations; his hobbies; his love of horses, piloting, motorcycling, his ex-wives, and his children; his friendships; his relationship with the people; the kind of king that he was; his strong faith; and his personality. She writes about him with the love and admiration of a student for her mentor: "I thought I had learned a great deal from my reading and from meetings with foreign correspondents who would come through the region, but with King Hussein I was receiving a doctorate degree" (81). Although the book contains much about the king, it is the queen's persona with which this chapter is more concerned.

Helen M. Buss argues that the "memoir form" has the "ability to bring together self and other, private and public history" (2002, 158). Queen Noor's memoir is an excellent embodiment of bringing the personal and the political together. Like the king, as portrayed by her, who was both a public figure with large-as-life ambitions and also a warm person as father, husband, and friend, Queen Noor developed a self in which the personal and the political, the private and the public, were reconciled. While maintaining her role as a loyal wife and devoted mother, she became a partner to the king in his political work but would also independently develop her own public responsibilities. The queen played this complex role in spite of all the challenges of the roller coaster she was to ride throughout her life with the king, as she would be forced to stretch in every direction.

SHREWD POLITICIAN

"It would be highly controversial in some circles for the wife of a head of State, especially an Arab state, to deliver a political address rather than focusing on more traditional subjects such as children or culture. Hussein would be accused of using me, but I was no puppet" (243). For a private person, the queen, a fast learner, quickly became very shrewd in her dealings with not only the public but also her husband. Supportive of political reform and freedom of expression, the king appointed Leila Sharaf minister of information in the 1980s. Sharaf would later resign over the king's letter to the prime minister in which he chastised reporters for their lack of professionalism and reliability in stories that were critical of the 1974 decision to merge tribal and civil laws (300). The queen was faced with a terrible dilemma, as Sharaf had been her best friend and adviser since the early days of her marriage. The issue caused a great fuss.

Appearing in public next to Leila showed her implicit personal support without the need to take a verbal public position against the government. On another occasion, the queen showed great diplomatic skills when, much to the king's surprise, she granted him his wish to cancel the women's *iftar,* the evening meal at the end of Ramadan days that she had decided to hold in order to "bring together influential and dedicated women from different parts of the country to exchange information and share in this communal ritual" (301). She knew she was going to reinstate the women's *iftar* the following year. Indeed, over the years these events were to grow, and attendants included "diplomats, students, orphans, and people from various organizations" (302). A fast learner, the young royal bride "began by observing: trying to understand, to tread softly and not upset the daily routine or question the way things were done" (149). She gradually began to express her opinions but could not avoid ruffling feathers (149).

As she became more confident in her role as queen, she created her own work to complement the work of her husband. She writes about her work with children as chair of Jordan's National Committee for the Child; her contribution to environmental issues with the Royal Society for the Conservation of Nature, founded by the king in 1966; her establishment of the Royal Endowment for Culture and Education in 1979; her role as a catalyst for consensus building and action at the Royal Scientific Society (187–96); and her support for local and traditional textile, dressmaking, and glass industries (205–6). In the chapter "The Edge of the Abyss," we are casually told that she was inaugurated as the global education movement's president, succeeding Prince Charles (441), and that she received the Eleanor Roosevelt Val-Kill Medal for peace together with Lea Rabin in 1996 (452).

Two issues meant a great deal to the queen: "honor killing" and freedom of speech and expression. The queen was frustrated "about our inability to remove the outrageous and legally protected practice of 'honor crimes' from Jordan's penal code, which essentially gave men license to kill wives or sisters or daughters whom they accused of having had illicit sexual relations, with little fear of legal consequences" (447). The queen could only pay tribute to Rana Hussein, a journalist who "single-handedly brought this problem to the attention of the public in a series of newspaper articles over a nine-year period" (448). She also criticized the government for its "simple lack of political will, despite the Constitution and the religious law known as *shariʿa,* both of which are patently opposed to the so-called honor killings and forbid the taking of the law into one's own hands" (448). Over the years, the queen argued for more freedom of the press in Jordan and lobbied her husband and his key officials to reconsider their sometimes restrictive attitude toward personal and institutional freedoms (299), while she herself was under media attack around the world. Although she decried the irresponsibility of certain Western journalists, she felt just as strongly that there should be an outlet in Jordan for differences of opinion. The press in Jordan, though privately owned, was effectively government controlled. Truly independent reporting did not exist (299).

TEXTUAL STRATEGIES

Although *Leap of Faith* is Queen Noor's memoir, the voice is not always hers throughout the book. The memoirs are based on a "journal" or "diary" that she kept, as is evident from comments on several occasions such as "I wrote in my journal" or "I noted in my diary."[8] She takes sole responsibility for the views expressed (ix) in her book but admits that these views have been refined in the course of many spirited conversations with friends and advisers, whom she acknowledges by name. In the course of the book, Queen Noor writes with a seemingly unified voice. However, it is not difficult to hear her own and the voices of her "advisers" or ghost/shadow writers. In this sense, the book suffers from a multiplicity of voices, even though the queen insists that all views in the book reflect her own. Nevertheless, one can understand that this book necessarily recounts the personal and the political in the queen's life that she wishes to disclose to readers. Her voice includes all personal information and reflections, but it is also evident in other parts of the book where the data are clearly historical and political but where the shadow voices are more dominant. What distinguishes the queen's political voice from the voices of the ghosts is the way in which politics and political data are personalized. For example, in chapter 3,

8. Queen Noor refers to the journal that she kept for twenty-five years (x) as the source of information on these pages: 45, 91, 313, 342, 344, 352, 376, 377, 384, 395, 405, 407, 419, 422, 425, 427, 431 twice, 433, 439, 472, 476 three times, 478, 485, 488, 493, 495.

"Tehran Journal," the queen offers her own personal reflections on the society and country in which she lived and worked for two years. In this section, she describes the social and political situation in Iran when she was actually there, from 1975 to 1977. Here, because she is recounting events she witnessed, the voice sounds authentic. Though the focus of this section is the politics of Iran, the voice is personalized to a great extent. We read politics, but we also get something of Queen Noor's own interpretation of events: "I observed these developments with interest. As a young professional, I was intrigued by the special challenges facing young women in their public and private lives, particularly highly visible and active women like the Shahbanou, who so often seemed to draw fire because of their opposition to their husbands and for the failings of their society" (46). We hear her voice again when she states, "After coming to know the city and its people, I became quite disturbed by the destructive environmental and social impact I imagined the mammoth Shahestan Pahlavi project would have" (48) and "My urban planning work in Tehran had exposed me to the social and cultural fabric of a major Middle Eastern Islamic country" (51).

Shadow voices are especially clear in the pages that, for example, offer a detailed history of Jordan (60–74) buried in chapter 4, "An Audience with the King." Ghost voices abruptly interrupt the narrative in chapter 6, "Honeymoon at Gleneagles." Twelve pages are included in a chapter that should sound very personal, but we are suddenly reading about Jordan's political challenges, the creation of the Palestinian Liberation Organization (PLO) and its relationship with Jordan, the conflict between the king and PLO leader Arafat, and the Syrian "invasion" of Jordan in 1970, before hearing the queen's voice again in the section about Gleneagles.

The ghost voices, necessary and common in political memoirs, do interrupt the narrative, probably confuse the reader, and sometimes distance the reader from the queen; however, the resulting effect is not without critical implications. As argued in this chapter, *Leap of Faith* is the memoir of a queen and her husband, the king: the personal and the political are expectedly present. They cannot be dichotomized in the monarchs' life any more than the private and the public may be separated. The personal and the political are interwoven in the book in a way that emphasizes that a queen's life is not her own; the political will rule the queen's life for good. The intrusion of politics on her honeymoon and the inclusion of political data in that chapter mirror the queen's realization that "politics had become our constant companion" (133) and that she would have to live with this fact until the end.

LACK OF CONFESSIONALISM

Queen Noor is aware that memoirs are expected to reveal what is hidden: "Memoirs are by definition a deeply personal undertaking requiring reflection and a measure of introspection" (x). Rick Shenkman dooms to failure a memoir that does not reveal enough to engage the reader:

> A memoir to be successful must be honest. No president can afford to be truly honest. He can't explain the deals he made, the compromises he accepted, the sacrifices of his principles on the altar of personal ambition. So instead of the truth we get the president AS HE WOULD LIKE TO BE REMEMBERED. This is death to a good memoir. For a person who has spent their life concealing who they are—and all politicians do this to an extent—the memoir is especially unsuited as a literary form to presidents. For the memoir depends on revelation. (2004, n.p.)

Has Queen Noor succeeded in meeting such expectations? Such a question may garner different responses according to the reader's expectation. However, one way in which to answer the question is by relating it to the purpose that Queen Noor had in mind when writing her memoirs. Her purpose is spelled out clearly on the first page. As a believer in building cultural bridges as a means of promoting "constructive dialogue," she hopes that her book "will inspire some of its readers to put those ideals into practice." Having written the book in the spirit of reconciliation, she hopes that it "will contribute to a greater awareness, especially in the West, of events that have shaped the modern Middle East, and encourage a deeper understanding of contemporary challenges facing the Arab world as well as an appreciation for the true values of Islam." To achieve this goal, she "tried to write accurately and from firsthand experience whenever possible" (ix).

Leap of Faith does not reveal much about the personal lives of the queen, her husband, and her children precisely because the queen has not intended for her memoirs to do so. If she sounds "guarded and aloof, particularly when it comes to her private life and to her children" (Bennet 2003, n.p.), it is because she never promised that her memoirs would reveal that aspect of her life. This highly political purpose partly explains the modest and gentle style of the book. However, Queen Noor's total admiration of her king is behind much of the book's sense of propriety and mild critical style. The book's lack of confessionalism is reminiscent of the style of Huda Shaarawi (1879–1947), an early-twentieth-century aristocrat, in her *Harem Years: Memoirs of an Egyptian Feminist* (1986). Nawar Al-Hassan Golley argues that "Shaarawi's genteel style of writing reflects herself in real life and also her practical feminist demands" (2003, 47).

Queen Noor's politeness is evident in her comments on tense situations and people that she did not necessarily want to reveal much about her relationship with, such as the Queen Mother, with whom, she confesses, she "never had a very intimate relationship" (353). Her politeness in difficult situations, as described in the following quotation, shows the tension between self-assertion and self-effacement: "When I first began attending the Sunday gatherings at Zahran [the Queen Mother's palace] I had no idea of what the family conventions were, or what their expectations were of me—I knew that I was, understandably, the subject of intense curiosity and comment. In the absence of guidance, I followed my own instinct and tried to be polite and respectful, but I had to also be myself; otherwise I would have gone mad" (154). On her marital affairs, Queen Noor would only and very gently confess that some political events such as Camp David had a dramatic influence on the twenty-one years of her married life and her husband's quest for peace (176), but she does not go into any detail. On only one occasion does she express her anger at the king, and even then with an attempt to justify his actions:

> I became quite angry with Hussein. . . . I looked at him, dumbfounded by his seeming non sequitur, but I was discovering a pattern of behavior that would hold throughout our marriage. His response to any personal concern I expressed would be to counter with some greater problem that he was suffering from, in order to put my problem into perspective. I also learned that this man, who had the biggest heart in the world, could not talk about things that were personally painful to him precisely because he felt that pain so deeply. He just could not handle it. (186)

Queen Noor may have not bared her soul in the way other memoirists, such as Virginia Woolf, have, but there is no reason to doubt her motives and honesty.[9]

INTENDED AUDIENCE

Queen Noor, like many Arab women discussed in this book, is clearly addressing Western readers in her memoirs. Like Leila Abouzeid in *Return to Childhood: The Memoir of a Modern Moroccan Woman* (see chapter 6 in this volume, "A Muslim Woman Writes Back," by Pauline Homsi Vinson), she states in the acknowledgments that she wishes to "contribute to a greater awareness, especially in the West, of events that have shaped the modern Middle East, and encourage a deeper understanding of contemporary challenges facing the Arab world as well as an appreciation for the true values of Islam" (ix). Using her position as an insider, Queen Noor then embarks on a project of cultural understanding and appreciation. Even if the queen had not declared her purpose in writing her memoirs, the narrative shows that the intended audience is Western and non-Arab. Several historical and political accounts in *Leap of Faith* include details that a non-Arab reader probably needs to know.[10] Occasionally, the queen gives some specific details that only the intended audience might need. For example, Ramadan, we are told, is "the Muslim holy month of fasting" (163); the hajj and Hijri calendar also need to be explained for a Western reader: "Hajj. . . . spans five days of the last month of the Islamic Hijri year, which is approximately eleven days shorter than the Gregorian calendar. . . . Every able Muslim is obligated to make the Hajj to Mecca once in his or her life" (181). She further explains, "Arabic is the language of the Quran, which all Muslims, whether in the Middle East, the Far East, Europe, or the United

9. In 1920, Virginia Woolf read to the Bloomsbury group, one of whose goals was "absolute frankness," "a shockingly revealing memoir about her half brother's . . . incestuous relationship with her and her sister," which was later published as *Moments of Being.* See Barrington 2002, 11.

10. We would like to thank our student Abeer Fahmi, an English major (2001–2005) at the American University of Sharjah, for tracing the following page numbers as examples of the political data in the book: 45–51, 60–74, 84–90, 134–44, 187, 245–51, 319–24, 345–52, 356–63.

States, need to learn in order to read and recite daily prayers" (207). "Halloween," in contrast, gets no explanation (471).

Having an audience in mind is no deficiency in a book. In fact, most of the narrative appeals to any reader. For example, when she writes about what drew her to Islam, the narrative does not particularly address a specific reader. Even some Muslims can do with this reminder, for example:

> Islam's emphasis on a believer's direct relationship with God, the fundamental equality of rights of all men and women, and the reverence for the prophet Muhammad as well as all the Prophets and messengers who came before him, since Adam, to Abraham, Moses, Jesus, and many others. Islam calls for fairness, tolerance and charity: "Let there be no compulsion in religion," the Quran commands (2:256). And "Not one of you is a true believer until he desires for his brother what he desires for himself," reads one of the sayings of the prophet Muhammad. I was attracted, too, by its simplicity and call for justice. Islam is a very personal belief system. There are prayer leaders and religious scholars but no intermediaries or bureaucrats, as in other monotheistic religions. No Muslim is better than any other Muslim except by piety. Honesty, faithfulness, and moderation are a few of the virtues that Islam calls for, and by which one Muslim can have merit over another. (111–12)

CONCLUSION

Queen Noor can be seen as a role model for women around the world. Her personal and political devotion to a new community, beyond the borders of the country in which she was raised, shows women's ability to transgress borders, resolve differences, absolve mistakes, and embrace the Other without totally losing all sense of individuality. Her contribution to women's lives in Jordan cannot be denied. She, in her usual modest way, refers to some of the areas where her support was instrumental in changing Jordanian women's lives. A believer that "whenever women engage as equal partners with men, development and progress accelerate and endure" (446), she supported women in Jordan and the world in many ways. The queen was instrumental in encouraging some political reform, but owing to her modest style, she does not credit herself so straightforwardly.

A good memoir, argues William Zinsser, "requires . . . integrity of intention. Memoir is the best search mechanism that writers are given. Memoir is how we try to make sense of who we are, who we once were, and what values and heritage shaped us. If a writer seriously embarks on that quest, readers will be nourished by the journey, bringing along many associations with quests of their own" (1998, 6). How does Queen Noor do in her *Leap of Faith* according to Zinsser's criterion? In spite of the book's technical shortcomings, the analysis given here of *Leap of Faith* emphasizes the nobility of Queen Noor's quest in our highly divided world. The wholehearted adoption of an Arab Muslim culture by an American is especially inspiring and reassuring to Arabs in a world characterized by utmost despair owing to the imperial role the United States of America is playing in the Arab world and elsewhere.

Inasmuch as writing personal narratives is an act of liberating the self, for women in particular, reading *Leap of Faith* is an act of self-empowerment, too.[11]

11. On the power of self-writing, see Nash 2004, esp. 23–29, 75, 130, 157–59.

12

Art, Autobiography, and the Maternal Abject

MIREILLE ASTORE

Through the mangroves, I give birth and choke on an aerial root the size of an umbilical cord.

—Mireille Astore

I give birth to myself amid the violence of sobs, of vomit.

—Julia Kristeva, *Powers of Horror*

I make art in order to understand the self and to contexualize personal experiences within the framework of contemporary art discourses. It is my way of bringing different life forces together, of combining the ordinary with the extraordinary, the normal with the abnormal, and the subject with its abject. Through my art, I explore what it is to be a woman, an Arab living in a Western culture, and an artist. Julia Kristeva states that "the 'woman effect' entails a specific relationship to both power and language. . . . [T]his particular relationship is based on . . . being a source of silent support, a useful backdrop and an invisible intermediary" (Guberman 1996, 104).

Through the Maternal Abject photographic series, I attempt to construct a visual narrative on contemporary nuclear motherhood. In my images, the dismantling of spontaneity, the systemic isolation, and the cultural invisibility merge with the surrender of the self, the self that has been painstakingly constructed from dispersed and in some instances lost realities. As such, inherent conflicts about motherhood and my search for what binds me and separates me from my own children are the compelling forces behind this photographic series.

THE ABJECT

Georges Bataille defines *abjection* as "the inability to assume with sufficient strength the imperative act of excluding abject things (and that act establishes the foundations of collective existence)" (1970, 217). His interest in heterogeneous elements constitutes a project to strip away ideological screens and to expose hypocrisies that try to conceal and make palatable a basically meaningless existence. As a result, Bataille considers "the vilest, most discouraging and corrupted things in the world" (Ades 1976, 12). He calls abjection the inability to come to terms with the imperative of excluding the repulsive. He places the abject at the heart of our collective existence and tests the hypocrisy of a social order. Bataille has much distaste for banning from view processes that are very much part of life. He gives the example of temples, which in times past were places of prayer and slaughter. Through Western modernity, the two functions have become separated to such an extent as to become antitheses to each other. It is as if "acts of purification" take place with the sole purpose of rejecting the abject and to relegate it to the unseen (Hollier 1992, xii). It is interesting to note, however, that through *Halal* (religious acceptance in Islam), this relationship between slaughter and prayer has been preserved.

According to Julia Kristeva, abjection is a state of crisis, of self-disgust and disgust toward others. It is not so much the physically repulsive but that which "disturbs identity, system, order" (1982, 4). It is something that simultaneously fascinates and repels, distresses and relieves. It does not exist outside the self, yet it threatens it. It is that which has emanated from the person's sense of order, be it biological, social, or spiritual. Abjection is not only the individual's relationship to the more acknowledged forms such as vomit, excrement, and the corpse but also a whole set of systems that nurture that relationship. In religion, for example, it manifests itself as taboo or sin, and in a social and legal framework it is not unlike corruption. Therefore, to be in a state of abjection is to merge the Other, that which is outside the self, with the self. Kristeva describes the abject thus: "We may call it border; abjection is above all ambiguity. Because while releasing a hold, it does not radically cut off the subject from what threatens it—on the contrary, abjection acknowledges it to be in perpetual danger" (9).

The all-encompassing world of abjection does fill me with a simultaneous sense of horror and peace. The knowledge that I can never contain the abject and that it is within me, and indeed within every human being, fuels my search to identify it in all its manifestations. It is, as Elizabeth Grosz expresses it, "the impossible desire to transcend corporeality" (1989, 72). In fact, it is this search that I yearn for and that constitutes my artistic process. As Kristeva says: "When one is in a state of abjection, the borders between the object and the subject cannot be maintained" (Penwarden 1995, 22).

MOTHERING

Mothering is invisible and castrated. Susan Maushart in her book *Mask of Motherhood* (1997) details the way women negate their experience. Artists, including myself, have tended to also make less of the actuality of mothering. Julia Kristeva states that "we should recognise the civilising role that mothers play. . . . Feminists have not stressed this enough and neither have the media, who usually portrays mothers as housekeepers. . . . Mothers perform a sort of miracle by separating themselves from the children while loving them and teaching them to speak. . . . [T]his gives [the children] a corporeal and sensory pleasure as well as an intellectual one" (Guberman 1996, 10).

My interest in the maternal abject is a search into some of the processes a woman undergoes when she becomes a mother and the subsequent mother-child separation that occurs in the child. Physical, semiotic, and social phenomena take place when the child separates from the mother and forms its own identity, and these issues, which have historically not been given much credence, stimulate my art and my need to give them a visual representation. I investigate the barriers and misconceptions that a woman faces when she enters motherhood in a Western culture. I also examine the way motherhood is relegated to the domestic and how it renders her invisible.

THE MATERNAL ABJECT

It is through the process of making art that I explore my own psyche. I search for my own identity as a mother and the identity of my children through the channels that link us as well as the ones that separate us. It is a process of trying to understand the nature of that most intense form of love that occurs between two human beings, a love whose roots stem from an abject relationship whereby a mother tries to keep herself bound to the child while at the same time working continuously at teaching her child to become independent, to acquire language, and, finally, to separate from her. John Lechte (1990, 29) interprets the role of this love as necessary for the child to exit the oral and anal phases and to enter the acquisition-of-language phase.

I believe that it is in the maternal that the abject is most prominent. If we were to itemize this form of abjection, the cycle begins at the onset of pregnancy with the woman's "nausea"—also known as morning sickness. There, the abject resides within the visceral substance of the lining of the womb for the duration of the pregnancy. Grosz interprets Kristeva's abject this way: "Like the abject, maternity is the splitting, fusing, merging, fragmenting of a series of bodily processes outside the will or control of the subject" (Grosz 1989, 79).

The abject surfaces again during the birthing drive with the painful convulsions of the womb known as contractions, the rupture of the membranes, and the gushing of the amniotic fluid. Abjection then intensifies with the emergence of a squirming, visceral infant possibly via a tear in the woman's flesh, as in an episiotomy or in a caesarean section. There, both mother and child face simultaneously yet not independently the life and death drives. The umbilical cord, another piece of flesh, is cut with a sharp instrument to initiate the transformation of one being into two. Finally, the placenta, which has been the life-giving force for the infant, is expelled from the woman's body.

Very soon after the birthing process, abjection presents itself with the cause-and-effect process: mother's breast milk and infant's feces. For the mother, the infant's excrement, as separate from the screams, becomes the most intimate way the child can communicate with her. Through its color, consistency, and frequency, the mother faces the abject and returns herself to the preverbal stage of signs in order to learn and interpret the child's needs. It is at the end of the phase of breast milk and infant's excrement that another form of abjection takes place: the child's separation from the mother, its acquisition of language, and the mapping of its body.

Rosalind Krauss explains: "The child's losing battle for autonomy is performed as a kind of mimicry of the impassability of the body's own frontier, with freedom coming only delusively as the convulsive, retching evacuation of one's own insides, and thus abjection of oneself" (1996, 89). In other words, Krauss alludes to the fact that as a child attempts to separate from its mother, it approaches the act of abjection in order to free itself from within. From the time of birth until the child enters its own subjectivity, it does not distinguish between its own body and its mother's body. Therefore, to the infant, the mother's body is an extension or a part of its own, and it remains so until the child recognizes first its own body parts, and then its unified body. As such, the child is driven to expel the mother in order for it to exist. It is as if the child instinctively feels that as long as the mother is within it, it will never grow and become a subject. Expulsion of the mother's body is the child's first act of noncorporal abjection such as sucking, screaming, excreting, or vomiting. Therefore, by attempting to understand our relationship to the maternal or indeed trace its origin, we are in fact trying to understand our state of abjection.

Kristeva explains how separation from the mother coincides with the acquisition of language through the negation of the image and the isolated object (Oliver 1997, 42). In effect, what Kristeva is saying is that the relationship between a preverbal infant's physical world, which constitutes its mother's body, and the infant's attempts at formulating language and entering the semiotic has to reach a state of crisis in order for the acquisition of language to occur. This crisis is abjection, and it is where the process of negating the maternal presence or separating from her becomes a prerequisite to the child's acquisition of language.

Kristeva goes even further and relates the authority of the semiotic, the system of written and spoken signs, to another very important aspect of a child's socialization: the mapping of the body. "Through frustrations and prohibitions, this authority shapes the body into a *territory* having areas, orifices, points and lines, surfaces and hollows, where the archaic power of mastery and neglect, of the differentiation of proper-clean and improper-dirty, possible and impossible, is impressed and exerted" (1982, 72). Therefore, this site is where the body's mapping process becomes the point upon which all social systems and orders are built. Again, Kristeva points out how the mother's body becomes the mediator of the symbolic law organizing social relations (Oliver 1997, 37).

Grosz also explains how abjection serves the separating child to connect different parts of its body (1989, 71). For example, it is necessary to make the child realize that its own toes are connected to its own leg and that the leg belongs to the self, also that the child's hands, which are touching its own stomach, are all parts of a unified subject called "my body." She further explains how understanding abjection involves examining the ways in which the inside and the outside of the body relate, such as with food, or air, and the means by which the child's body becomes a unified whole.

Melanie Klein's psychic analysis of the child's separation from the mother is based on a field of objects to be fused or split, possessed or destroyed by means of fantasies produced by bodily drives. According to Klein, the first object of aggression, for example, is not the mother or father, but a series of part-objects (breasts, milk, penis, children, and so on) to which the infant fantasizes the connection of other part-objects (mouth, teeth, urine, and excrement) (Nixon 1995, 70). Therefore, through these fantasies, the body is mapped and a social order is built.

ABJECTION IN THE ARTISTIC PROCESS

I have looked at theories of abjection through Kristeva and the interpretive writings of Grosz: the role of the maternal in abjection theory and the relationship between acquisition of language, a child's separation from the mother, and the mapping of the body, the latter being a signifier in social orders, taboos, and sin. Through this search to understand my fascination with the abject and its manifestation in my own art practice, I examine the relationship between the artistic process and the maternal abject. First, I study Kristeva's analysis of the artistic process, or *text*—whether in literature or art:

> If there exists a "discourse" that is not a mere depository of thin linguistic layers, an archive of structures, or a testimony of a withdrawn body, and is, instead, the essential element of a practice involving the sum of

> unconscious, subjective, and social relations in gestures of confrontations and appropriation, destruction and construction—productive violence, in short—it is "literature" or, more specifically, the *text.* Although simply sketched out, this notion of the text already takes us far from the realm of "discourse" and "art." The text is a practice that could be compared to political revolution: the one brings about in the subject what the other introduces into society. (Oliver 1997, 30)

Hence, the body, the *text,* and the social order are linked into what the subject brings into society. *Text* is not merely a literary reference but rather a semiotic mode of reading and writing verbal as well as nonverbal signs. Kristeva further explains that the aesthetic process is a form of pursuit to resolve or harmonize the conflict between the semiotic and the forces that gyrate the person toward the mother's body through the drives: "Drives involve pre-Oedipal semiotic functions and energy discharges that connect and orient the body to the mother. We must emphasise that 'drives' are always already ambiguous, simultaneously assimilating and destructive; this dualism . . . makes the semiotized body a place of permanent scission" (37; see also 44).

In an interview on the Tate exhibition Rites of Passage: Art for the End of the Century, she explains that the artworks have a cathartic value and that the artists who produce them are in a temporary state of harmony while experiencing a malaise. However, she states, the artistic process "does not seal the [malaise] off or ignore it" (Penwarden 1995, 23).

The abject is by its very nature the permanent scission or crisis that resides in the life of the individual. This scission has its roots in the time the infant separates from its mother and performs its first act of noncorporal abjection. It is also the time the body of the infant is mapped through the teaching of language and the initiation of what is taboo and what is not. Through this mapping, the individual is introduced to the particular social structure in which it will grow. For example, in some Islamic cultures, a baby girl who is not yet verbal learns through signs and while acquiring language that hair on a woman's head must be covered, whereas hair on the body is considered unclean and must be removed. Therefore, a woman's hair becomes a signifier for a range of prohibitions that form the basis of that particular social order. However, a baby boy's circumcision is performed as a ritual and forms for the boy the basis of what is clean and unclean within this social and religious order. At a particular time in history and in a certain social hierarchy, a Chinese girl's feet had to remain small and were bound, restricting the girl's (woman's) movement. A girl's or woman's feet therefore were a signifier for a complete set of social rules and expectations.

These examples illustrate how the mapping of an infant's body is the building block of social structures and the possible site of scission or malaise in an artist. Shirin Neshat is an Iranian artist who illustrates well how the body is mapped through the veil and how this mapping becomes a malaise or a scission in her life. In her work *Rapture* and many of her previous works, she focuses on the meaning of the hidden female body in an Islamic culture through the veil. James Rondeau says: "Neshat maintains a critical distance that has allowed her to locate both the poetics and the power of the veil" (2000, 92). Therefore, Neshat shows us how when she expresses her abject experience in a particular social or religious order she inadvertently refers to the maternal abject that, as previously mentioned, constitutes the mapping of the body (in this instance, the covering of a woman's hair), separation from the mother, and acquisition of language.

Kristeva postulates that there exists in the life of the artist an oscillating continuum between the production of art and the coming to terms with the presence of a scission or separation. It then follows that in order for the artist to exist, she or he has to experience a state of conflict echoing the original abject experience that begins at the time the child tries to separate from its mother. The maternal abject with its scission and malaise therefore is that particular energy that drives my art practice.

CONSTRUCTION OF THE MATERNAL ABJECT SERIES

In the Maternal Abject series, I explore three major areas. The artworks consist primarily of photographic images that have been scanned, layered, and digitally manipulated. Each layer represents an idea or a reference. The layers are then merged together in one image in order to create a dense landscape of visual dialogue (fig. 1).

There are three major themes running through this series. First, the visual representation of the mother's body is quite pronounced owing to the fact that

1. *DeadBird Mary.* Photograph courtesy of Mireille Astore.

apart from the icon of the Madonna and child in Western art, women as mothers are very rarely seen in art. I note their absence and crave their presence.

Second, I incorporate the naked body of the mother in all images in order to highlight the vulnerability and strength of her body and to focus on the physical nature of a mother's work. It was a conscious, deliberate, and labored decision given the widespread exploitative visual representation of the female body and its subsequent objectification. Danielle Knafo (1996, 1) points out that a shift to a new female aesthetic has taken place in the past decade precisely because female artists have chosen to use the female body to signify their own experiences.

In essence, I use the body as an encoded message to extract the voyeur in the viewer but only to reflect and subvert his or her voyeurism. In order to do so, I merge with the body threatening structures such as spikes, metallic constructions, and rocky surfaces. At times, such as in *Body Map* (fig. 2), I strip the skin and attempt to expose what lies beneath, such as veins and organs. In doing so, I aim to construct a performance of pain.

Paradoxically, these painful representations serve a different purpose. The hard labor a woman faces right from the beginning of her journey into motherhood, at the onset of the birthing process, through to the time the child is walking, talking, and toilet trained, is often hugely underestimated. Except for the birthing process, the toll on her body is very rarely acknowledged. Through the use of these threatening objects, I attempt to give to these ephemeral intruders a material presence that then acts on the naked and vulnerable body.

Finally, I use aesthetic processes such as a glossy and delicate surface of rich colors in a darkened background. I do so in order to draw the viewer inside the work. Thus, the images are denser and offer complexity as well as density.

THE PERSONAL IS POLITICAL

Artists whom I position within the circuit of my own art production, such as Mona Hatoum and Shirin Neshat, focus on various forms of the personal and invoke the political. This idea of the personal versus the political holds an important place in my work.

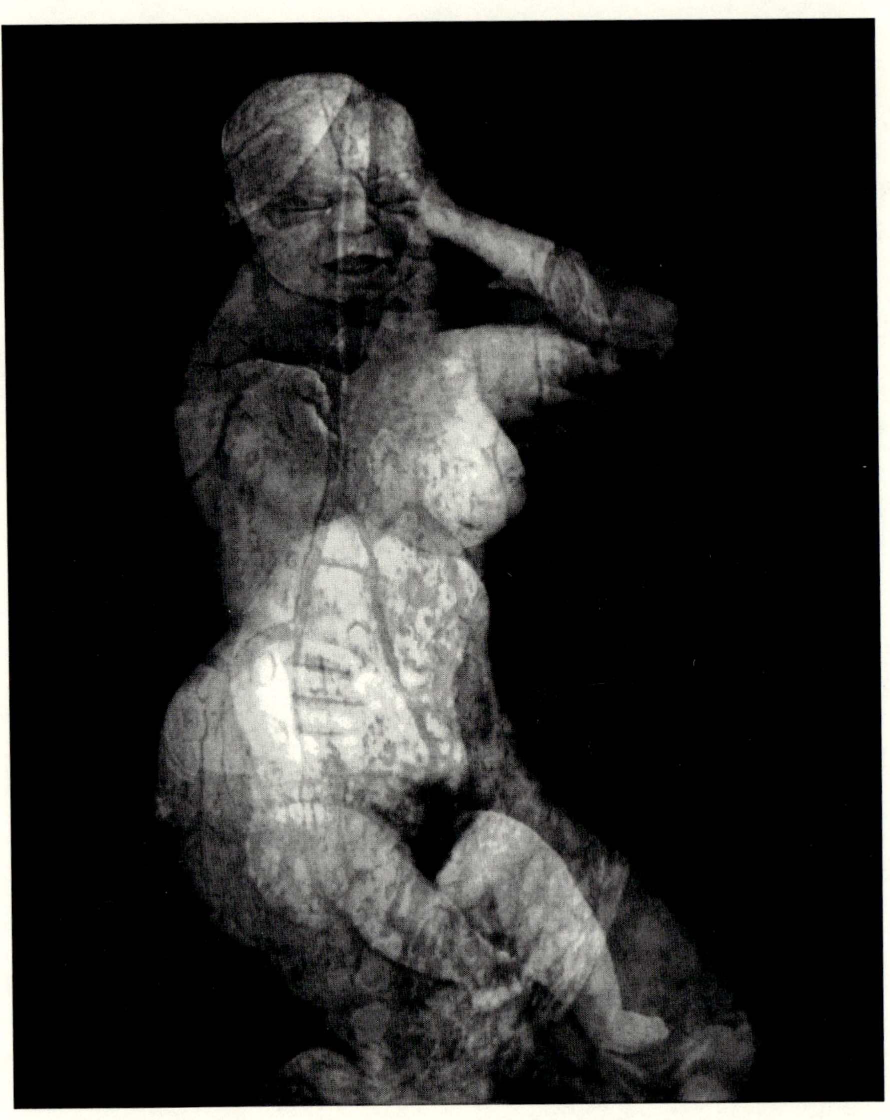

2. *Body Map.* Photograph courtesy of Mireille Astore.

One intriguing issue that persists in my work and is the driving force in all my artistic pursuits is the belief that all my experiences are not particularly unique. Indeed, my desire to articulate, demonstrate, and exhibit my inquiry into the self stems from a strong belief that I am not alone in my experience. However, my experiences lead me to believe that the self is mostly misunderstood or effaced in order to negate, as Georges Bataille (1970) writes, the presence of the all-encompassing abject experience. He disregards the hypocrisy of exclusion and the hiding of abject processes that are very much part of life. It is as if the inherited social order is the inertia or gravity from which the self cannot escape and that acts as the agent to destroy the abject within the self. The question that drives my inquiry is, then, how can a social order continue to exist if it negates the existence of the abject within itself? One method, I believe, is the relegation of the abject to the private sphere and the public dismembering of its existence.

The festering anger, the silent sobs, the closed doors all merge and are confined to the home, which becomes a sanctuary for these abject processes. The abject, however, is no less a public function of the human experience than a natural spring spewing water from the earth. The earth, which is the recipient of abject objects such as corpses and excrement, is at the same time the nurturer of seeds and trees. Therefore, by exposing and framing the abject publicly in my artwork, I am exposing that which is hidden in the self. Piero Manzoni talks about art production as a deep exploration of the self (Hatoum 1997, 108). He says that being subjective while being inventive is the only means of discovering objective realities and that it is the only possible means to communicate. He explains that subjective invention through the production of art emanates from the self and that objective realities are the public manifestations of that art. Communication is certainly an essential part of why I produce visual art and my need to bring the personal to the public sphere.

Returning to the reading of contemporary maternal abjection, I will now look at and explore the relegation of the maternal to the personal or private sphere. In effect, when a woman surrenders to the biological demands of the cultural construction of Western nuclear motherhood, she enters the sphere of the private, her home, where the only social or public interactions she has take place either through the father of her child or her child's support agencies. Here she is not seen, and a social blindness takes place. The unquestioned fact that a mother's daily work has no monetary value translates as peripheral or private in all social manifestations. It would appear puzzling how the tasks of a mother such as planning, analyzing, supervising, cooking, feeding, nursing, cleaning, purchasing, educating, counseling, documenting, preserving, liaising, and budgeting are not ascribed distinct monetary values. Yet all these tasks performed outside the home do indeed have wide-ranging salaries and associated benefits such as retirement plans as well as social status. Nighttime, in particular, is the site of much conflict in mothers, whether physical or mental or both. Exhaustion, anxiety over the well-being of the infant or child, and sleep deprivation ironically act as catalysts for a heightened level of awareness of what it means to be a mother. Kate Figes says that the exhaustion that mothers experience can be so profound that it makes them more susceptible to other problems common after childbirth such as "ill-health, depression, lowered self-esteem, angry outbursts, and poorer social or sexual relationships" (2000, 110).

Therefore, the maternal function, through a series of historical, biological, social, and economic realities, has been relegated to the private sphere where it is allowed to merge with the abject silently, away from the public sphere. Rita Felski (1989, 72) explains how the slogan "The personal is political" serves to emphasize that child care, rape, abortion, and the gendered division of labor are, in fact, political issues. She adds that these supposedly "personal" problems, which have particularly affected women, are fundamental questions of power and underpin the most deeply rooted aspects of social organization.

Although the maternal experience has of course been present from the beginning of time, its female expression in art is minuscule in comparison to other issues, a notable example being the sexual. Felski (1989, 25) proposes that the whole notion of the female aesthetic and the artistic process is inherently an autobiographical function. If so, where then can a mother with the previously listed tasks find the time to practice a maternal aesthetic? This lack of time indeed adds to the isolation of the mother and the enforced domestication of her work. It is as if the weight of her role serves to deny its self-expression and becomes publicly scarce and private: abject.

To quote the Victorian feminist critic and writer Anna Jameson: "You must change the physical organization of the race of women before we produce a Rubens or a Michelangelo" (Holcomb 1987, 15). In other words, we must change a whole set of values and social structures for women to be able to dedicate a good proportion of their life to the production of art and to produce lasting masterpieces such as the works of Rubens or Michelangelo. Then, once they have been able to produce works of such grandeur, a further issue is to keep the author's identity from disappearing through male-dominated historical channels.

In *Endoscopic Journey* (fig. 3), the viewer is invited to go down a well in the dark where mystery and intensity merge in order to create a sense of loss and ambiguity. The child in my images is often acting on the mother's body and mind. I attempt to portray a sense of relentless attachment. Either on the breast, on the stomach, or on the feet, the child is omnipresent.

In *Body Map* (fig. 2), the child even takes over the whole head of the mother, and they become one. The symbiotic relationship is symbolized with the merging of the two bodies. At times, as in *Endoscopic Journey* (fig. 3), the child is in the same image but at a different age. This double appearance is to accentuate the perpetual demands a child makes on the mother and to highlight the different roles the mother is meant to perform. The imposed isolation is not only the product of her home-centered experience but also of the Western mother-unfriendly environment outside the home. From nonsloping footpath curbs to a total absence of seats in supermarkets, these public indicators communicate a social or economic taboo for women as mothers and push them further back in the realm of the hidden and private. Figes concludes: "The outside world seems at times so hostile and difficult to navigate with a small baby that many women retreat into isolation" (2000, 210). And indeed this isolation feeds on itself and becomes a terrain fraught with anxiety, low self-esteem, and depression.

THE "PERSONAL IS POLITICAL" IN THE WORKS OF MONA HATOUMI

A clear example of the political nature of the personal can best be illustrated in Mona Hatoum's performance *Pull* and the two installations *Recollection* and *Mother and Child.*

In the two-hour performance *Pull,* the viewer was invited to pull a hank of hair hanging down in a specially constructed niche below a TV screen at

3. *Endoscopic Journey.* Photograph courtesy of Mireille Astore.

the Küntslerwerkstatt, Munich. When the hair was pulled, the artist's face on the screen registered a feeling of pain or discomfort. The hank of hair was, in fact, attached to Hatoum, despite the illusion of the TV screen above it. The TV screen and the viewer acted as the public sphere, and the artist's face and body physically behind the screen acted as the personal sphere. In this performance Hatoum placed her actual face and body behind a TV screen rather than making a filmed recording representing it. She did so in order to draw the spectator's attention to the private versus public dichotomy and to invite the participating viewer to question the realm of the public media and the private bodily experience of pain. In *Pull,* Hatoum also signifies the disjuncture between the images of violence seen almost daily on TV screens and the personal experience of those individuals being subjected to the reality of this violence.

In *Recollection,* where hundreds of hair balls are strewn on the floor of a room, she confronts the viewer's revulsion with a personal bodily item: hair. Hair invokes contradictory reactions, from fascination to abjection, particularly when detached from the body. A detached hair on a shoulder is brushed away, whereas a mass of hair on a shoulder acts as an attractor. Catherine de Zegher (Hatoum 1997, 88) extrapolates Kristeva's systemic abject through Hatoum's works by explaining how the connotation of beauty and identity, and the delicate, eroticized, and lasting of human materials, is also considered unclean. De Zegher believes that through this work, Hatoum leads us directly into symbolic systems of purity and abjection and, consequently, toward issues of power and oppression. She says that Hatoum's work is "a complex reflection on bodily pollution, involving the relation of order to disorder, being to non-being, form to formlessness, and life to death." According to de Zegher, this work affirms the way in which social ordering is based on behavioral patterns of dirt affirmation and dirt avoidance. In choosing a personal bodily item and placing it in a public room for viewing, Hatoum has successfully highlighted the political nature of the personal object.

Mother and Child holds a specific interest for me through its implied symbiosis and the piece's relationship to the maternal abject. Here, I am interested in Hatoum's relationship with her own mother. The piece is meant to deal with violence on the personal level, and Hatoum referred to it as *Mother and Child.* She says: "The two chairs have an unequal but inescapable relationship. They are angular, cold, and cage-like, but at the same time there's a symbiotic relationship between them because they are similar" (1997, 23). The two chairs are facing each other and positioned too close for comfort. If one were to imagine a person sitting on the smaller chair representing the child, the body on the large chair representing the mother would simply engulf or squash the person sitting on the small chair. It seems as if Hatoum in this piece has come as close as she could to materializing and symbolizing her maternal abject through her separation from her mother and the conflict she feels as an artist within this separation.

These three examples of Hatoum's work relate to my own work in the way they render the personal abject experience public. Emotions and gestures that typify the private mothering experience such as the breast-feeding infant, the cuddles, the entrapment, the claustrophobia, the birthing pains, the visceral infant, the dread, the self-doubt, the sleeplessness I render public in my work. It is not unlike the way Hatoum explored the facade of the public rendered private with the performance piece of hair pulling, the viewer's and her own relationship to hair, her cagelike chairs and relationship to her own mother.

CONCLUSION

Abjection is the hypocrisy of social hygiene conveniently relegated to the private sphere where it is allowed to merge with all that is unwanted by a particular social order. It is the site of conflict, crisis, sin, and war. It has no borders. More specifically, maternal abjection is the point at which the infant separates from the mother, acquires language, and maps its body. Paradoxically, the maternal abject is intrinsic to the aesthetic process, a process that seeks to synchronize a conflict whose roots stem from the phase of mother-child separation. It is through the maternal abject that the artist brings abjection to center stage in order to harmonize the social order he or she finds himself or herself in. The maternal abject therefore is the entity that resides within the self and the site where the self is in a constant state of negotiating order and disorder, implosions and explosions, life and death.

R E F E R E N C E S

I N D E X

References

Abbas, Ihsan. 1956. *Fan al-Sira.* 2d ed. Beirut: Dar al-Thaqafa.

Abdi, Abdul A. 1999. "Frantz Fanon and Postcolonial Realities: A Temporal Perspective." *Wasafiri* (Autumn).

Abdo, Nahla. 1994. "Nationalism and Feminism: Palestinian Women and the Intifada—No Going Back." In *Gender and National Identity,* edited by Valentine Moghadam, 148–73. London: Zed Books.

Aboulela, Leila. 1999. *The Translator.* Edinburgh: Polygon.

Abouzeid, Leila. 1989. *The Year of the Elephant: A Moroccan Woman's Journey Toward Independence.* Translated by Barbara Parmenter. Austin: Univ. of Texas Press.

———. 1998. *Return to Childhood: The Memoir of a Modern Moroccan Woman.* Translated by Heather Logan Taylor. Austin: Univ. of Texas Press.

Abu-Lughod, Ibrahim. 1988. "Territorially-Based Nationalism and the Politics of Negation." In *Blaming the Victims,* edited by Edward Said and Christopher Hitchens, 193–206. London: Verso.

Accad, Evelyne. 1995. "Arab Women's Literary Inscriptions: A Note and Extended Bibliography." *College Literature* 22, no. 1: 172–80.

Ades, D. 1976. "Web of Images." In *Dada and Surrealism Reviewed,* by D. Ades. London: Arts Council of Great Britain.

Adnan, Etel. 1982. *Sitt Marie-Rose: A Novel.* Translated by Georgina Kleege. 1978. Reprint, Sausalito, Calif.: Post-Apollo Press.

———. 1985. *The Indian Never Had a Horse, and Other Poems.* Sausalito, Calif.: Post-Apollo Press.

al-Afghani, Sayyid Jamal al-Din. 1968. *An Islamic Response to Imperialism: Political and Religious Writings of Sayyid Jamal al-Din al-Afghani.* Translated and edited by Nikki R. Keddie. Berkeley and Los Angeles: Univ. of California Press.

———. 1970. *The Emergence of the Modern Middle East: Selected Reading.* Translated and edited by Robert G. Landen. New York: Van Nostrand Reinhold.

Aflaq, Michel. 1982. "The Arab Personality Between Past and Present." In *Islam in Transition: Muslim Perspectives,* edited by John J. Donohue and John L. Esposito. Oxford: Oxford Univ. Press.

Ahmad, Muneer. 2002. "Homeland Insecurities: Racial Violence the Day after September 11." *Social Text* 72: 101–15.

Ahmed, Leila. 1978. *Edward W. Lane: A Study of His Life and Works and of British Ideas of the Middle East in the Nineteenth Century.* London: Longman.

———. 1982. "Western Ethnocentrism and Perceptions of the Harem." *Feminist Studies* 8: 521–34.

———. 1989. "Feminism and Cross-Cultural Inquiry: The Terms of the Discourse in Islam." In *Coming to Terms: Feminism, Theory, Politics,* edited by Elizabeth Weed. New York: Routledge.

———. 1992. *Women and Gender in Islam.* New Haven: Yale Univ. Press.

———. 1999a. *A Border Passage: From Cairo to America—a Woman's Journey.* New York: Penguin Books.

———. 1999b. "Growing Up Muslim: One Woman's Story." Interview and review by Susan Geller Ettenheim. *Cybergrrl,* June 11. http://www.cybergrrl.com/fs.jhtml?/fun/bookgrrl.

al-Ali, Nadje Sadig. 1994. *Gender Writing/Writing Gender: The Representation of Women in a Selection of Modern Egyptian Literature.* Cairo: American Univ. in Cairo Press.

Alloula, Malek. 1981. *Le harem colonial: Images d'un sous-erotisme.* Geneva and Paris: Éditions Slatkine.

———. 1986. *The Colonial Harem.* Translated by Myrna Godzich and Wlad Godzich. Minneapolis: Univ. of Minnesota Press.

Andrea, Bernadette. Forthcoming. *Women and Islam in Early Modern English Literature.* Cambridge: Cambridge Univ. Press.

Antonius, George. 1939. *The Arab Awakening: The Story of the Arab National Movement.* Philadelphia: J. B. Lippincott.

Antonius, Soraya. 1983. "Fighting on Two Fronts: Conversations with Palestinian Women." In *Third World: Second Sex,* edited by Miranda Davies. London: Zed Books.

Armah, Ayi Kwei. 1995. *Osiris Rising.* Dakar: Per Ankh.

Ashcroft, Bill. 2001. *On Post-colonial Futures.* London: Continuum Press.

Ashcroft, Bill, Gareth Griffiths, and Helen Tiffin. 1989. *The Empire Writes Back.* London: Routledge.

Ashrawi, Hanan Mikhail. 1991. "Principles, Politics, and Pronouns." In *Israel/Palestine: The Quest for Dialogue,* edited by Haim Gordon and Rivca Gordon. New York: Orbis Books.

———. 1995. *This Side of Peace: A Personal Account by Hanan Ashrawi.* New York: Simon and Schuster.

Atiya, Nayra. 1982. *Khul-Khaal: Five Egyptian Women Tell Their Stories.* Syracuse: Syracuse Univ. Press.

Aziz, Barbara Nimri. 2004. Foreword to *Scheherazade's Legacy: Arab and Arab American Women on Writing,* edited by Susan Muaddi Darraj, xi–xv. Westport, Conn.: Praeger.

Badran, Margot. 1995. *Feminists, Islam, and Nation: Gender and the Making of Modern Egypt.* Princeton: Princeton Univ. Press.

Bakhtin, Mikhail M. 1981. *The Dialogic Imagination: Four Essays.* Edited by Michael Holquist and Vadim Liapunov. Translated by Vadim Liapunov and Kenneth Brostrom. Austin: Univ. of Texas Press.

Balibar, Etienne. 1994. *Masses, Classes, Ideas: Studies on Politics and Philosophy Before and After Marx.* London: Routledge.

Barber, Benjamin. 1993. *Jihad vs. McWorld: How Globalism and Tribalism Are Reshaping the World.* New York: Ballantine Books.

Bardenstein, Carol. 1998. "Threads of Memory and Discourses of Rootedness: Of Trees, Oranges, and the Prickly-Pear Cactus in Israel/Palestine." *Edebiyat: The Journal of Middle Eastern Literatures* 8, no. 1: 1–36.

Barrington, Judith. 2002. *Writing the Memoir: A Practical Guide to the Craft, the Personal Challenges, and Ethical Dilemmas of Writing Your True Stories.* 2d ed. Portland, Ore.: Eighth Mountain Press.

Barthes, Roland. 1968. *Writing Degree Zero.* Translated by Annette Lavers and Colin Smith. 1953. Reprint, New York: Hill and Wang.

Bataille, Georges. 1970. "L'abjection et les formes misérables." In vol. 2 of *Essais de Sociologie: Oeuvres Complètes.* Paris: Gallimard.

Bauman, Zygmunt. 2003. *Liquid Love: On the Frailty of Human Bonds.* Cambridge: Polity.

al-Bazzaz, Abd al-Rahman. 1982. "Islam and Arab Nationalism." In *Islam in Transition: Muslim Perspectives,* edited by John J. Donohue and John L. Esposito. Oxford: Oxford Univ. Press.

Ben, Myriam. 1986. *Sabrina, ils t'ont volé ta vie.* Paris: L'Harmattan.

Benjamin, Walter. 1968. *Illuminations: Essays and Reflections.* New York: Schocken Books.

Bennett, Elizabeth. 2003. "A Slice of Royal Life: Queen Noor Recalls a Tough Transition." *Houston Chronicle,* May 9. http://www.chron.com/cs/CDA/ssistory.mpl/ae/books/reviews/1901968.

Beyala, Calixthe. 1996. *L'assèze l'Africaine.* Paris: J'ai Lu.

Bhabha, Homi. 1986. "Remembering Fanon: Self, Psyche, and the Colonial Condition." Foreword to *Black Skin, White Masks,* by Frantz Fanon. Translated by Charles Markmann. London: Pluto Press.

———. 1994. *The Location of Culture.* New York: Routledge.

Boehmer, Elleke. 1995. *Colonial and Postcolonial Literature.* Oxford: Oxford Univ. Press.

Boer, Inge C. 1995. "Remastering the Master Narrative; or, Feminism as a Travelling Theory." In *Changing Stories: Postmodernism and the Arab-Islamic World,* edited by Inge Boer, Annelies Moors, and Toine van Teeffelen. Amsterdam: Rodopi.

Bouraoui, Nina. 2000. *Garçon manqué.* Paris: Stock.

———. 2002. *La vie heureuse.* Paris: Stock.

Burnett, Paula. 2001. "Ahdaf Soueif: Talking about *The Map of Love.*" *EnterText* 1, no. 3 (Autumn): 97–112. http://people.brunel.ac.uk/~acsrrrm/entertext.

Buss, Helen M. 2002. *Repossessing the World: Reading Memoirs by Contemporary Women.* Toronto: Wilfrid Laurier Univ. Press.

Cainkar, Louise. 2002. "No Longer Invisible: Arab and Muslim Exclusion after September 11." *Middle East Report* 224: 22–29.

Camus, Albert. 1951. *L'homme révolté.* Paris: Gallimard.

Cixous, Hélène. 1976. "The Laugh of the Medusa." Translated by Keith Cohen and Paula Cohen. *Signs* 1: 875–93.

cooke, miriam. 1998. "*Ayyam min hayati:* Prison Memoirs of a Muslim Sister." In *The Postcolonial Crescent: Islam's Impact on Contemporary Literature,* edited by John Hawley. New York: Peter Lang.

———. 2001. *Women Claim Islam: Creating Islamic Feminism Through Literature.* New York: Routledge.

Cosslett, Tess, Celia Lury, and Penny Summerfield, eds. 2000. *Feminism and Autobiography: Texts, Theories, and Methods.* London and New York: Routledge.

Croucher, Sheila L. 2004. *Globalization and Belonging: The Politics of Identity in a Changing World.* Lanham, Md.: Rowan and Littlefield.

Dajani, Souad. 1995. *Eyes Without Country: Searching for a Palestinian Strategy of Liberation.* Philadelphia: Temple Univ. Press.

Daly, Mary. 1973. *Beyond God the Father: Toward a Philosophy of Women's Liberation.* Boston: Beacon Press.

Danielson, Virginia Louise. 1998. *"The Voice of Egypt": Umm Kulthum, Arabic Song, and Egyptian Society in the Twentieth Century.* Chicago: Univ. of Chicago Press.

Darraj, Susan Muaddi. 2004. Introduction to *Scheherazade's Legacy: Arab and Arab American Women on Writing,* edited by Susan Muaddi Darraj, 1–4. Westport, Conn.: Praeger.

de Beauvoir, Simone. 1974. *The Second Sex.* Edited and translated by H. M. Parshley. New York: Vintage Books.

de Beauvoir, Simone, and Gisele Halimi. 1962. *Djamila Boupacha: The Story of the Torture of a Young Algerian Girl Which Shocked Liberal French Opinion.* Translated by Peter Green. New York: Macmillan.

de Certeau, Michel. 1984. *The Practice of Everyday Life.* Translated by Steven Rendall. Berkeley and Los Angeles: Univ. of California Press.

de Lauretis, Teresa. 1997. "Aesthetic and Feminist Theory: Rethinking Women's Cinema." In *Feminisms,* edited by Sandra Kemp and Judith Squires. Oxford: Oxford Univ. Press.

Djebar, Assia. 1980. *Femmes d'Alger dans leur appartement.* Paris: Des Femmes.

———. 1985. *L'amour, la fantasia.* Paris: Albin Michel.

———. 1992. *Women of Algiers in Their Apartment.* Translated by Marjolijn de Jager. Charlottesville: Univ. Press of Virginia.

———. 1993. *Fantasia: An Algerian Cavalcade.* Translated by Dorothy Blair. Portsmouth, N.H.: Heinemann.

———. 1999. *So Vast the Prison.* New York: Seven Stories Press.

Donadey, Anne. 2000. "Portrait of a Maghrebian Feminist as a Young Girl: Fatima Mernissi's *Dreams of Trespass.*" *Edebiyat* 11: 85–103.

Donahue, Deidre. 2003. "Noor Sheds Light on Her Life." *USA Today,* Mar. 17. http://www.usatoday.com/life/books/reviews/2003-03-17-noor.

Donohue, John J., and John L. Esposito, eds. 1982. *Islam in Transition: Muslim Perspectives.* Oxford: Oxford Univ. Press.

Douglas, Carol Anne. 1990. "Separatism: When and How Long?" In *Love and Politics: Radical Feminist and Lesbian Theories,* 250–77. San Francisco: ISM Press.

Dower, Nigel. 2003. *An Introduction to Global Citizenship.* Edinburgh: Edinburgh Univ. Press.

Efrati, Noga. 2006. "Negotiating Rights in Iraq: Women and the Personal Status Law." *Middle East Journal* (Summer): 595.

Enderwitz, Susanne. 1998. "Public Role and Private Self." In *Writing the Self: Autobiographical Writing in Modern Arabic Literature,* edited by Robin Ostle, Ed de Moor, and Stefan Wild, 75–81. London: Saqi Books.

Fanon, Frantz. 1952. *Peau noire, masques blancs.* Paris: Seuil.

———. 1961a. *Les damnés de la terre.* Paris: Maspéro.

———. 1961b. *The Wretched of the Earth.* New York: Grove Press.

———. 1975. *Pour la révolution africaine.* Paris: Maspéro.

———. 1986. *Black Skin, White Masks.* Translated by Charles Markmann. London: Pluto Press.

Faqir, Fadia. 1998. *In the House of Silence: Autobiographical Essays by Arab Women Writers.* Reading, Pa.: Garnet.

Farah, Christopher. 2004. "Beyond Bling-Bling." *Jerusalem Report,* May 31.

Fay, Mary Ann, ed. 2002. *Auto/Biography and the Construction of Identity and Community in the Middle East.* New York: Palgrave Macmillan.

Fayad, Mona. 1996. "Reinscribing Identity: Nation and Community in Arab Women's Writing." *College Literature* 22, no. 1: 147–60.

Felski, Rita. 1989. *Beyond Feminist Aesthetics.* London: Hutchinson Radius.

Figes, Kate. 2000. *Life after Birth.* London: Penguin Books.

Foucault, Michel. 1984. "Nietzsche, Genealogy, History." In *The Foucault Reader,* edited by Paul Rabinow, translated by Donald Bouchard. New York: Pantheon Books.

Franklin, H. Bruce. 1978. *The Victim as Criminal and Artist: Literature from the American Prison.* New York: Oxford Univ. Press.

Freud, Sigmund. 1963–1964. "Lecture XXXIII: Femininity." In vol. 22 of *The Standard Edition of the Complete Psychological Works of Sigmund Freud,* edited by James Strachey. London: Hogarth and the Institute of Psychoanalysis.

Friedman, Susan Stanford. 1988. "Women's Autobiographical Selves: Theory and Practice." In *The Private Self: Theory and Practice of Women's Autobiographical Writing,* edited by Shari Benstock, 34–62. Chapel Hill: Univ. of North Carolina Press.

Gamal, Wael. 2003. "Riding for a Fall." *Al-Ahram* 646 (July 16).

Gandhi, Leela. 1998. *A Critical Introduction to Postcolonial Theory.* New York: Columbia Univ. Press.

Gilmore, Leigh. 2005. "Autobiography's Wounds." In *Just Advocacy? Women's Human Rights, Transnational Feminisms, and the Politics of Representation,* edited by Wendy Hesford and W. Kozol. New Brunswick, N.J.: Rutgers Univ. Press.

Gilroy, Paul. 1993. *The Black Atlantic: Modernity and Double Consciousness.* London: Verso.

Glavanis-Grantham, Kathy. 1996. "The Women's Movement, Feminism, and the National Struggle in Palestine." In *Women and Politics in the Third World,* edited by Haleh Afshar, 171–85. London: Routledge.

Gluck, Sherna Berger. 1995. "Palestinian Women: Gender Politics and Nationalism." *Journal of Palestine Studies* 24, no. 3: 5–15.

Golley, Nawar Al-Hassan. 2003. *Reading Arab Women's Autobiographies: Shahrazad Tells Her Story.* Austin: Univ. of Texas Press.

Grace, Daphne. 2004. *The Woman in the Muslin Mask: Veiling and Identity in Postcolonial Literature.* London: Pluto Press.

———. 2006. Interview of Haifa Zangana. London, July 10.

Graham-Brown, Sarah. 1988. *Images of Women: The Portrayal of Women in Photography of the Middle East, 1860–1950.* New York: Columbia Univ. Press.

Grosrichard, Alain. 1979. *Structure du sérail: La fiction du despotisme Asiatique dans l'Occident classique.* Paris: Éditions Seuil.

———. 1998. *The Sultan's Court: European Fantasies of the East.* London: Verso.

Grosz, Elizabeth. 1989. *Sexual Subversions.* Sydney: Allen and Unwin.

Guberman, R., ed. 1996. *Julia Kristeva: Interviews.* New York: Columbia Univ. Press.

Hamami, Rima, and Eileen Kuttab. 1999. "The Palestinian Women's Movement: Strategies Towards Freedom and Democracy." *News from Within* 15, no. 4: 3–9.

Hammad, Suheir. 1996. *Born Palestinian, Born Black.* New York and London: Harlem River Press.

———. 1997. "Drops of Suheir Hammad: A Talk with a Palestinian Poet Born Black." Interview by Nathalie Handal. *Al-Jadid,* May 5. http://www.aljadid.com/interviews/DropsofSuheirHammad.html.

———. 2001. "First writing since." *Middle East Report* 221: 2–3.

———. 2006a. *Drops of This Story.* 1996. Reprint, New York: Writers and Readers Press.

———. 2006b. *ZaatarDiva.* 2005. Reprint, New York: Rattapallax Press.

Hardt, Michael, and Antonio Negri. 2004. *Multitude: War and Democracy in the Age of Empire.* New York: Penguin Books.

Harkabi, Yehoshofat. 1972. *Arab Attitudes to Israel.* Translated by M. Louvish. London: Ballantine.

Harlow, Barbara. 1987. "From the Women's Prison: Third World Women's Narratives of Prison." In *A Poetics of Women's Autobiography: Marginality and the Fictions of Self-Representation,* edited by Sidonie Smith. Bloomington: Indiana Univ. Press.

———. 1989. "Narrative in Prison: Stories from the Palestinian Intifada." *Modern Fiction Studies* 35, no. 1: 29–46.

Hassan, Mahmoud Abd el-Ghana. n.d. *Al-Tarajim wa al-Sir.* 2d ed. Cairo: Dar al-Ma'arif bi Masr.

Hassan, Waïl S. 2002. "Arab-American Autobiography and the Reinvention of Identity: Two Egyptian Negotiations." *Alif: Journal of Comparative Poetics* 22: 7–35.

Hatoum, Mona. 1997. *Mona Hatoum.* London: Phaidon Press.

Head, Dominic. 1997. *J. M. Coetzee*. Cambridge: Cambridge Univ. Press.

Hesford, Wendy, and W. Kozol, eds. 2005. *Just Advocacy? Women's Human Rights, Transnational Feminisms, and the Politics of Representation*. New Brunswick: Rutgers Univ. Press.

Holcomb, Adele M. 1987–1988. "Anna Jameson on Women Artists." *Woman's Art Journal* 8.

Hollier, D. 1992. *Against Architecture: The Writings of Georges Bataille*. Cambridge: MIT Press.

Hoodfar, Homa. 1997. "The Veil in Their Minds and on Our Heads." In *The Politics of Culture in the Shadow of Capital*, edited by Lisa Lowe and David Lloyd. Durham: Duke Univ. Press.

Hourani, Albert. 1988. *Arabic Thought in the Liberal Age, 1798–1939*. Cambridge: Cambridge Univ. Press.

———. 1991. *A History of the Arab Peoples*. New York: Warner.

Hovsepian, Nubar. 1994. "Universal Versus Particular Identity: Reflections on a Visit to Palestine." *Arab Studies Quarterly* 16, no. 1: 43–54.

Hull, Gloria T., and Patricia Bell-Scott. 1982. *All the Women Are White, All the Blacks Are Men, but Some of Us Are Brave: Black Women's Studies*. Old Westbury, N.Y.: Feminist Press.

Huntington, Samuel P. 1996. *The Clash of Civilizations and the Remaking of World Order*. New York: Simon and Schuster.

Husayn, Taha. 1954. *The Future of Culture in Egypt*. Translated by S. Glazer. Washington, D.C.: American Council of Learned Societies.

al-Husri, Sati. 1982. "Muslim Unity and Arab Unity." In *Islam in Transition: Muslim Perspectives*, edited by John J. Donohue and John L. Esposito. Oxford: Oxford Univ. Press.

al-'Id, Yumna. 1998. "The Autobiographical Novel and the Dual Function." In *Writing the Self: Autobiographical Writing in Modern Arabic Literature*, edited by Robin Ostle, Ed de Moor, and Stefan Wild, 157–77. London: Saqi Books.

Irigaray, Luce. 1974. *Speculum de l'autre femme*. Paris: Éditions de Minuit.

———. 1985a. *Speculum of the Other Woman*. Translated by Gillian Gill. Ithaca: Cornell Univ. Press.

———. 1985b. *This Sex Which Is Not One*. Translated by Catharine Porter. Ithaca: Cornell Univ. Press.

Jad, Islah. 1995. "Claiming Feminism, Claiming Nationalism: Women's Activism in the Occupied Territories." In *The Challenge of Local Feminisms*, edited by Amrita Basu, 226–48. Boulder: Westview Press.

Jay, Paul. 2005. "Globalization and the Postcolonial Condition." In *Modern Language Association,* Dec. http://www.home.comcast.net/~jay.paul/pc.htm.

Jelloun, Ben. 1987. *La nuit sacrée.* Paris: Seuil.

Jordan, June. 1989. "Moving Towards Home." *Political Essays.*

Joseph, Suad. 1999. "Against the Grain of the Nation: The Arab." In *Arabs in America: Building Towards a New Future,* edited by Michael W. Suleiman, 257–71. Philadelphia: Temple Univ. Press.

Kadi, Joanna, ed. 1994. *Food for Our Grandmothers: Writings by Arab-American and Arab-Canadian Feminists.* Boston: South End.

Kahf, Mohja. 1999. *Western Representations of the Muslim Woman: From Termagant to Odalisque.* Austin: Univ. of Texas Press.

———. 2000. "Packaging 'Huda': Sha'rawi's Memoirs in the United States Reception Environment." In *Going Global: The Transnational Reception of Third World Women Writers,* edited by Amal Amireh and Lisa Suhair Majaj, 148–72. New York and London: Garland.

———. 2003. *E-mails from Scheherazad.* Univ. of Central Florida Contemporary Poetry Series. Gainesville: Univ. Press of Florida.

———. 2004a. "Lustrous Companions." *Muslim Wakeup!* Apr. 9. http://www.muslimwakeup.com/sex/archives/2004/04/000687print.php.

———. 2004b. "Poetry Is My Home Address." In *Scheherazade's Legacy: Arab and Arab American Women on Writing,* edited by Susan Muaddi Darraj, 7–20. Westport, Conn.: Praeger.

Kanafani, Ghassan. 1987. *Al-adab al-filastini 'l-muqawim tahta 'l-ihtilal, 1948–1968* [Palestinian Resistance Literature under Occupation, 1948–1968]. Nicosia, Cyprus: IAR.

———. 1998. *Men in the Sun, and Other Palestinian Stories.* Translated by Hilary Kilpatrick. 1962. Reprint, Boulder: Lynne Rienner.

Kandiyoti, Deniz. 1994. "Identity and Its Discontents: Women and the Nation." In *Colonial Discourse and Post-colonial Theory,* edited by Patrick Williams and Laura Chrisman, 376–91. New York: Columbia Univ. Press.

Khalidi, Rashid. 1989. "Consequences of the Suez Crisis in the Arab World." In *Suez, 1956: The Crisis and Its Consequences,* edited by Roger Louis and Roger Owen, 377–92. Oxford: Oxford Univ. Press.

Khatibi, Abdelkebir. 1983a. *Amour bilingue.* Paris: Éditions Fata Morgana.

———. 1983b. *Maghreb pluriel.* Paris: Denoel.

———. 1990. *Love in Two Languages.* Translated by Richard Howard. Minneapolis: Univ. of Minnesota Press.

Knafo, Danielle. 1996. "In Her Own Image: Self-Representation in the Art of Frida Kahlo and Ana Mendieta." *Art Criticism* 11, no. 2.

Krauss, Rosalind. 1996. "'Inform' Without Conclusion." *October* (Cambridge, Mass.) (Fall).

Kristeva, Julia. 1982. *Powers of Horror.* New York: Columbia Univ. Press.

Kureishi, Hanif. 2002. *Gabriel's Gift.* London: Faber and Faber.

LaCapra, Dominick. 2001. *Writing History, Writing Trauma.* Baltimore: Johns Hopkins Univ. Press.

Langer, Jennifer. 2004. "Writing Diasporas." In *Crossing the Border: Voices of Refugee and Exiled Women Writers.* Nottingham: Five Leaves Publications, 2000. http//www.swan.ac.uk/conferences/transcom/htm.

Lazreg, Marnia. 1994. *The Eloquence of Silence.* New York: Routledge.

———. 2000. "The Triumphant Discourse of Global Feminism: Should Other Women Be Known?" In *Going Global: The Transnational Reception of Third World Women Writers,* edited by Amal Amireh and Lisa Suhair Majaj, 29–38. New York and London: Garland.

Lebdai, Benaouda. 2002. "Voix narrative enigmatique dans *La nuit sacrée:* Rêves et réalités." In *Langages au Féminin* (Presses Université d'Angers) (June): 71–86.

Lechte, John. 1990. *Abjection, Melancholia, and Love.* London: Routledge.

Lejeune, Philippe. 1989. "The Autobiographical Pact." In *On Autobiography,* edited by James Olney. Minneapolis: Univ. of Minnesota Press.

Lentin, Ronit. 2000. *Israel and the Daughters of the Shoah: Reoccupying the Territories of Silence.* New York: Berghahn Books.

Levie, Smadar, and Ted Swedenburg, eds. 1996. *Displacement, Diaspora, and Geographies of Identity.* Durham: Duke Univ. Press.

Lorde, Audre. 1984a. "An Open Letter to Mary Daly." In *Sister Outsider: Essays and Speeches,* 66–71. Freedom, Calif.: Crossing Press.

———. 1984b. "Poetry Is Not a Luxury." *Sister Outsider: Essays and Speeches,* 36–39. Freedom, Calif.: Crossing Press.

Lowe, Lisa. 1991. *Critical Terrains: British and French Orientalisms.* Ithaca: Cornell Univ. Press.

———. 1996. *Immigrant Acts: On Asian American Cultural Politics.* Durham: Duke Univ. Press.

Lukacs, Yehuda. 1992. *The Israeli-Palestinian Conflict: A Documentary History.* Cambridge: Cambridge Univ. Press.

Majaj, Lisa Suhair. 2000. "Arab-Americans and the Meanings of Race." In *Postcolonial Theory and the United States: Race, Ethnicity, and Literature,* edited by Amritjit Singh and Peter Schmidt, 320–37. Jackson: Univ. Press of Mississippi.

Makdisi, Jean Said. 2005. *Teta, Mother, and Me: An Arab Woman's Memoir.* London: Saqi Books.

Makdisi, Saree. 1995. "Postcolonial Literature in a Neocolonial World: Modern Arabic Culture and the End of Modernity." *Boundary* 2, no. 22 (Spring): 85–115.

Malak, Amin. 2000. "Arab Muslim Feminism and the Narrative of Hybridity: The Fiction of Ahdaf Soueif." In *Alif: Journal of Comparative Poetics* (Elias Modern Press, Cairo) 20: 140–83.

Mandela, Winnie. 1985. *Part of My Soul Went with Him.* Harmondsworth, Middlesex: Penguin Books.

Manganaro, Elise. 1989. "The Politics of Public Disclosure: Race and Gender in Raimonda Tawil's *My Home, My Prison.*" In *Biography East and West,* edited by Carol Ramelb. Honolulu: College of Languages, Linguistics, and Literature, Univ. of Hawaii, and East-West Center.

Manisty, Dinah. 1998. "Negotiating the Space Between Private and Public: Women's Autobiographical Writing in Egypt." In *Writing the Self: Autobiographical Writing in Modern Arabic Literature,* edited by Robin Ostle, Ed de Moor, and Stefan Wild, 272–82. London: Saqi Books.

Mason, Mary G. 1980. "The Other Voice: Autobiographies of Women Writers." In *Autobiography: Essays Theoretical and Critical,* edited by James Olney, 207–35. Princeton: Princeton Univ. Press.

Matthes, Melissa. 1999. "Shahrazad's Sisters: Storytelling and Politics in the Memoirs of Mernissi, el-Saadawi, and Ashrawi." *Alif: Journal of Comparative Poetics* 19: 68–96.

Maushart, Susan. 1997. *Mask of Motherhood.* Milsons Point, New South Wales: Random House Australia.

Medina, Tony, and Louis Reyes Rivera, eds. 2001. *Bum Rush the Page: A Def Poetry Jam.* New York: Crown.

Melman, Billie. 1992. *Women's Orients: English Women and the Middle East, 1718–1918.* Ann Arbor: Univ. of Michigan Press.

Mernissi, Fatima. 1985. *Beyond the Veil.* London: Saqi Books.

———. 1987. *Beyond the Veil: Male Female Dynamics in Modern Muslim Society.* Rev. ed. Bloomington: Indiana Univ. Press.

———. 1988. *Doing Daily Battle: Interviews with Moroccan Women.* Translated by Mary Jo Lakeland. London: Women's Press.

———. 1991. *The Veil and the Male Elite.* Translated by Mary Jo Lakeland. Reading, Mass.: Perseus Books.

———. 1995. *Dreams of Trespass: Tales of a Harem Girlhood.* Cambridge, Mass.: Perseus Books.

———. 1996. *Women's Rebellion and Islamic Memory.* London and Atlantic Highlands, N.J.: Zed Books.

———. 2001. *Scheherazade Goes West: Different Cultures, Different Harems.* New York: Washington Square Books.

Metlitzki, Dorothee. 1977. *The Matter of Araby in Medieval Europe.* New Haven: Yale Univ. Press.

Millet, Kate. 1969. *Sexual Politics.* New York: Ballantine.

Mohanty, Chandra Talpade. 1991. "Cartographies of Struggle: Third World Women and the Politics of Feminism." Introduction to *Third World Women and the Politics of Feminism,* edited by Chandra Talpade Mohanty, Ann Russo, and Lourdes Torres, 1–47. Bloomington: Indiana Univ. Press.

Montagu, Lady Mary Wortley. 1992. *Letters.* New York: Alfred A. Knopf.

Moraga, Cherríe, and Gloria Anzaldúa. 1981. *This Bridge Called My Back: Writings by Radical Women of Color.* Watertown, Mass.: Persephone Press.

Muaddi Darraj, Susan, ed. 2004. *Scheherazade's Legacy: Arab and Arab American Women on Writing.* Westport, Conn.: Praeger.

Murphy, Julian. 1995. "Beauvoir and the Algerian War: Toward a Postcolonial Ethics." In *Feminist Interpretations of Simone de Beauvoir,* edited by Margaret A. Simons, 263–97. Univ. Park: Pennsylvania State Univ. Press.

Naber, Nadine. 2000. "Ambiguous Insiders: An Investigation of Arab American Invisibility." *Ethnic and Racial Studies* 23, no. 1: 37–61.

Nafisi, Azar. 2003. *Reading "Lolita" in Tehran.* New York: Random House.

Nandy, Ashis. 1989. *The Intimate Enemy: Loss and Recovery of Self under Colonialism.* Oxford: Oxford Univ. Press.

Narayan, Uma. 1997. *Dislocating Cultures: Identities, Traditions, and Third World Feminism.* New York: Routledge.

Nash, Robert J. 2004. *Liberating Scholarly Writing: The Power of Personal Narratives.* New York: Teachers College Press.

Nietzsche, Friedrich. 1974. *The Gay Science.* Translated by Walter Kaufmann. New York: Vintage Books.

Nixon, Mignon. 1995. "Bad Enough Mother: Psychoanalytic Study of the Use of the Body in Contemporary Feminist Art." *October* (Cambridge, Mass.) 71: 70–92.

Noor, Queen. 2003. *Leap of Faith: Memoirs of an Unexpected Life.* New York: Miramax Books.

Nye, Naomi Shihab. 2002. Introduction to *19 Varieties of Gazelle: Poems of the Middle East.* New York: Greenwillow.

Oliver, Kelly, ed. 1997. *The Portable Kristeva.* New York: Columbia Univ. Press.

Ostle, Robin, Ed de Moor, and Stefan Wild, eds. 1998. *Writing the Self: Autobiographical Writing in Modern Arabic Literature.* London: Saqi Books.

Oufkir, Malika. 2000. *Stolen Lives.* Translated by Ros Schwartz. New York: Hyperion.

Parmenter, Barbara. 1994. *Giving Voice to Stone.* Austin: Univ. of Texas Press.

Pateman, Carol. 1988. *The Sexual Contract.* Stanford: Stanford Univ. Press.

Peirce, Leslie P. 1993. *The Imperial Harem: Women and Sovereignty in the Ottoman Empire.* New York: Oxford Univ. Press.

Penwarden, Charles. 1995. "Of Word and Flesh: An Interview with Julia Kristeva." In *Rites of Passage: Art for the End of the Century,* by Stuart Morgan and Frances Morris. London: Tate Gallery.

Penzer, N. M. 1937. *The Harem: An Account of the Institution as It Existed in the Palace of the Turkish Sultans with a History of the Grand Seraglio from Its Foundation to the Present Time.* Philadelphia: J. B. Lippincott.

Peteet, Julie. 1991. *Gender Crisis, Women, and the Palestinian Resistance Movement.* New York: Columbia Univ. Press.

Pike, Martha Conant. 1908. *The Oriental Tale in England in the Eighteenth Century.* New York: Columbia Univ. Press.

Reagon, Bernice Johnson. 1982. "My Black Mothers and Sisters; or, On Beginning a Cultural Autobiography." *Feminist Studies* 8: 81–95.

Reynolds, Dwight F. 2001. *Interpreting the Self: Autobiography in the Arabic Literary Tradition.* Berkeley and Los Angeles: Univ. of California Press.

———, ed. 1997. "Arabic Autobiography." Special issue, *Edebiyat: A Journal of Middle Eastern Literature* 7, no. 2.

Rich, Adrienne. 1979. *On Lies, Secrets, and Silence: Selected Prose, 1966–78.* New York: W. W. Norton.

Robbins, Ruth. 2000. *Literary Feminisms.* New York: St. Martin's Press.

Rondeau, James. 2000. *Biennale of Sydney, 2000.* Sydney: Biennale of Sydney.

Rooke, Tetz. 1997. "In My Childhood: A Study of Arabic Autobiography." Ph.D. diss., Stockholm Univ.

Ruby, Robert H., and Herman J. Viola. 1989. *Dreamer-Prophets of the Columbia Plateau: Smohalla and Skolaskin.* Norman: Univ. of Oklahoma Press.

el-Saadawi, Nawal. 1980. *The Hidden Face of Eve.* Translated by Sherif Hetata. London: Zed Books.

———. 1983. *Woman at Point Zero.* London: Zed Books.

———. 1986. *Memoirs from the Women's Prison.* London: Women's Press.

———. 1997. *The Nawal el-Saadawi Reader.* London: Zed Books.

———. 1998. *A Daughter of Isis.* London: Zed Books.

———. 1999. *Daughter of Isis: The Autobiography of Nawal el-Saadawi.* Translated by Sherif Hetata. London: Zed Books.

———. 2002. *Walking Through Fire: A Life of Nawal el-Saadawi.* Translated by Sherif Hetata. London: Saqi Books.

Sabbagh, Suha. 1989. "Palestinian Women Writers and the Intifada." *Social Text* 22: 1–19.

Said, Edward. 1978. *Orientalism.* New York: Pantheon Books.

———. 1986. "On Palestinian Identity: A Conversation with Salman Rushdie." *New Left Review* 1 (Nov–Dec.).

———. 1992. "The Anglo-Arab Encounter," *The Times Literary Supplement,* June 9.

———. 1993. *Culture and Imperialism.* London: Chatto and Windus.

———. 1994a. *Culture and Imperialism.* New York: Vintage Books.

———. 1994b. *The Politics of Dispossession.* New York: Pantheon Books.

———. 2001. "The One-State Solution." In *The End of the Peace Process: Oslo and After,* 312–21. New York: Vintage Books.

Said, Edward, and Christopher Hitchens, eds. 1988. *Blaming the Victims.* London: Verso.

Salaita, Steven. 2006. *Anti-Arab Racism in the USA: Where It Comes from and What It Means for Politics Today.* London: Pluto Press.

Sartre, Jean-Paul. 2004. *What Is Literature? and Other Essays.* 1948. Reprint, Cambridge: Harvard Univ. Press.

Scott, Joan W. 1993. "The Evidence of Experience." In *The Lesbian and Gay Studies Reader,* edited by Henry Abelove, Michèle Aina Barale, and David M. Halperin, 397–415. New York: Routledge.

Seaman, Donna. 2003. Review of *E-mails from Scheherazad,* by Mohja Kahf. *Booklist* (Mar. 1).

Sebbar, Leila. 1982. *Sherazad.* Paris: Stock.

Serageldin, Samia. 2000. *The Cairo House: A Novel.* Syracuse: Syracuse Univ. Press.

Shaaban, Bouthaina. 1988. *Both Right and Left Handed: Arab Women Talk about Their Lives.* London: Women's Press.

———. 1991. *Both Right and Left Handed: Arab Women Talk about Their Lives.* Bloomington: Indiana Univ. Press.

Shaarawi, Huda. 1986. *Harem Years: The Memoirs of an Egyptian Feminist (1879–1924).* Edited by Margot Badran. New York: Feminist Press.

Shammas, Anton. 1995. "Palestinians in Israel: You Ain't Seen Nothin' Yet." *Journal of the International Institute* (Univ. of Michigan) 3, no. 1.

Sharoni, Simona. 1995. "Gendered Identities in Conflict: The Israeli-Palestinian Case and Beyond." *Women's Studies Quarterly* 3, no. 4: 117–35.

Shehade, Raja. 1988. *Occupier's Law.* Washington, D.C.: Institute for Palestine Studies.

Shenkman, Rick. 2004. *Bill Clinton's Memoirs.* History News Network, June 15. http://www.hnn.us/blogs/26.html.

Shereen, Faiza W. 2003. "The Diasporic Memoirist as Saidian Itinerant Intellectual: A Reading of Leila Ahmed's *A Border Passage.*" *Studies in the Humanities* 30: 108–30.

Shohat, Ella. 1992. "Notes on the Postcolonial." *Social Text* 5, no. 31–32: 99–113.

Showalter, Elaine. 1977. *A Literature of Their Own: British Women Novelists from Brontë to Lessing.* Princeton: Princeton Univ. Press.

Simmons, Russell. 2003. *Russell Simmons Def Poetry Jam on Broadway . . . and More.* New York: Atria.

Smith, Sidonie. 1987. *A Poetics of Women's Autobiography: Marginality and the Fictions of Self-Representations.* Bloomington: Indiana Univ. Press.

———. 1998. "Autobiographical Manifestos." In *Women, Autobiography, Theory: A Reader,* edited by Sidonie Smith and Hulia Watson. Madison: Univ. of Wisconsin Press.

———. 2005. "Belated Narrating: 'Grandmothers' Telling Stories of Forced Sexual Servitude During World War II." In *Just Advocacy? Women's Human Rights, Transnational Feminisms, and the Politics of Representation,* edited by Wendy Hesford and W. Kozol. New Brunswick, N.J.: Rutgers Univ. Press.

Soueif, Ahdaf. 1992. *In the Eye of the Sun.* New York: Anchor Books.

———. 1999. *The Map of Love.* London: Bloomsbury.

———. 2004. *Mezzaterra: Fragments from the Common Ground.* London: Bloomsbury.

Spacks, Patricia Meyer. 1975. *The Female Imagination.* New Haven: Yale Univ. Press.

Spivak, Gayatri Chakravorty. 1987. *In Other Worlds: Essays in Cultural Politics.* New York: Methuen.

———. 1992. "Acting Bits/Identity Talk." In "Identities." Special issue, *Critical Inquiry* (Univ. of Chicago Press) 18, no. 4: 770–803.

———. 1996. "Echo." In *The Spivak Reader,* edited by D. Landry. New York: Routledge.

Sprinker, Michael. 1980. "The End of Autobiography." In *Autobiography: Essays Theoretical and Critical,* edited by James Olney, 339–42. Princeton: Princeton Univ. Press.

Stewart, Susan. 1984. *On Longing: Narratives of the Miniature, the Gigantic, the Souvenir, the Collection.* Baltimore: Johns Hopkins Univ. Press.

Suleiman, Yasir. 2004. *A War of Words: Language and Conflict in the Middle East.* Cambridge: Cambridge Univ. Press.

al-Tahtawi, Rifaa Badawi Rafi. 1982. "Fatherland and Patriotism." In *Islam in Transition: Muslim Perspectives,* edited by John J. Donohue and John L. Esposito. Oxford: Oxford Univ. Press.

Tawil, Raimonda Hawa. 1980. *My Home, My Prison.* New York: Holt, Rinehart, and Winston.

Terry, Ellen. 1985. *Ellen Terry and Bernard Shaw: A Correspondence.* Folcroft, Pa.: Folcroft Library Editions.

Thiong'o, Ngugi wa. 1981. *Decolonizing the Mind: The Politics of Language in African Literature.* Portsmouth, N.H.: Heinemann.

Turhan, Filiz. 2003. *The Other Empire: British Romantic Writings about the Ottoman Empire.* New York: Routledge.

Wassef, Hind. 1998. "The Unblushing Bourgeoisie." *Cairo Times* 2, no. 5 (Apr. 30).

Weir, Allison. 1996. *Sacrificial Logics: Feminist Theory and the Critique of Identity.* London and New York: Routledge.

Whitlock, Gillian. 2000. *The Intimate Empire: Reading Women's Autobiography.* London: Cassell.

Woodhull, Winifred. 1993. "Feminism and Islamic Tradition." *Studies in Twentieth Century Literature* 17 (Winter): 27–44.

Woolf, Virginia. 1977. *A Room of One's Own.* 1929. Reprint, London: Triad Grafton.

Zabus, Chantal. 2006. "The Empire Writes Back to and from the Centre." http://www.eng.fju.edu.tw/worldlit/empire.htm.

Zangana, Haifa. 1991. *Through the Vast Halls of Memory.* Translated by Paul Hammond and H. Zangana. Paris: Hourglass.

———. 2002. "Bombs Will Deepen Iraq's Nightmare." *Guardian,* Sept. 17.

———. 2004a. "I, Too, Was Tortured in Abu Ghraib." *Guardian,* May 11.

———. 2004b. "Quiet, or I'll Call Democracy." *Guardian,* Dec. 2.

———. 2005. "Colonial Feminists from Washington to Baghdad: Women for a Free Iraq as a Case Study." *Al-Raida* 22 (Spring–Summer): 109–10.

———. 2006. "The Right to Rule Ourselves." In *Not One More Death,* by John le Carré, Richard Dawkins, Brian Eno, and Michael Faber. London: Verso.

Zimra, Clarisse. 1995. "Disorienting the Subject in Assia Djebar's *L'amour, la fantasia*." Edited by Lynn Huffer. *Yale French Studies* 87.

Zinsser, William, ed. 1998. *Inventing the Truth: The Art and Craft of Memoir*. Boston: Houghton Mifflin.

Index

Italic page number denotes illustration.